PELICAN BOOKS

A207

THE AMERICAN UNION

H. G. NICHOLAS

THE AMERICAN UNION

H. G. Nicholas

PENGUIN BOOKS
HARMONDSWORTH · MIDDLESEX

FIRST PUBLISHED 1948
PUBLISHED IN PELICAN BOOKS 1950

*To my father
and mother*

MADE AND PRINTED IN GREAT BRITAIN
FOR PENGUIN BOOKS LIMITED
BY WYMAN AND SONS LTD

CONTENTS

PREFACE

THIS history was written during the war years and in intervals snatched from other duties. While it makes no pretence of being based on a fresh study of original source materials, I hope that it may serve as an introduction to the main lines of American historical development and as a basis for a better understanding of the present-day United States.

H.G.N.

CHAPTER I

Virginian Beginnings

ON a modern map the continent of North America presents the rough appearance of a triangle standing on its apex. Each side of the triangle rebuffs the intruder from the sea – the long range of the Rockies along the west and the more broken, but still formidable, rampart of the Appalachians in the east. There are two side doors to the interior – at the triangle's northern corner where the St Lawrence opens into the North Atlantic, and in the south-western indentation, where the Mississippi spills into the Gulf of Mexico. But the first of these is only open for half the year, when the summer heats keep the ice at bay; and the second is broken up into an intricate delta of fever-infested waterways. Consequently, even after Columbus and Amerigo Vespucci had proved to the world that a continent of America existed, and Cabot had found the St Lawrence, and Drake the coast of California, European sailors and settlers remained for a long time indifferent to those areas of North America now comprised by Canada and the United States.

Instead, it was the Caribbean and Central America which first attracted Europeans. Its climate was hostile, but the old-established civilization of the Aztecs offered an easy prey to the adventurous invader. When Cortez landed at Vera Cruz in 1519 he was not long in subduing the Aztec Kingdom and looting its coffers for Spain. Sixteenth-century Europe was so dazzled at these new-found riches of the tropics that for a century after Columbus no one even thought of making a settlement north of Florida. The rich fishing-banks of Newfoundland attracted fleets from Britain, France and Portugal, but these were summer visitors who, having made their catch, returned to sell it in their home markets. The long Atlantic coastline which stretched south from Newfoundland to Florida seemed an inhospitable country which offered no prospect of the quiet and easy fortunes of the Caribbean or the Spanish Main.

But as the sixteenth century proceeded and the impulse to colonization developed in Britain, it was necessarily to this part of North America that attention turned—if only because the Spaniards had a virtual monopoly of the Caribbean. The earliest efforts were not successful. It was in 1585 that Sir Walter Raleigh sent out his first expedition to colonize 'Virginia'. One winter in the New World was enough for these ill-prepared pioneer immigrants. When Drake, returning from one of his raids on the Spanish Main, stopped at Roanoke Island, the survivors of the colony seized the opportunity to return with him to England. A second attempt was made in 1587 when Raleigh despatched a further company of 150 to the same ill-fated island. This venture, like the last, proved to have been made with too little forethought. The colonists were left to face their first winter without adequate stocks: John White, their leader, went back to England for provisions, but by the time he returned all trace of the colony had disappeared, without a shred of evidence remaining to show whether famine, cold, disease or hostile Indians had been responsible. Twenty years had to elapse before the next attempt at British colonization in the New World.

From Raleigh's ventures it was apparent that a colony in order to succeed needed to be a planned and well-financed enterprise. The body of merchants, knights and gentlemen who in 1606 invested their capital in the 'London Company' learnt from Raleigh's failures. The party they despatched in three small vessels in December 1606 was considerably better equipped than its predecessors. Even so, it had a hard time of it. When, after a voyage lasting more than four months, they landed at what is now Jamestown, Virginia, their numbers were already reduced to a little over one hundred, sixteen men having died on shipboard. The port, storehouse, church and row of huts which they constructed represented a very weak outpost of European civilization in an inhospitable wilderness. The Indians were hostile, fevers broke out and food ran short, until at one time the colonists sank to eating mice and snakes to keep themselves from starving. Before long, the colony, to quote the words of one of them, looked like 'the ruins of any ancient fortification ... the gates torn from their hinges, the church ruined and unfrequented, empty houses ... rent up and burnt, the living not able, as they pretended, to step into the woods to gather other firewood: and it is true the Indian as fast killing without as the famine and pestilence within'. So bad was their plight that they decided in despair to abandon the settlement and even went so far as to take ship for England, but, as they were sailing down the river to the sea, they were met by a ship coming in from England, the first of three under Lord De La Warr,* that brought new colonists and fresh provisions from Britain. At this they took new heart, returned to Jamestown and began again. Although there were many hard times still ahead of them, the worst was now passed, and within ten years of the original landing the colonists were able to report of themselves that 'They sow and reap their corn in sufficient proportion ... their kine multiply already to some hundreds, their swine to many thousands, their goats and poultry in great numbers; every man hath house and ground to his own use.'

Above all, they profited by growing one plant in particular, tobacco. Thirty years earlier Sir Walter Raleigh had introduced it into England, and now the habit of smoking had grown so much in Europe that there was a ready market for all that Virginia could grow. Soon the chief export of the colony was its tobacco: the best tobacco the New World could supply.

But though the colony thus learnt how to overcome the dangers of disease and starvation, there was one threat which was always present, the Indians. The Indians regarded white settlements as encroachments on their terri-

* Who gave his name to the River Delaware north of Virginia.

tory; the Europeans in return regarded the Indians as savages and enemies. From the long, sad story of conflict between the Indians and the 'palefaces' one exception stands out, the romantic story of Pocahontas. In the early days of the colony, Captain John Smith, the colonists' buccaneering leader, was captured by Indians while exploring the river behind the settlement. He was taken before the chief, Powhatan, and, as he says, sentenced to death and dragged to the execution block. But just as the Indians were making ready, at the given signal, to beat out his brains with their clubs, Powhatan's young daughter, Pocahontas, sprang forward and with her own body sheltered his. Her heroism saved his life; he was released, accepted by the Indians as one of themselves and allowed to go back to the camp. Gifts were exchanged and for a time there was peace and amity. But soon quarrels and bloodshed were provoked again. In the wars that followed the British caught and kidnapped Pocahontas, to hold her as a hostage for an Indian peace. Pocahontas, however, was soon a willing prisoner because she fell in love and married John Rolfe, a young gentleman of the colony. Their marriage was Powhatan's pledge of peace, a peace that lasted after his death. Two years later John Rolfe took his bride to England, where she made a great sensation, people flocking to see 'the Indian princess,' 'La Belle Sauvage.' But at Gravesend, just as they were about to take ship back to Virginia, Pocahontas was attacked by smallpox and died. There at Gravesend she lies buried, the first native American to marry an Englishman.

CHAPTER II

The Puritan Colonists

THE settlers of Jamestown having proved that, given certain conditions, a colony in North America could very well be successful, it was not long before others followed in the trail they had blazed. The Virginia colonists had been attracted by expectations, in varying degrees, of New World success and adventure. As the seventeenth century went on another powerful motive was provided for colonization – religious persecution in the homeland and the prospect of religious independence overseas. From the loins of the Reformation there had sprung the Protestant Church of England. From that Church in turn there branched off the different varieties of Dissent; Protestants, mainly of the Calvinist persuasion, who disagreed with either the theology or the systems of worship or government of the established Church. The penalties for Dissent were sharpened as Elizabeth's long and, on the whole, tolerant reign drew to its close, and with the opening of the seventeenth century it became increasingly difficult for Puritanical Dissenters to worship publicly in accordance with their beliefs. This led one such group of 'Independents' from East Anglia to emigrate in 1607 to the Netherlands, where toleration was extended to all varieties of Protestant belief. But although they found at Leyden the freedom of worship they desired, they were conscious of being in a foreign country where their children would be likely to grow up ignorant of the ways and speech of England. The only land which offered them a prospect of a home of their own where they could live as Englishmen and yet have religious freedom was America. So though they were a small and poor community they determined to face the perils of the Atlantic and stake everything on the uncertainties of the wilderness.

First they returned to Britain, where they picked up

some others of their persuasion from their old homes in Nottinghamshire, Lincolnshire and Yorkshire. Then they embarked the assembled party on two small vessels, the *Speedwell* and the *Mayflower*. But the *Speedwell* twice sprang a leak and the vessels had twice to put back into port, until at last it was decided that the *Mayflower* would have to go on alone, bearing all the passengers and cargo. On September 16th, 1620, she set sail from Plymouth, a tiny ship of 180 tons, slow, square and overcrowded, with 101 passengers, of whom many were children – twenty boys and eleven girls. It was a long, stormy voyage and food was neither abundant nor good; five passengers died on board. After four months of uncertain navigation they reached, not the Virginia for which they had aimed, but a spot on the shores of Massachusetts, to which they gave the name Plymouth, in memory of their port of departure.

There they landed, and their first act was to give thanks to God for having brought them safely to the new land. They chose a site for their settlement and on Christmas Day began to build the first house on the site of an old Indian cornfield. In spite of the difficulties of the winter and of disease, it was not long before each family had built itself a house, with a garden and field behind, arranged in rows each side of a single street. The Indians, fortunately, were friendly; one of them, Squanto, came to live in the colony, learnt English and acted as interpreter and with his tribe the colony soon made a treaty of peace. The Narragansets, a more warlike tribe, sent a challenge of a snakeskin filled with arrows, to which the Pilgrims replied by sending the skin back filled with gunpowder and shot. The Narragansets took the hint.

The little colony then settled down in peace, and learnt how to adapt their English skills and customs to life in North America. When in the third summer after their landing they experienced one of those long droughts accompanied by great heat which are not uncommon along the Atlantic seaboard, their crops, on which the very existence of the colony depended, looked like being burnt up for lack of rain. 'Upon which,' says Governor Bradford, 'they set apart a day of humiliation, to seek the Lord by humble and fervent prayer in this great distress ... Towards evening it began to overcast, and shortly after to rain, with such sweet and gentle showers, as gave them cause of rejoicing and blessing God.' Their crops were saved, and with the crops the colony. 'For which mercy,' Bradford goes on to say, 'they also set apart a day of thanksgiving' – the origin of that Thanksgiving Day still celebrated in the United States on the last Thursday of November with the traditional New England dishes of turkey with cranberry sauce and pumpkin pie. Surviving such early vicissitudes, Plymouth Colony soon grew in strength with the addition of fresh immigrants who brought new skills and additional labour.

The colonists governed themselves. Before going ashore from the *Mayflower* they had met, forty-one of them, in the cabin of the vessel and drawn up and signed a solemn agreement by which, as they said, they combined themselves 'together into a civil body politic.' They chose their own governor and his assistant and, as the colony grew in numbers, they chose delegates to represent them in the assembly. Thus they established for themselves not only freedom of worship, but also a free government.

Their Covenant was that they would make just and equal laws and would yield obedience to the same. It was a remarkable application to civil affairs of the principle of self-government which these Independent groups were already applying to their religious organizations. The government so established was essentially democratic. Once a year all the freemen of the colony met in an assembly known as the General Court, where they elected the Governor and other officials, levied taxes, made laws and acted as a court of justice. And as the Colony grew in numbers they chose delegates to represent them in the General Court.

Other colonies were to surpass Plymouth in size, wealth, enterprise and leadership. But the Pilgrim Fathers were pioneers in the great migration of Puritans from Old England to New, and their memory is deservedly revered for the heroism of their enterprise and the constancy of their faith.

If James I had persecuted Dissent with whips, Charles I persecuted it with scorpions, and it was not long before the example of the Pilgrim Fathers was followed by other groups who were chafing under the High Church policies of Archbishop Laud. Not outright separatists only, but even mild Puritans who revered the Church of England, asking only that it should be 'purified' of any 'popish' tendencies, were finding it impossible to square their tenets with the religious practices enforced by the Crown. Representative of this type of Puritan was John White, a kindly well-to-do clergyman of Dorchester, who had long been interested in exploration and fishing enterprises in North America. He became the prime mover in the formation of a joint stock company, the Massachusetts Bay Company, which, like its predecessors of Plymouth and Virginia, was designed to finance a New World colony. Under these auspices in 1630, and under the leadership of John Winthrop – a squire of the manor of Groton, Suffolk – a party of Puritan emigrants about a thousand strong set out in a fleet of eleven vessels to settle on the coast of New England around the mouth of the Charles River. Although this settlement was by far the largest and the most carefully organized of all up to date, it did not escape the usual misfortune of the first American winter. The colonists arrived too late to plant crops and had to live largely on the scanty and stale supplies they had brought with them. Over two hundred of their number died, 'so that in every family', as one of them said, 'lamentation, mourning and woe was heard, and no fresh food to be had to cherish them.' Not until fresh supplies arrived from Britain and the colonists were able to fish and harvest their own crops was the danger point passed.

From that time on the colony steadily grew. Emigration from England was carefully planned by the Massachusetts Bay Company, and care was taken to see that the wants of the settlers were adequately provided for. The immigrants came mostly from the Eastern Counties of England, but others were by no means excluded. Their places of origin in Britain are well indicated on any early map of Massachusetts, where may be found, amongst others, the townships of Cambridge, Lynn, Salisbury, Boston, Hull, Dorchester and Weymouth.

Under the Governorship of John Winthrop the Massachusetts Bay Company enjoyed a far less democratic form of government than its neighbour at Plymouth. Control of affairs was in the hands of a relatively small number of settlers and particular care was taken to see to it that the Puritan character of the colony was preserved by restricting votes to those persons who were church members.

Not only was Winthrop hostile to any democratic theory which implied political equality, but he and his fellow-churchmen were firmly of the conviction that it was contrary to scripture and sound Christian doctrine to entrust political power to anyone who did not hold the right theological views and follow the right religious practices. Church and State were, in their opinion, one, and the same tests of fitness were applied to those seeking admission to either. Furthermore, having fled to New England in order to establish a commonwealth such as they believed in, they were not going to have it endangered by admitting to power (or even to residence) persons of a different faith. That this would make them as intolerant in New England as Charles I had been in the old, did not disturb them; the idea of toleration was still in its infancy in the 1630's. Nevertheless, from their intolerance there soon flowed surprising consequences.

In the winter of 1635 an eloquent young Minister who held a prominent place among the settlers of Massachusetts was summoned before the General Court of the colony and sentenced to banishment. His name was Roger Williams and his crime was that he believed and eloquently proclaimed that control of the church and control of the government ought not to be in one and the same hands, as they were in Massachusetts.

Rocky Mountains
Cascade Range
Columbia R.
Missouri R.
Sierra Nevada
Sacramento R.
Gt Salt L.
Colorado R.
Rio Grande
Red R.

U.S.A.

St Lawrence R.
Erie Canal
Hudson R.
Mississippi R.
Missouri R.
Ohio R.
Plains
Mississippi R.
Land over 1000 feet

PHYSICAL

Expelled from the colony in the depths of winter, Williams would almost certainly have died from cold and exposure had not the kindly Narraganset Indians, whose language he had learned and whose friendship he had cultivated, given him refuge and shelter. Finally, in the spring of 1636, he and five of his friends reached the site of the present city of Providence. There with the help of the Indians and the addition of other deserters and outcasts from Massachusetts Bay, Roger Williams began to build up the settlement of Rhode Island. The keystone of the little community was the principle of religious toleration. Ahead of most men of his generation, Roger Williams, a saintly, generous and courageous spirit, had grasped the truth that a man can only have true freedom for himself if he is prepared to grant the same rights to others, and that a State should not coerce the citizen's beliefs but should allow for differences of honest opinion, provided that those who differ do not try to settle their differences by force. He accordingly insisted that in Rhode Island no one should be persecuted or excluded from a share in the government merely on account of his religious beliefs. Members of different sects, Baptists or Quakers or Catholics, were equally welcome provided they kept the peace and respected their neighbour's faith. Later it was written into the charter of Rhode Island Colony that no one should be 'in any wise molested, punished, disquieted or called in question for any differences of opinion in matters of religion.' Thus it was in Rhode Island that for the first time in modern history the ideals of liberty of conscience and toleration were put into operation in the government of a state and Roger Williams may claim to rank as the first great American champion of liberty.

While Rhode Island was being settled by men who could not accept the theocracy of Massachusetts, Connecticut was coming into being as an overflow for those settlers in the Bay Colony who, without harbouring any religious grievances, were attracted by the opportunities offered by Connecticut's fertile river valleys. Pushing westwards in Massachusetts, they came to the upper reaches of the river

Connecticut, and in 1635 made their first encampment on the spot where Hartford, Connecticut's capital, stands today. Soon other Puritans landed from the sea; at New Haven, Saybrook, and other spots with good harbours and prospects of reasonable fertility. For strength and mutual aid the settlements banded together: in 1662 a royal charter was granted confirming their independence from Massachusetts and giving royal sanction to their form of government – a government in all important respects akin to that of Massachusetts Bay.

CHAPTER III

The Middle and Southern Colonies

WHILE Puritans were settling in New England and Virginia was growing into a large colony, the intervening parts of the seaboard were being filled up by other groups. Although the government of Charles I was hostile to the Puritans, Englishmen in general were far from well disposed to the Catholics who represented the other extreme of religious belief. In fact, ever since Guy Fawkes had attempted his desperate and foolish Gunpowder Plot the Catholics had been viewed with growing suspicion and distrust by most of their fellow Englishmen, until they, too, began to look to the New World for safety and freedom for the exercise of their religion. To Lord Calvert, a wealthy Catholic nobleman, Charles I made a generous grant of all the land between the River Potomac and the 40th degree of latitude. Charles called the territory Maryland, in honour of his wife, Henrietta Maria. (The present State of Maryland still keeps the old Potomac boundary, but has been trimmed on the North and West by Pennsylvania and Delaware.) In 1633 Lord Calvert sent out his first batch of settlers, two to three hundred of them. They sailed up the Potomac – as one of them said, 'The sweetest and greatest river I have ever seen, so that the Thames is but a little finger to it' – and settled at St. Mary's, not far from the spot where the Potomac flows into the Chesapeake. It was a healthy spot, with good soil, and the neighbouring Indians were friendly. From the start the colony did well and before very long Maryland was even attracting colonists from Virginia. This was principally due to the wise and generous handling of Lord Calvert, who from the outset adopted a policy of religious toleration, promising that no settler should be denied the 'free exercise' of his religion. This had a great appeal to all the Puritans who had come to Virginia and found that colony rigidly and intolerantly Church of England, and between 1644 and 1649 they emigrated to Maryland in large numbers.

But the British were not the only colonists on the Atlantic seaboard. As early as 1609 the Dutch had sent their explorers, beginning with Henry Hudson, an Englishman in Dutch employ who, searching for the North-West Passage to China, discovered and sailed up the river that bears his name. On the heels of his discovery came the Dutch settlers seeking to trade in furs with the Indians. Their first post was in 1614 on Manhattan Island; nowadays the crowded skyscrapers of downtown New York stand on the spot where the Dutch traders erected their wooden huts and stockade. But it was not until ten years later that a proper team of colonizers was sent out and it was in 1626 that the Governor Peter Minuit made the historic purchase of the island of Manhattan from the Indians. For about twenty-four dollars he bought the territory which in three hundred years has become the congested and wealthy centre of the city of New York. Here, at New Amsterdam, Peter Minuit made the capital of the colony which the Dutch called New Netherland and which extended from the Delaware to the Connecticut. It was not long before neighbours came to live at the edge of both these boundaries.

In seventeenth-century Europe Sweden was a great power, vigorous and expanding. It was consequently no matter for surprise that, when Peter Minuit, who had been forced out of his position of Governor at New Amsterdam, offered to lead a Swedish expedition to America, the offer should be promptly accepted. Where Wilmington now stands in Delaware, the Swedes made their first colony of Fort Christina in 1638, and from there spread down the river. For ten years the Swedes lived in peace, a few of them by farming, but most by trade with the Indians. As long as in Europe the Thirty Years War lasted, Holland and Sweden, who were allies, imposed a similar rôle on their colonists overseas. The war once over, however, the bonds of alliance were loosened and in 1655 the Dutch of New Amsterdam under their autocratic, vigorous Governor, Peter Stuyvesant, carried out their long-cherished plan and annexed the territory of their much weaker Swedish neighbours without even the expense of firing a shot. This gave the Dutch stations on the mouths of two of the great inland waterways, at New York and Philadelphia, and control of the coastline from Long Island Sound to the River Delaware. The result was that they not only divided in two the British colonies along the seaboard; they were also in a good position for penetrating into the interior of the continent.

Therefore it was scarcely surprising that when Britain and Holland, as the two rival sea powers of the seventeenth century, came to blows, the issue was joined not only in European waters, but also on the American continent. Charles II, recruiting volunteers from New England, despatched a strong force against New Amsterdam and demanded the surrender of the town. The fortifications were in poor repair; the Dutch Governor, Peter Stuyvesant, had alienated the loyalty of the settlers by his harsh administration, and as a result the city was in no position to resist. It yielded without bloodshed, and under its new proprietor, the Duke of York (later James II), changed its name from New Amsterdam to New York. The Dutch were not, however, molested. There was toleration of their religion and respect for their property. The vitality and capability of these Dutch settlers is demonstrated by the place their descendants still hold in the life of New York State and of the nation. The blood of the New Netherlands colonists still flows in the veins of the Vanderbilts, the Van Cortlands and, of course, the Roosevelts. The Dutch founders of New York were part of the rich mingled strains which have gone to make up America.

Meanwhile Virginia had been developing from a group of struggling settlements into a vigorous and enterprising colony. It had not been founded, like Plymouth and Massachusetts Bay, by colonists whose main ambitions were as much religious and political independence as they could get. From the first, Virginia had been principally a commercial enterprise, a colony run by a company whose headquarters were in London. Nevertheless, it was not long before Virginians began to lay claim to the rights of free-born Britons everywhere, to have a say in their own government. In fact it was in Jamestown, Virginia, that the first parliamentary body in America met, when in 1619 the Governor called together two representatives from each plantation to meet in the log church (it was the only building big enough to accommodate them) to deliberate on laws for the colony. This House of Burgesses, as it was called, became the Virginia counterpart of the House of Commons in Britain. The colonists were bringing to the New World the political ideas of their homeland: transplanted amidst new conditions, these ideas were to undergo strange changes until the colonists would claim as the rights of Britons more freedom than the mother country would be willing to give.

1619 saw another event, almost as important in the history of Virginia and America. 'About the last of August,' a Virginian wrote in his diary, 'came a Dutch man-of-war that sold us twenty niggers.' These were the first Negro slaves to be imported into English America. In the seventeenth century there was nothing about black slavery which offended the morality of either Puritan or Anglican, and it was only the unsuitability of the climate and the greater skill and experience required to farm in northern latitudes that prevented the northern colonies from importing slaves as well. In the south, however, the warm climate and the large plantations devoted to one simple crop, tobacco, made slave-owning possible and profitable, and the traffic in human flesh and blood begun by the Dutch warship in 1619 became a regular practice until it developed into the greatest organized and compulsory immigration in history. Virginia and the South grew to regard slavery as not merely natural, but also necessary, as they relied more and more on slave labour to work their farms and plantations.

It was these great plantations that gave life in Virginia its distinctive quality. Unlike the northern colonies, Virginia developed few towns. The line of settlement was along the great rivers which provided the natural means of communication. On their banks the settler laid out his tobacco plantation, so that he could easily ship his crop down to Jamestown, from there to export it to its final destination in England. The planter lived in his 'big house' surrounded by his Negro slaves in their cluster of rudely-built cabins. It might be twenty or thirty miles to the nearest white neighbour, so each plantation became self-sufficient for sustenance and defence, rather like the baron's manor of the Middle Ages.

Thus, although there was nothing particularly well-born about the colony's settlers, it was natural for Virginia to breed an aristocracy. The king gave land grants to those who won his favour. And when the strife in England between the King and Church on one side and Parliament and Puritan on the other reached the point of open civil war, ending in defeat for the king, it was to Virginia that many of the defeated party fled. In Virginia the Church of England was still the ruling religion and in Virginia an Englishman who had lost his estates could easily carve some more out of the spacious wilderness. So the restoration of 1660 was nowhere more popular than in Virginia, the colony whose loyalty to the crown had earned it the title of 'the old Dominion.'

But all this time the colony was growing, and as it grew it was developing its own problems and conflicts, different from those of old England. All along the flat plains of the seaboard the great plantations were multiplying, but as more and more settlers came in, often poor men with nothing to live on save what their own hands wrested from the soil, there was a greater demand for free lands and soon the small farmers pushed westwards beyond the plains into the 'Piedmont,' the foothills. Here there grew up a new class of colonials with interests different from those of the planters. The farmer of the Piedmont was not so concerned about the English tobacco market, because he lived off the produce of his own farm. What worried him was the risk of attack from the Indians whom his settlements were pushing back farther and farther each year. This conflict of interests came to a head in 1676 in Bacon's Rebellion, when the aristocratic Governor, Sir William Berkeley, attempted to penalize Nathaniel Bacon for having led the frontiersmen in an 'unauthorized' attack on the Indians. The rebellion was a failure, Bacon being struck down with a fatal fever, and his followers falling away for lack of a leader. But it attained some of its objects. It secured a revision of voting rights, giving the frontiersmen a larger share in the representation in the House of Burgesses, and it served notice that henceforward there were other elements in Virginia besides Royalists and patricians.

CHAPTER IV

The Proprietary Colonies

FEW religious groups suffered such persecution in seventeenth-century England as the Quakers. Their habit of holding sessions of silent contemplation instead of formal church services, their belief in a man's right to be guided by his own judgment and conscience alone, their eccentric mode of address, their refusal to pay tithes or taxes to support the Church of England and their opposition to war in every form – all this made them unpopular and often exposed them to hardship and cruelty. One of their converts was William Penn, a well-to-do young man in good standing at the court of Charles II. His father, Admiral Penn, had earned the king's gratitude for his influence in restoring him to his throne: he had also owing to him a debt of £16,000 which the king had incurred and never paid.

The Admiral's death, in 1681, gave William Penn the opportunity he was looking for. He exchanged his father's claim against the Crown for a grant of land in North America with the name of Pennsylvania and with powers which made William Penn both ruler and landlord. It was an enormous tract, almost as large as England and Wales combined: its size may be judged from the modern state of Pennsylvania, which is smaller by some 10,000 square miles than Penn's original grant. It was practically uninhabited and contained some of the richest lands in North America.

Thanks to Penn's wealth and organizing ability, the colony made an excellent start. Although he designed it primarily as a haven for the Quakers, he was eager to have any colonists who would work hard and live peaceably together. He therefore advertised his colony in a pamphlet which was translated into Dutch, French and German. It was a practical handbook which shows how sensibly Penn went about the business of planning his colony and how much he had profited from the experience of earlier settlers. 'They that go must wisely count the cost, for they must either work themselves or be able to employ others. A winter goes before a summer (this was what all the earlier settlers had learnt to their cost) and the first work will be country labour, to clear ground and raise provision; other things by degrees.'

In response to Penn's announcement many colonists offered themselves: not only Quakers from England and Wales, but also Germans of similar beliefs from the Rhineland and elsewhere. By the summer of 1683 three thousand immigrants had arrived. The Quakers lived up to Penn's precepts and were excellent colonists – hard-working, thrifty and peaceable. The last quality played an important part in the colony's success, since from the beginning Penn determined to try and live at peace with the surrounding Indians. He made a treaty at the outset which he and his fellow Quakers scrupulously kept. He treated them fairly, and was careful neither to sell them the white man's 'fire water', nor cheat them in business deals. As a result, while other colonies were constantly harassed by Indian wars, Pennsylvania enjoyed peace until in 1755 our war with France brought in the Indians as agents of each side.

The same wealth, carefulness and enterprise which organized the immigration remained in evidence when the colony got under way. It was not long before Philadelphia, laid out by Penn himself to be the capital of his colony, and symbolizing in its name his Quaker ideals, was a town of nearly four hundred houses, mostly of handsome brick surrounding spacious squares and served by good docks and a good anchorage. The plan of the city remains to this day virtually unchanged.

Before leaving Britain, Penn prepared a constitution and a set of laws for his colony. In 1682 he presented them to an assembly of freemen in Philadelphia who accepted them as 'The Great Law of Pennsylvania'. The 'Great Law' embodied many Quaker ideals which were much in advance of the normal practices of the period. It provided that prisons should be places for work and reform rather than mere houses of punishment. It allowed liberty for all religious beliefs, and gave no especial privileges for any one faith. In the government the people had a strong voice. All property holders could elect members to represent them in the council, a small body which proposed the laws, and the assembly, a larger body which passed them. At the head was the proprietor, Penn himself, but he often chose to be represented by a governor who had three votes in the council, but had no power of veto. The whole was a surprisingly humane and democratic government: Penn called it a 'Holy Experiment' – an experiment in Quaker ideals.

Between Virginia and Spanish Florida lay a vast tract of land almost unsettled. Spain laid claim to it, but had done nothing more. It had a difficult coastline, poorly provided with harbours, save at river mouths where great swamps infested with mosquitoes bred disease in the hot and humid summer months. It was unsuitable for colonization by individual pioneers or by poor groups who could not finance a large venture. But a group of well-to-do noblemen at the court of Charles II saw possibilities in the region. To eight of these, who included Lords Clarendon and Ashley, Charles II, first of all in 1663, and more extensively in 1665, granted all the land from Virginia to Florida.

This territory, the Carolinas, was regarded by these proprietors very much as a private estate, to be run for profit, leased to tenants or farmed by hirelings or slaves. They set out to recreate in Carolina in exaggerated form the system of a landed aristocracy which operated in Britain, with a church established according to the principles of the Church of England. John Locke, the English philosopher, was employed to draw up a ridiculous set of 'Fundamental Constitutions', which did more credit to his interest in the past than to his common sense or his knowledge of America. He attempted to cut up the colony into mediæval manors, each to be run on a feudal system, with a system of government so complicated and unworkable that his entire plan had to be scrapped.

In the practical business of settling and building the proprietors fortunately showed themselves to be more able. In the north, where North Carolina abuts on Virginia, an independent settlement was already existing, an overflow from Virginia, at Albemarle Sound. This slowly expanded southward and in 1690 was joined by a band of refugees from France, Huguenots who settled along the Pamlico river, thus contributing a new element to the varied races of British America. The first settlements actually organized by the proprietors were on the mouth of the Charles River, South Carolina, in 1670 and after ten years on a trial location moved to the site of the present Charleston in 1680. The town grew rapidly on its beautiful situation, a land-locked harbour where the rivers Ashley and Cooper meet. By 1682 an eye-witness wrote: 'The Town is regularly laid out into large and capacious streets ... In it they have reserved convenient places for building of a Church, Town House, and other public structures, an Artillery Ground for the exercise of their militia and Wharves for the convenience of their trade and shipping.' Charleston fulfilled its founders' promise and even to-day, when its commercial importance is largely a thing of the past, it retains in its streets and buildings the beauty of its original design. Much of the prosperity of the town was due to the Huguenots who early made their homes there. Their thrift and ability soon earned them a dominant place in the colony and many family names still prominent in South Carolina go back to these French settlers of 1680.

In South Carolina the climate and the soil made the production of two crops especially easy and profitable. The first of these was rice, which was grown along the river sides, in fields fertilized by flooding during the growing season. Only Negroes could work in such malaria-infested swamps; the result was the establishment of a system of large plantations even more splendid than those of Virginia, where a relatively few land-holders farmed their property with imported Negro slaves. In the 1740's indigo was introduced as a second staple crop, only slightly less profitable and equally suited to cultivation by slave labour. North Carolina, with cooler climate and fewer coastal swamps, was better suited to other crops, in particular tobacco. Here the small farmer could more easily make a living, but rivalry was keen with Virginia, who denied North Carolina tobacco growers the use of harbours for export.

CHAPTER V

The New England Way

WHILE these planned settlements of the South were being made under the smile of royal favour, the Puritan colonies of New England were developing a distinctive way of life of their own, as different from that of the other American colonies as from that of the old country.

Two things determined the New England way, the land and the religion. The land of New England is seldom fertile: in the main it consists of rocky, poor soil on which the farmer has to work hard to make a living. But it has a coastline that abounds in good harbours giving on to a sea that is rich in fish. Consequently the New Englander soon learnt that to make a living he must either be a thrifty, hard-working farmer or else he must become a sailor and find his food in the ocean. Both are hard lives that breed thrift, courage and independence, but leave little leisure for play or elegance. Out of his practice as fisherman the New Englander soon added a third occupation to these two, that of trader, when he found that ships which were strong enough to stand the gales off the coast of Maine could also sail to the West Indies or to Europe. But the habits formed on the farm or the fishing banks stayed with him when he went into commerce.

The New Englander was very conscious of his religion. It was to preserve it that he had crossed the Atlantic and he drew from it a set of principles which guided his everyday life, outside the church as well as within it. He believed that the Scriptures told him not merely in general principles but also in detail how God would have him behave. He applied them literally, word by word, and tried to set up a church and a government which would exactly duplicate those described in the Bible. He understood the Bible to say that Church and State should be one and he was convinced that only so could you make sure that the laws would be in accordance with what he understood the teaching of the Bible to be. Consequently in seventeenth-century Massachusetts no one could vote who was not a church member, and only those could become church members whom a church recognized as being godly persons and who, after careful apprenticeship, gave evidence of accepting the beliefs of the church. Such a faith bred an intolerance capable of nursing susperstition, and stimulating persecution. It bred a crop of legislation, founded often on misapplications of Old Testament texts, which could be harsh and narrow, such as the famous 'Blue Laws' of Massachusetts which banned the drama and made it an offence on the Sabbath 'to make mince pies, dance, play cards or play any instrument of music, except the drum, trumpet, and Jew's harp'.

But despite these shortcomings, the New Englander drew great strength from his religion. One result of his tendency to identify Church and State was that he applied the tests of right and wrong to his public affairs as well as his private ones, and demanded that governments should obey the law and respect the principles of justice just as much as their subjects. Moreover, if the New Englander was intolerant, he was also courageous and independent. It was largely the strength he drew from his rigid Calvinism that gave him the courage to face the threats of the Indian, the wilderness and the winter. Nor did his belief in the literal truth of the Scriptures lead him to neglect learning. On the contrary, within seven years of the founding of Massachusetts Bay Colony, the settlers had established the college of Harvard, a great achievement for so small and so poor a group. They followed this up with a system of schools, one in every village of fifty householders, so that soon every part of the colony was served by some kind of school, and New England became the leader of American education, 'the schoolmaster of America'.

Although the Massachusetts system of restricting votes to church members was a good deal less than democratic there was one important New England institution which gave a great training in self-government. Outside the one or two urban centres like Boston the usual form of settlement in New England was the 'township' or 'town' – that is to say a community large enough to feed and provide for itself, but not too large for the inhabitants to come together to the common centre of worship and, when the Indians attacked, to the stockade which could protect their cattle and their lives. This 'town' had a common pasture on which the inhabitants turned out their cattle, while the rest of the land was divided up on an equitable basis, according to size of family and the citizen's importance. There were thus no great landholdings like those in the South and no great extremes of wealth and poverty. Living together and working together, the pioneers developed a rough equality and for the settlement of their common concerns formed the habit of assembling in 'town meeting' and there, in debate and discussion, deciding at first hand how their own local government should be run. Thus at a time when the central government of colonies like Massachusetts or Connecticut was still far from democratic the farmers and pioneers were getting practice in managing their own immediate concerns for themselves, an experience in working democracy which was to stand them in good stead in the future.

It was not surprising that a state so highly individual as Massachusetts, which was also the most powerful of all the New England colonies, should soon find herself in difficulties with the mother country. Strongly Puritanical and independent in outlook, the colony was very suspicious of any control by Charles II and persistently broke the laws which the English parliament laid down for the control of trade with the colonies. Englishmen, for their part, with the new-found tolerance of the Restoration, watched with dismay the 'New England way' in religion with its persecution of rival faiths. In the Massachusetts of the 1650's it had led to the execution of four Quakers for 'heresy' and in the 1690's it sanctioned the ignorant and primitive hysteria which demanded over a score of executions in the witch-hunt at Salem.

Already in 1684 Massachusetts' indifference to the

Navigation Laws had led Charles II to annul her charter which had guaranteed a certain amount of self-government to the colony. In 1686 James II, who had come to the throne the previous year, decided to go a step further. These independent colonies in New England offended his sense of efficiency as well as impeding his ambitions for an absolutist régime in Britain. So, at one stroke, he abolished the popular assemblies in every colony and appointed Sir Edmund Andros to be Governor, not only of New England but also of New York and New Jersey, his new territory to be called the Dominion of New England.

Over this area Andros imposed an unpopular and oppressive government. He tried to introduce the Anglican church into Puritan New England and set out to raise taxes without the consent or even the cognizance of the popular assemblies. But his autocracy was short-lived; in 1688 he shared the fate of his royal master at home. With James's fall, Andros went, and the Dominion of New England broke up and governmental powers reverted to each colony. The disappearance of all central control was not without its drawbacks, because for certain purposes the colonies badly needed the benefits of combination – notably for defence – and the moment Andros was removed they just became separate and rather jealous units again. Even so, when Massachusetts, in 1691, got back her Charter, it was not as generous as the old one; she was allowed a good deal of self-government, but care was taken to see that the king kept certain powers of veto and appointment.

CHAPTER VI

Wars with Neighbours

By the end of the seventeenth century the planting of most of the British colonies along the Atlantic seaboard had been accomplished. A fringe of settlements, all under the British flag, ran from Maine to the Carolinas. But to the north, south and west of this fringe other European powers held varying degrees of sway. Spain, who by right of discovery still thought of herself as the proper claimant to both of the Americas, was in possession of Florida and an uncertain area along the top of the Gulf of Mexico. France, a more serious rival, had entered the American continent by way of that spacious river highway, the St Lawrence.

Early in the sixteenth century, Jacques Cartier, a Frenchman from St Malo, had explored the estuary of the St Lawrence, but it was not until the seventeenth century that the French, like the British, succeeded in making a permanent settlement on American soil. Their leader was a pilot by the name of Samuel de Champlain and it was he who in 1608 founded Quebec on a high, easily defensible cliff above the St Lawrence River. It was Champlain too whose explorations discovered the Great Lakes and so opened up to French settlers and traders the whole St Lawrence basin.

At first the development of French Canada proceeded only slowly. But in 1672 Colbert, the energetic Minister of Louis XIV, removed the colony from the control of the 'Hundred Associates', as its proprietors were called, and sent out Frontenac to be a vigorous and able Governor. Frontenac strengthened the French hold on the Great Lakes by constructing a chain of forts wherever the British might be likely to attack. Even more important was his enterprise in sending a Jesuit priest, Father Marquette, and an explorer, Joliet, to open up the Western territories. Their wanderings led them to the southern tip of Lake Michigan and then overland to the Mississippi. Once this link was discovered the next step was obvious; and five years later another French explorer, La Salle, sailed, in a ship of his own making, all the way down the Mississippi to its mouth.

By this voyage La Salle changed the whole basis of French power in America. In place of a thinly-populated settlement along the banks of the St Lawrence, cut off from Europe during all those months of winter when the St Lawrence is frozen over, La Salle opened up the prospect of a great

Western Empire extending in a huge arc from the estuary of the St Lawrence to the delta of the Mississippi and thus provided with two outlets to the sea, as well as a great system of waterways for its internal communications. To Spain this meant a threat to her hold on the Gulf of Mexico, but to Britain it might mean even more – the establishment of a French frontier at the back of all her Atlantic settlements which would restrict their growth as a dam holds back a stream.

All the same, if the settlement of North America had been left to its own impetus, it would probably have been a long time before New France and New England came into conflict. There was still land in plenty for both, and the frontiersmen, French and English alike, were not worrying much about the future of empires so long as their own day-by-day livelihood was unmolested. But in Europe the parent countries were always on the point of conflict, and the repercussions of their strife were immediately felt in America. Thus when in 1689 the War of the Rhenish Palatinate broke out in Europe, with Britain opposed to Louis XIV, Frontenac followed his royal master's orders and set out to conquer New York. Both sides, to their shame, stirred up the Indians to fight for them; much of the savagery and ruthlessness of the frontier wars is due to this fact. The war in Europe and America petered out in 1697 without any decisive issue, and the Treaty of Ryswick which concluded it restored all American boundaries. But by 1702 Britain and France were fighting again, this time in the War of the Spanish Succession, and again their colonists in America took up the struggle. The British suffered from the reluctance of the colonies to work together in common defence, Pennsylvania in particular contending that the war, which was fought mainly along the borders of New York and New England, was none of her concern. The British forces did, however, succeed in capturing Nova Scotia and this, together with Hudson's Bay and Newfoundland, was confirmed as British territory by the Peace of Utrecht in 1713.

But while Britain secured these gains in New England, French development proceeded apace in the West, particularly in the Mississippi valley. In 1718 they founded New Orleans and from there French settlers pushed their way up the river until Louisiana, as the French called it in honour of their king, became a vast, if thinly-populated, area of French domination.

The rivalry with which France and Spain menaced British America produced one beneficial result. In 1732 George II granted a Charter to a generous-hearted, enterprising Englishman, General Oglethorpe, to settle the area below South Carolina. Oglethorpe's desire was to do something for those unfortunates who had been sentenced to imprisonment for debt. A recent lightening of the laws had set a great many at liberty but, being without any money, they were little better out of prison than in it. Oglethorpe's colony of Georgia was designed to offer these a fresh start in life, with a little land of their own – fifty acres a head – and a liberal-minded government, which guaranteed religious toleration. However, the colony's growth proceeded at the expense of Oglethorpe's original plan: slaves were introduced, large plantations developed, as in South Carolina, and soon the yeoman farmers turned into frontiersmen and pushed inland for a living.

From the point of view of the British Crown, of course, the principal value of the colony was initially as a bulwark against the Spanish power in the New World. The 'War of Jenkins' Ear' broke out in 1739 between England and Spain and the border of Georgia and Florida soon became one of the battlefields of the rival powers. The Anglo-Spanish war soon merged in the larger conflict known to Europeans as the War of the Austrian Succession and to the colonists as King George's War, in which France joined Spain as a rival to British power in North America. This extended the area of conflict to the whole length of the Western frontier. New England was attacked and, counter-attacking in turn, captured the French fortress of Louisbourg, on Cape Breton Island, which commanded both the St Lawrence and the

Newfoundland fisheries. When the Treaty of Aix-la-Chapelle, which terminated the war in 1748, obliged the colonists to return this strategic stronghold to the French, they felt, not without justification, that their interests were being subordinated to the exigencies of European diplomacy. However, they did not have to wait very long for their revenge.

Of all the British colonies none was so ambitious for western development as Virginia. New England and New York were hemmed in by French Canada and in any event their surplus population could find an outlet on the sea, in fishing and in trading. The colonies of the 'deep' South were walled off from the interior by the formidable barrier of the Appalachians: moreover they had still land in plenty, in proportion to their small population. In Virginia the mountain passes, though difficult, were not impenetrable and on the further side of them the valleys of the Ohio and its tributaries offered land of tempting fertility. The plantation magnates of Virginia also had capital with which to explore and open up the country; in 1749 the Ohio Company, which they formed for this purpose, received from the British Crown a grant of a large and vaguely delimited tract beyond the mountains. But when the Virginians came to take up their territory they found that others had come before them; the French were already stationed on the banks of the great Ohio tributary, the Monongahela.

Virginia first of all tried polite measures, and a young Virginian, Major George Washington, a handsome youth of twenty-one, was deputed to inform the French that they were trespassing. The French, however, claimed as much right to the wilderness as the Virginians and stubbornly refused to move. Washington proceeded to try force, but the French were too strong for him; they captured his unfinished fort and built one of their own, Fort Duquesne, on the site of later-day Pittsburgh. War between Britain and France had broken out again – but begun, this time, not in Europe but in the forests of North America. Indeed, it took two years for the war to cross the Atlantic: it was not until

1756 that the Seven Years' War formally began with Britain and Prussia lined up against France, Austria and Russia.

Early in 1755 the British sent over General Braddock to be Commander-in-Chief in America, and under his command an effort was made to recover Fort Duquesne. But General Braddock refused to realize that war in North America, in trackless forests and against Indian braves, called for different tactics from the formal battles of Europe, in which each side drew up its troops in battle array and gave fight in the open. He refused to listen to American advice: as a result his force was ambushed and destroyed and he himself was killed. The French, now under the able command of Montcalm, improved their position by capturing all the forts commanding the approaches from New York State to the St Lawrence basin. Only young Washington's able generalship held back the tide.

At last, however, William Pitt succeeded to control in Britain, and under his direction a new and more vigorous policy was taken up. This led up to the campaign of 1759 in which year two British armies converged, the one up the Hudson and the other up the St Lawrence. While Amherst's forces were winning back the forts at Niagara, Crown Point, and Ticonderoga, James Wolfe conducted his daring raid on Quebec and, by his victory on the Plains of Abraham, struck a blow at the French power in Canada from which it never recovered. Thus by 1760 the war in North America was virtually over, though elsewhere Britain and France, with their respective allies, remained fighting until 1763. By the Peace of Paris in that year France surrendered all her possessions in North America, and Spain, who had joined France in time to share in her beating, also surrendered Florida, being compensated by the territory of Louisiana, made over to her by the French. Over the whole of the rest of America, from the Atlantic to the Mississippi, the British were left in sole control.

CHAPTER VII

After the Seven Years' War

THE obvious answer in 1763 to the question, 'What was the most important result for North America of the Seven Years' War?' was, certainly, 'The expulsion of the French'. But in fact the war had set in train many other developments which were to be even more significant for the future history of America. During the war an extra heavy strain had been imposed on the colonies and on the British Empire as a whole, and this laid bare much that both colonists and Englishmen had hitherto overlooked.

It had been possible, for example, for the colonists to keep throughout the war a flourishing commerce with the French both in Canada and in the West Indies. To trade with the enemy in wartime was little short of treasonous behaviour and as such gave great offence in Britain. But it gave offence for another reason, too. The eighteenth century held firmly to the 'mercantilist' theory that the way for a state to become commercially powerful was to restrict its trade as much as possible within its own dominions and to forbid colonies to do any business outside the Empire. Despite its obvious failure to do justice to the two-sided character of trade this 'mercantilist' theory held firm sway amongst the rulers of most eighteenth century European states. France enforced it very strictly, England rather less so, largely because the whole British system of colonial government was much laxer, allowing, as in North America, a great deal of self-government to the colonists. But even so Britain had passed several laws to regulate colonial trade in accordance with mercantilist principles, the most important being the Molasses Act of 1733 which placed a tremendously heavy duty on imports of sugar and sugar products from the French West Indies and so protected the British colonial sugar growers.

In peace these laws had been very loosely enforced, but

during the war enforcement had been tightened up, to the great annoyance of the colonists and in the face of their vigorous protests. Having had their attention drawn to the problem by these wartime breaches of the law, the British set to after the peace to tighten it up. The steps they took in this direction between 1763 and 1776 were, as we shall see, one of the chief reasons for the colonists' revolt.

Problems of trade were not the only worries left behind by the war. The war had cost a great deal of money. As a result of it the British national debt had doubled, from £70,000,000 to £140,000,000. Britain had borne most of the cost of the war in North America and most of the colonies had not paid even that share which they had agreed to. In New Jersey and Pennsylvania the Quakers had objected to the war on grounds both of religion and trade; colonies such as New Hampshire, Georgia and North Carolina had pleaded poverty, while others like Rhode Island thought the war none of their business because it did not actually touch their frontiers. But all had benefited from the removal of a powerful enemy and serious rival. Since the war had shown that the colonists could not be relied upon to volunteer funds for their joint defence, the British government felt obliged to devise some system of general taxation which would raise an adequate revenue – because, though France was beaten, the Indian menace remained. For this defence of North America the British government estimated that 10,000 troops would be needed, costing about £300,000 a year. How was this to be raised?

One other question was posed by the peace – what was to be done with the new territory west of the Appalachians which the peace transferred to Britain? For years, the colonists had been looking keenly westwards and Britain had encouraged westward expansion as a defence measure against the French. Such defence was no longer needed; in the changed post-war circumstances Britain feared that expansion would only provoke costly wars with the Indians for which Britain might have to pay, while the fur trade, which was what most interested British investors in the West, could be perfectly well carried on without extending the boundary of settlement. Finally, it was strongly felt in London that whatever policy was followed in settling the West it was essential that it should be a common policy, and the only place where that could be made, so long as you had thirteen separate colonies, was in Westminster.

With these problems on their hands, it would have taken all the patience and wisdom of both the Americans and the British combined to find a solution satisfactory to both. But in each country the ablest men had their attention distracted by internal political troubles: consequently the post-war problems of North America either suffered from neglect or became mixed up with other sources of strife within the thirteen colonies or within Britain itself. The truth was that on both sides of the Atlantic big changes were taking place: in America they were proceeding very fast – so fast indeed as to be properly called revolutionary, and certainly too fast for any calm and patient elucidation of difficult problems.

In Britain a struggle was developing between the king and all those leaders of opinion who resented his attempts to bring Parliament directly under his control. They did not want, save for a few 'Radicals', to go to the logical extreme and make Parliament completely and genuinely representative of all classes in the nation but they did feel, as Mr. Dunning emphatically stated, 'that the power of the Crown has increased, is increasing, and ought to be diminished'. They disliked the whole system of patronage and 'influence' by which the king tried to secure that only those members should be returned to Parliament who would support his policies and carry out his orders. In opposing this system the Whigs naturally opposed the policies that went with it. One of the subjects which bulked large in George III's policies was, of course, North America. The Whigs were, generally speaking, right about North America, and George III was wrong, but one of the results of their strife was that neither side studied the problem on anything approaching its merits – most of the time it was simply a pawn in the bitter contest for control of the British constitution.

In America, too, there were divisions. Just as in Britain, there was wide dissatisfaction at the existing system. In most of the colonies both the right to vote and the right to hold office were restricted to a minority of the inhabitants, those who possessed a fair amount of property. These were, in the main, the business men and the planters, with the business men more important in Pennsylvania and points North, and the planters dominant in Maryland and points South. Massachusetts, New York and Pennsylvania were the states in which commerce and industry counted for most. Here were the principal industries of young America, shipbuilding, distilling, iron and steel. Here, too, were the main centres of American commerce – Salem, Boston, New York, Philadelphia – from which American merchantmen put out in increasing numbers to carry American products overseas or to bring home purchases made abroad or, very often, to act as carriers for other people's trade, the good ships and good seamanship of the Americans having made them very popular as the middlemen of the North Atlantic. South of Pennsylvania industries and seafaring counted for less. Here, notably in Virginia and South Carolina, the great staple crops of tobacco, rice and cotton were the backbone of the planters' wealth: upon the success of these crops and the price they fetched in overseas markets depended the prosperity of these colonies.

In the Northern and Middle colonies the principal cleavage in political power was between the well-to-do investors and traders on the one hand and the poor of the cities or the hinterland on the other. In the Southern colonies the line of cleavage was also a territorial division. The planters, in the main, inhabited what was known as the Tidewater, the flat, fertile strip between the sea and the hills (running inland as far as the tide ran up the rivers' sluggish estuaries). Behind them rose the Piedmont, the foothills of the Appalachians, where the small farmer, the frontiersman, was trying to make a living. Unlike the planter, he did not rely on producing one staple crop for export so much as on trying to grow enough of everything to be self-supporting. He probably was not a slave-owner, at any rate not on a large scale. His eyes were fixed not so much on markets overseas as on the prospects of new lands in the West.

But it would be a mistake to think that these internal differences prevented the colonists from acting together when circumstances required it, or that the issues over which they quarrelled overshadowed those on which they agreed. While in Virginia, for example, planter and piedmonter quarrelled over their representation in the House of Burgesses, both agreed in not wanting the House to be controlled by decisions made in London. In this sense the differences within the colonies were much less serious than those in Britain. In Britain the ardent Whigs who, like Barré, fought tooth and nail against the personal rule of George III, felt so bitterly opposed to the king's party that they openly welcomed the 'rebellious' colonists as allies in a common cause, preferring to see the Empire break up than have the power of the Crown consolidated. In America, on the other hand, north and south, rich and poor, came by degrees to forget their differences and unite in a common resistance to 'the tyrant George'.

CHAPTER VIII

Tea and Taxes

THE first point on which the plans of the British government and the wishes of the colonists came into conflict was the disposition of the western lands, the great territories, formerly French, which passed under the British flag as a result of the Treaty of Utrecht. One or two colonies, like Delaware, whose frontiers did not give upon this new hinterland, were uninterested in the prospects of expansion westwards, were indeed opposed to it for fear that it would drain off their population, as in fact it did. But the great majority of Americans were of one mind – they wanted to see the

West 'opened up'. It was their El Dorado – whether they planned to settle, or hunt, or trap or merely explore, they all felt a common passion to 'go West'.

Not so the British government. They were worried in the first place by the risks of arousing the Indians. No sooner had the war ended than the Indians of the Ohio, goaded by what they felt to be the menace of the white man to their lands and their hunting, united under their talented chieftain, Pontiac, to wipe out the white intruders along the whole frontier from New York to Virginia. The damage they inflicted was severe and, as the British truly pointed out, it took the king's redcoats to suppress the rising which the colonists themselves were unequal to meeting. The British did not want to provoke any similarly costly onslaughts.

To meet the immediate problem it was decided to stop further settlement until the Indians were pacified and a definite land policy could be worked out. So in 1763 a Royal Proclamation stopped all settlement west of the crest of the Appalachians and wiped out all previous land grants. Shelburne, the British minister responsible for the Act, intended it as a merely temporary measure until a proper scheme of colonization could be worked out, but within a few months of the enactment Shelburne was forced out of office and his successors accepted it as permanent. The colonists were convinced that it was merely a device for robbing them of their western lands in order to benefit land speculators in London, and from the first they determined to ignore it. In their twos and threes, or their two hundreds and three hundreds, settlers with axe and musket took to the trail, making new tracks through the mountain passes and new foes among the Indian tribes, and caring not a button for laws drafted in the remote offices of Whitehall.

To protect the frontier of 1763 against further 'conspiracies of Pontiac' the Imperial government had to have more money. Some of it, the English argued, ought to come from those colonists for whose safety the debts of the Seven Years War had been incurred. The colonists, on the other hand, said they were already paying as much as they could afford.

In 1764 the Sugar Act was passed, putting new customs duties on sugar and luxury goods imported into North America. The colonists disliked paying extra duties, but they disliked even more the stringent regulations of the Act which made it much harder to dodge payment than it had previously been. The Act introduced no new principle: it was in line with the long-standing mercantilist policy. But hitherto that policy had been so loosely enforced that the colonists had not felt it. Now, for the first time, practice was coming into line with theory and the profits from the rich trade with the West Indies would be reduced in fact as well as in name. It particularly affected the big distilling trade of New England and all those who in tavern or at home refreshed themselves with its products. That was why, as John Adams said later, 'rum was an essential ingredient in the American Revolution'.

The next Act, a year later, had the same disastrous characteristic of falling on everybody and on all sections of the country alike. The Sugar Act having failed to bring in more than about one-seventh of the sum needed, Grenville, George III's new Chancellor of the Exchequer, had the idea of imposing a tax, to be collected by means of stamps, on all newspapers, licences, bills, legal documents, etc. – rather as bank cheques bear 2d. stamps – representing a tax paid to the government. There were few people with votes or property whom this did not touch: lawyers and journalists, persons especially skilled in politics and the arts of public persuasion, were particularly affected. The Act provoked an immediate outburst of popular rage. It was not merely that mobs rioted and in Boston burnt down the Governor's mansion and despoiled his library. Respectable men formed themselves into groups of resistance, organized a stoppage of business as a protest, and openly violated the terms of the Act.

The storm burst first in Virginia. Young Patrick Henry, who had gained political skill and reputation as a spokesman in the House of Burgesses for the claims of the upstate farmers against the Tidewater planters, now came forward as the leader of the whole colony against the British Government. On May 30th, 1765, he introduced in the House of Burgesses seven resolutions against the Stamp Act and supported them by a flow of oratory which immediately caught the nation's ear. 'Cæsar', said Patrick Henry to the Burgesses, 'had his Brutus, Charles I his Cromwell, and George III ...' – there were cries of 'Treason!' from the Speaker and from members – 'and George III', continued Patrick Henry, 'may profit by their example. If that be treason, make the most of it.'

If it was not treason it was certainly a battle-cry around which public indignation gathered. Henry's denunciation of the Stamp Act as an outrageous attempt at taxation without representation evoked immediate echoes all over the colonies. The next step was taken by Massachusetts, which sent a circular letter to all the colonies inviting them to send delegates to New York to discuss the problem. They met in the October of the same year, a historic occasion, because for the first time the colonies were taking counsel together, recognizing that although they might be separate colonies they nevertheless had certain interests in common. Gadsden, the delegate from South Carolina, drove the point home forcibly. 'We should stand upon the broad common ground of national rights ... There ought to be no New England man, no New Yorker, known on the continent, but all of us Americans'. The delegates of nine colonies met in joint session and made their common protest, in terms similar to those of the Virginia House of Burgesses – 'no taxation without representation'.

From New York the argument shifted to London, where Parliament debated on the troubles the Stamp Act had aroused, and the king's men wrangled with his opponents as to whether the colonists were within their rights or no. The official British argument was that, while it was true that the colonists did not directly elect members to the Parliament at Westminster which was taxing them, yet they were for all that, as the phrase went, *virtually* represented – the theory being that members of parliament underwent some miraculous change in the moment of their election by which, when they entered the House, they became guardians of the interests not of any particular place, but of the whole commons of England – and so, by extension, of the king's subjects overseas. To which the colonists had a short reply – that whatever the theory their interests were sadly neglected in practice.

The defenders of the colonists, like Pitt, for the most part without asserting that Parliament could never tax the colonies, argued that the Stamp Act was an *internal* tax such as only the colonial legislatures could levy and that in passing it Parliament was exceeding its proper powers. In strict law, no doubt, there was something to be said on each side, but the fate of the Act was decided not by the debate in Parliament, but by the action of the colonists. When the ships bearing the stamps arrived at Philadelphia flags were flown at half-mast and bells tolled as for a day of mourning. In New York the citizens organized a Watch Committee to see that no stamps were bought, and to threaten possible purchasers with reprisals. Along the whole Atlantic seaboard there was no one who dared to try and collect the tax.

The colonists went even further. Forming themselves into organizations called 'Sons of Liberty', they everywhere agreed to boycott all British imports. So effective was their policy that merchants in Britain soon saw their livelihood threatened and bombarded Parliament with petitions for the repeal of the Act. The king meanwhile had been forced to accept a Whig Minister, Lord Rockingham, who was far more sympathetic to the colonists' case than Grenville. So in March, 1766, the hated Act was repealed. The colonists hailed the repeal with loyal gratitude and enthusiasm. Statues of George III and Pitt were erected to celebrate the event. It was a moment when mother-country and colonists seemed to be speaking the same language of affection again. Could each side have shown restraint and understanding the moment might have lasted. But events were to turn out otherwise.

The Rockingham Ministry which had repealed the Stamp Act was too weak to survive for long. Its place was taken by a government headed by Pitt, now the Earl of Chatham. Pitt was, of course, a good friend of the colonists, but here again bad fortune intervened. Pitt was taken ill and the administration of the colonies drifted into the hands of the Chancellor of the Exchequer, Charles Townshend, who had no understanding of the colonial point of view. In order to make the Ministry popular at home, he reduced the British land tax; to make up the deficit, he placed new import duties in America on a number of articles, such as lead, paper and tea, and, to see that the duties were not evaded, he put additional customs officers in the American ports and gave them wide powers of search. Worst of all, he used some of the money so obtained to pay the royal governors and royal judges in the colonies. The colonists felt that this cut at the very root of their liberties. Hitherto, though the king had appointed these officials, it had been the colonial assemblies who paid them. In this way the colonists could keep some control over their governors: under Townshend's scheme this control would be lost.

Indeed, it soon became evident that even the assemblies themselves, the parliaments of the colonies, were not safe. When in 1768 Massachusetts and Virginia protested, by circular letters, against the Townshend Acts, the governors dissolved the assemblies. This was what Charles I had done to his Parliament, and the colonists, many of them descendants of the seventeenth-century Roundheads, noticed the analogy with alarm. When British troops arrived in Boston to assist the Customs officers in carrying out their duties, they were met with hostility. In March of 1770 this broke out into an open clash between the troops and a Boston crowd. Four Bostonians were killed: it was not a large number, but it was the first encounter of its kind; tempers were running high, and the general disposition was to exaggerate the incident. In a few days indignation had spread all over New England at what immediately became known as 'The Boston Massacre'.

Once again the British Government bowed before the storm it had provoked. Lord North, who was now in power

– a willing tool of George III – repealed all the Townshend Duties except, 'for the sake of principle', a 3d. per lb. tax on tea. The repeal, plus a welcome trade revival in New England, quietened the agitation of the colonists. But that tax on tea was to prove costly indeed, and the 'principle' was going to lose a continent.

For three years there was calm. There was a fair measure of prosperity, the British government refrained from further measures, and the moderate elements in the colonies were not anxious to see matters pushed to a point where further disturbances must result. But in 1773 Parliament, packed with the king's creatures and submissive to Lord North, interested itself again in the fatal question of tea. The East India Company had been given a monopoly on all tea exported to the colonies and, in order to sell it cheaply in North America, the Company decided to sell it through its own agents instead of through the colonial merchants, as before. The effect was to deprive the colonial merchants of a good deal of business. Reflecting on the blow, they asked themselves, 'If the British do this to our tea, what will they do to the rest of our trade?' Everywhere there was resentment, but in Massachusetts, where there was a well-organized group of extremists eager to translate resentment into violence, a band of young men disguised as Mohawk Indians went aboard the tea ships as they lay in Boston harbour and dumped their contents into the sea. Their 'tea party' had two characteristic results. It made it harder for the moderates in the colonies to control events; more and more the extremists had things their own way. And in England inflamed official opinion became determined to meet violence with repression. The punishment for the crime, since the young men could not be identified, was laid on Boston as a whole: the port was closed until the cost of the tea was paid for. To check the unruly spirit of Massachusetts, the colony's charter was revised, and the government was brought much more closely under royal control. Lastly, since the local courts could not be trusted to convict officials who had opposed the Crown, an Act was passed by which they could be taken out of the colony and tried in Britain. These Acts, passed in the spring of 1774, seemed to mark the end of self-government in the colony. Their popular name, the 'Intolerable Acts', reflected the colonists' feelings. What could not be borne, men said, must be ended.

All over the American colonies a wave of support and sympathy for Massachusetts was felt. In Virginia, when the Governor dismissed the House of Burgesses at Williamsburg for their anti-British expressions, the Burgesses merely moved the scene of their deliberations to the nearby Raleigh Tavern and from there sent out a call to all the colonists to send representatives to a congress in September.

By the time the Congress met the colonists had another grievance to add to the rest. To provide for the government of Canada, with its French-speaking population, Parliament passed the Quebec Act. The Quebec Act was in many ways an excellent measure: it guaranteed to the French the right to their religion, which was Catholicism, and to their own laws. But the colonies were worried because it did not grant the French a legislature of their own – in the light of the recent Intolerable Acts they asked themselves whether this meant that Britain was hostile to all legislatures in America – and they also resented the boundaries which the Act fixed, extending Canada as far as the Ohio and the Mississippi. Was not the Act another device for excluding Americans from the West? It was in this spirit of suspicion and resentment that the delegates met in Philadelphia on September 5th, 1774, for the first 'Continental Congress'.

CHAPTER IX

From Protest to Independence

At the Continental Congress all the colonies except Georgia were represented, and the delegates they sent included some of the ablest men in America. But the Massachusetts radicals soon got control of the proceedings and what came out of the Congress was a good deal more extreme than many delegates intended when it began. What came out of the Congress was first of all a protest against the Coercive Acts and a Declaration of Rights and Grievances, secondly new agreements to stop all trade with Britain and all consumption of British goods as long as the Coercive Acts remained in force, and thirdly, 'The Association'. 'The Association' provided for a system of committees in every district whose job it was to see that the boycott on British goods was observed and that merchants who broke it were denounced. 'The Association' was, of course, not a constitutional body, but something which worked outside the regular machinery of colonial governors and assemblies. This very fact made it easier for extremists to gain control of it, and it did much to force the pace, compel moderates to swim with the current and conservatives to think twice before resisting.

Meanwhile in Britain the friends of America – the Chathams, the Shelburnes and the Burkes – were out of office and helpless. The king and his willing servant Lord North were determined to make no concessions. 'The die is now cast', the king had said, 'the Colonies must either submit or triumph', and the British reply to the Continental Congress was a retort in kind, the New England Restraining Act, which, in reply to America's refusal to trade with Britain, forbade Britons to trade with America. But before copies of the Act could reach American soil the quarrel had passed from words to blood. The long-smouldering resentment against the British redcoats quartered in Massachusetts to enforce the 'Intolerable Acts' broke into fire. For some time Massachusetts men had been secretly arming and training in anticipation of hostilities. They called themselves 'minute men', because they held themselves ready to set off and fight at a minute's notice. One night in April, 1775, the notice came. Word had reached General Gage, the British Commander, that the Massachusetts patriots had collected arms and stores at Concord, a village outside Boston: he sent his men to seize them. But Paul Revere, one of the minute men, got in ahead of him. He rode through the Massachusetts countryside all night giving the signal to his colleagues, with the result that when the redcoats, after a night of marching, appeared in Lexington in the morning they found the Massachusetts men barring the road to Concord. Shots were fired and eight Americans were killed. The War of Independence had begun. As Emerson reflected fifty years later:

> Here once the embattled farmers stood
> And fired the shot heard round the world.

The redcoats never got through to Concord. As they withdrew to Boston the farmers sniped at them from every hedgerow, killing and wounding almost 250 men.

A month later the second Continental Congress met, again in Philadelphia, to consider the new situation. It responded to the stirring appeal of Patrick Henry, 'It is vain, sir, to extenuate the matter. Gentlemen may cry "peace, peace", but there is no peace. The war is actually begun! ... Our brethren are already in the field! Why stand we here idle?' Congress agreed with him, recognized the irregulars of Massachusetts as the nucleus of an army, and appointed Colonel George Washington as Commander-in-Chief. But even before he arrived to take up his command further engagements had been fought. Bunker Hill, outside Boston, which saw the next engagement, might be a defeat for the patriots, but it disproved the assumption that a farmers' army could not stand up to the regulars. And further north an enterprising young leader, Ethan Allen, with his 'Green Mountain Boys', recruits from his own state of Vermont, assisted by dashing young Benedict Arnold, seized Fort Ticonderoga and Crown Point, the important posts of Lake Champlain. By the spring of 1776 Washington was able to force the last redcoat to evacuate Boston, leaving by sea for Halifax.

So far Americans had been fighting not for independence, but merely for what they felt to be their rights as British subjects. As late as the spring of 1776 the officers in George

Washington's mess were loyally drinking the toast of 'the King'. It had been felt that if only George III would repeal his oppressive Acts, if only Parliament would recognize the right of the colonists to manage their own affairs, it would not be too late to patch up the quarrel. But although this might have been possible ten years earlier, those who hoped for it in 1776 were closing their eyes to the facts. So much had happened since the quarrel began. At first the matters of dispute had seemed just legal questions – could the British Parliament tax the colonies, could it fix boundary lines and revoke charters? But beneath the surface of these legal arguments big changes had been taking place in the thinking of most Americans.

In the first place they had come to think of themselves as *Americans*. They had begun to have a sense of unity, of being one nation instead of being thirteen colonies. Along with this they had rather lost their sense of being Britons. Britain had always been a long way off: it often took six months to get an answer to a letter. That did not matter so much when the colonies were small, weak and isolated and had no choice but to look to the mother country, however distant, for protection. Now, however, with the French menace removed, the colonies had much less to fear, and furthermore they had learnt, during those dozen years of struggle with Britain, that, united, they were no longer so weak, that in fact they were strong enough to resist Britain with some success. At the same time as they ceased to be *dependent* on Britain, they also began to feel *different* from her. As Americans they were thinking differently and behaving differently from their kinsmen in the old country. Some of these differences, though important, were not serious enough to drive a wedge between the two countries. But, as the struggle between America and Britain deepened, one difference began to count for more and more.

The England of the eighteenth century was an aristocratic country, that drew a hard line of distinction between the nobleman and the commoner, and in the main concentrated wealth, political power and privilege in the hands of a very small number of people. By contrast with other European countries the rule of the English aristocracy was humane, just, and even generous, but seen through the spectacles of an American, it appeared harsh, proud and oppressive. America had its aristocrats, but they never attained to the power of the great Whig and Tory families of England. When consequently there broke out all over Europe the new and revolutionary theories of political equality there was no country in which the seed of the democratic idea so quickly took root as in America. Throughout the colonies there were very few old-established families with claims to leadership like those of Britain. There were few great inherited estates, and in any case, with plenty of land always available on the frontier, there was no class of economically dependent agriculturists. The idea that all men were equal took on a new reasonableness in a country of easy movement and free land. What in Britain was being demonstrated by political theory and argument in America won the immediate acceptance of a natural law – at least wherever vested interests had not entrenched themselves in the contrary assumption.

Then in 1776, at the crucial moment, there appeared in America a short pamphlet which bore the name *Common Sense.* Its author was Thomas Paine, a discharged customs officer who had emigrated from England to Pennsylvania two years before. The pamphlet sold 100,000 copies within four months and its effect was tremendous. To thousands of Americans it proved beyond dispute that this new ideal of democracy, of the rights of man, could never be realized as long as America was under the rule of a British king and a Parliament principally composed of placemen or aristocrats. If Americans would be free and equal, Paine said, they must also become independent. For the first time the ideas of independence and equality were put together, and in Paine's crisp, stirring language they proved irresistible. As they read men found their doubts vanish. Their minds were made up: since George III would not let them be free there was nothing for it – they must win independence.

The new urge for independence immediately found expression in the Congress. Virginia's delegate, Richard Henry Lee, at the instructions of his home state, proposed the motion, 'That these United Sates are, and of right ought to be, Free and Independent States'. His motion was carried and a committee was appointed to act upon it. Out of this committee, and from the pen of the principal member, Thomas Jefferson, came the Declaration of Independence. Congress adopted it on July 4th, 1776, a day forever after to be commemorated as Independence Day, traditionally celebrated by fireworks and jubilation.

Without the Declaration of Independence, for all its factual inaccuracies, the history of the United States cannot be understood. In a few hundred words of forceful, sonorous and majestic English prose it presents the American case for independence – what the overwhelming majority of Americans felt the facts to be in 1776. Here are set out what they felt to be their grievances, which impelled them to break away from a government too 'tyrannical' to grant them their rights. These grievances, some real, some imagined, have now been forgotten, and had the Declaration been merely a catalogue of these it would have been a forgotten document, too. But by a stroke of genius the first two paragraphs of the Declaration contain a statement of the positive aims of the new United States, in language so eloquent and at the same time so directly comprehensible as to exercise a compelling influence on the whole course of American history.

'We hold these truths to be self-evident, that all men are created equal, that they are endowed by their Creator with certain unalienable Rights, that among these are Life, Liberty and the pursuit of Happiness. That to secure these rights Governments are instituted among Men, deriving their just powers from the consent of the governed. That whenever any Form of Government becomes destructive of these ends, it is the Right of the People to alter or to abolish it, and to institute a new Government, laying its foundation on such principles and organizing its powers in such form, as to them shall seem most likely to effect their Safety and Happiness.'

These words expressed then and still continue to express the ideals that lie behind American democracy. Abraham Lincoln was speaking the truth not merely about himself, but also about a great mass of American democrats, when he confessed, 'I have never had a feeling, politically, that did not spring from the sentiments embodied in the Declaration of Independence'.

Jefferson did not realize in the fury of his resentment against the 'tyranny' of George III, how much his Declaration was in the truly British tradition of self-government. His ideas were in fact a development of the thoughts of the British seventeenth-century philosopher, John Locke, the apologist for the peaceful Revolution of 1688. What Jefferson was doing was carrying these thoughts one stage further and applying them to the actions of a British government which had forgotten its own ideals. He was in fact reminding Britons as well as Americans of their own political traditions, and liberal-minded men in Britain as well as in America hailed Jefferson's Declaration as a new call to freedom.

Just as in Britain there were Britons outside the government who were sympathetic to the ideals of the Declaration of Independence, so in America there were Americans, a numerous minority though with little say in Congress, who opposed it. They were the Loyalists, who felt either an old-fashioned blind loyalty to the king, irrespective of what his policy might be, or else opposed the movement towards democracy as such, or else clung to the belief that, though George III was in the wrong, there were other ways for the colonists to establish their rights than by making war. These Loyalists, though principally consisting of the well-to-do and the well-born, were by no means confined to that class. There was a large number of them, ranging from the extremists, who fled to Canada rather than acquiesce in the Revolution, to the mere passive resisters, who without openly opposing the war refused to assist it and always threw their weight on the conservative side of any political issue. But their existence is a further proof of the fact that the American War of Independence was really a civil war, a war in which the two opponents were divided not by the Atlantic Ocean, but by ways of thinking about how men ought to live and how they ought to be governed. On this issue the majority opinion in America was ahead in 1776 of the majority opinion in Great Britain, and in consequence the war took the form of a struggle for American independence from British rule. But on both sides of the Atlantic there was division, and the fighting between 'colonials' and 'redcoats' was paralleled inside America by the quarrels of Republicans and Loyalists and in Britain by the controversies between King's men and Reformers.

This had, of course, a direct effect on the actual conduct of the war. Had George III been able to call upon the full resources and loyal support of his country he would have had little difficulty in reducing the Americans to subjection. So reluctant were the British to enlist for the American war that the king had no choice but to hire German mercenaries, while many British officers were resigning their commissions rather than fight their fellow-countrymen overseas. Although his own control of the corrupt political machinery enabled him to keep a voting majority in Parliament, George III had to face throughout the war, both in the Commons and the Lords, a continuous fire of opposition from such weighty Parliamentary figures as Chatham, Fox and Burke, men who felt, not only that Americans had much justice on their side, but also that if George III won his American war the next victim of his lust for power would be the British Parliament itself. Many people felt that if Americans were subjugated, Englishmen would not long remain free.

The presence of Loyalists in America operated as a similar kind of drag on the American war effort. Some of the Loyalists formed themselves into actual regiments for the king – particularly in New York City and State, where they outnumbered the insurgents. Often, moreover, Loyalists who were not actually fighting would aid the British by acting as spies and informers. From this arose an intense bitterness of feeling, republican Americans regarding such behaviour as the lowest form of treason.

But in organizing his army Washington suffered as much from apathy as from hostility among his fellow Americans. There were some whose minds were just not on the war at all, like the frontiersmen in the West, who were more excited about following Daniel Boone into the new lands of Kentucky than in defeating the redcoats along the Tidewater. There were others – and these were the great majority – who were prepared to turn out and fight the British when their own state or county was invaded but who could not realize that if Virginia was to be safe it could only be when Massachusetts or New Jersey were also cleared of the enemy. It was taking the colonists a little while to think of themselves as Americans first and Virginians or New Yorkers only second. And this tendency was strengthened by the dislike almost everyone had for a standing army. To turn out when the danger was acute and disband when it was over, or when the weather became too bad for campaigning – that was the kind of soldiering the Americans were disposed to, and it took all Washington's powers of leadership, plus several bad defeats, before they realized that a professional army like King George's could not be beaten on part-time soldiering.

CHAPTER X

The War of Independence

STRUNG loosely along the length of the Atlantic seaboard, the thirteen rebellious colonies or, as they now called themselves, the United States, were separated by vast distances and hampered by poor communications. The weakest link in the chain was New York, where the Loyalists were numerous and where the British, who seized the city with very little difficulty in the summer of 1776, were in a strong position for both sea and land warfare. New York City commanded the southern end of the great Hudson waterway which, by the way of Lake Champlain in the north, was the natural route to Canada. If the British could dominate the Hudson valley they would split New England from the Middle and Southern States and could then by their command of the seas reduce each half independently. In 1776, with Canada and New York City already in their hands, they seemed in a very good position to do this. Burgoyne was sent to Canada, with instructions to move south by way of Lake Champlain, and General Howe from New York was to advance northwards and meet him at Albany.

Unfortunately for the British, General Howe tried to do more than this. He thought he would strike at the main army in the Middle States first, the army which in the summer of 1777 was under Washington's command in Pennsylvania. He succeeded to some extent in this. Washington was beaten at Brandywine and Congress had to flee from Philadelphia, the city which the United States had made their capital. But the price of Howe's victory was a loss of time. Burgoyne, advancing south from Canada, as arranged, found no one coming up to meet him, and by the time he reached Saratoga in upper New York State he was forced, by reason of inferior numbers, to surrender.

This was a great victory for American arms, but the results were not immediately apparent. What most observers saw in the winter of 1777-78 was a much more depressing picture. Howe was wintering comfortably in Philadelphia while Washington's army, ill-clothed, unpaid and underfed, was shivering in the fields of nearby Valley Forge. Congress, the official government of the United States, was ignominiously taking refuge in the town of York, torn by internal jealousies and fears. Only Washington's own high character kept the army in being during these difficult months.

Later legend has fastened many stories, like that of the famous cherry tree, on to Washington's name which can claim only the slenderest basis of fact. What these stories do show is the impression Washington's honesty, wisdom and courage made on those who knew him. He came of a prominent Virginian family, whose ancestors, defeated Royalist country gentlemen, had emigrated to America after the Civil War and started the family fortunes anew. While quite young he had had to assume the responsibilities of managing a large estate, owing to his father's early death; at twenty-one he was a Major entrusted with the difficult task of negotiating with the French in western Pennsylvania, just before the Seven Years' War. His notable success in that conflict, as commander of the Virginia Militia, prepared him for his greater rôle later on, but when Congress appointed him to lead the army of the new republic he came not as a professional soldier, but as a Virginia landowner reluctantly giving up his quiet country life in response to the call of his country.

Few generals have done so much with so little. The army he commanded at Valley Forge was pathetically small, numbering not much more than 5,000 men. They were all volunteers, paid, not by Washington or by Congress, but by their own separate states or even towns. Consequently Washington had very little power of control over his forces beyond the discipline inspired by respect for his own character. If a state decided to withdraw the troops from his army he had no power to refuse to let them go.

This, in turn, proceeded from the weakness of the Congress. The thirteen states had rushed into war without very much thought of the kind of government they would need to conduct it. The Congress consisted of delegates from each of the states: it had very little power of its own and was much more like a conference than a government. It could only *ask* the individual States to subscribe to the cost of the war, or to send troops to Washington's army. It was entirely up to them to obey or refuse as they wished. Thus for everything he wanted, men, money, arms and supplies, Washington had to come to Congress and beg, and Congress in turn had to beg of its component states. Washington had to be not only a general in the field, but a pleader and a politician at home.

At last the snows at Valley Forge melted, and Washington's army, whose general had shared every privation of the winter with his soldiers, looked out on a world in which his confidence was shown to be justified. Benjamin Franklin, the United States ambassador at Paris, had persuaded the French that the victory of Saratoga proved that the new nation would be a worth-while ally, and in March 1777 France took the opportunity to declare war on Britain. This not only gave George III a new and serious enemy: it also helped the Americans where they were weakest, on the sea. The British could now no longer move their troops from point to point along the Atlantic coast with impunity. The French, besides supplying a fleet of their own, lent the Americans vessels for them to sail themselves. For the first time there was an American navy, and such daring seamen as Captain Paul Jones began to strike at the British in the element of their traditional supremacy, the sea.

Despite this aid, success for the Americans was slow in coming. Though the British had been foiled in their attempts either to seize the Hudson Valley or to knock out Washington's force in the Middle States, they were able to land a considerable force in the South and capture and hold Savannah. At last in 1780 two new factors of strength were added to the American cause. The severity of the British blockade added a new member to the anti-British coalition, when Holland, objecting that the British right of search interfered with her trade, allied herself with France and Spain. The despotic Louis XVI, who had been a little lukewarm in the aid he was giving the republican Americans, was at last persuaded to send troops as well as ships and money. This was due principally to the influence of Lafayette, a young French nobleman who, fired by admiration for the ideals of the young republic, had offered his services to Washington and immediately became his devoted friend.

The Americans still had difficulties and disappointments to contend with, the greatest of which was the treason of one of their ablest generals, Benedict Arnold, who offered to sell West Point, the fort on the Hudson, to the British, thereby making his name a byword in American history for unpatriotic behaviour. But in spite of this the Americans now had the ingredients necessary for victory. Washington had now made a real army, French aid had assumed substantial proportions, and the British were at war in too many oceans to keep their dominance in the North Atlantic. Thus it came about that when the British general Cornwallis, after a successful march northwards from South Carolina, was hemmed in by Washington on that peninsula of Virginia in Chesapeake Bay which ends in the port of Yorktown, it was not the British fleet that came to rescue him, as he had planned, but the French who cut off his last hope of escape by sea. Cornwallis surrendered and his men marched out while the American bands played 'The World Turned Upside Down'.

With Cornwallis's surrender British power south of the St. Lawrence was broken. Fighting continued in New York and Charleston, where British armies were beleagured, but the issue was no longer in doubt. 'O God! it is all over!' cried North when he heard the news, and realized that this was the end of the war he had precipitated and mismanaged. North resigned and the Whigs, who had always opposed the war, came in to negotiate the peace. That took time, while the differing claims of France, Spain and the United States were harmonized, and it was not until 1783 that the Treaty of Paris was signed. The British, anxious to end hostilities and recover their troops, gave generous terms. The boundary with Canada was fixed along the St. Lawrence and the Great Lakes, but left vague at both the north-east and the far west, while Spain insisted on retaining Florida (which had been occupied by Spanish troops fighting as allies of the colonists), and also all the territory west of the Mississippi. The poor Loyalists who had fled into Canada got only a promise from Congress that it would 'recommend' to the several states that they should restore confiscated property, and an equal weakness marked the clauses which dealt with the debts that Americans had incurred in Britain before the war. But the war was over. In Britain the king's power had received a shock from which it never recovered and the Empire a lesson from which it greatly benefited, while in America a new nation turned to its own internal problems, and to the prospect of its own future.

CHAPTER XI

The Confederation: Reforms and Problems

IN freeing themselves from the British, the colonists had undergone many internal changes. When they got rid of their royal governors, they had to work out a new form of government to take their place. Each colony won a separate solution to the problem of how to govern itself. But certain features were common to all the new state governments from Georgia to Maine. They almost all retained the old division between a legislative assembly and a governor, save that the governor was now elected by the colony instead of being appointed by the king. The exact degree of democracy they imparted to these institutions differed considerably from state to state. In Pennsylvania, for example, any one could vote or hold office who paid a quite small state tax. On the other hand in South Carolina votes were restricted to men who held fifty acres freehold, while to hold office you had to be a very wealthy landowner indeed. In the main the southern states all tended to be more aristocratic in their new constitutions than did the states of the middle and north. It is also true to say that while almost every state made votes dependent on ownership of some amount of property this was not, in the main, as undemocratic as might be supposed, because of the relative ease with which, in a frontier or pioneer state, land could be obtained.

The same reforming spirit which showed itself in extending the franchise also worked to do away with other privileges which British control had previously preserved. The Crown Lands and the princely estates of Loyalists like Lord Fairfax of Virginia were confiscated and largely redistributed to small farmers and discharged soldiers. The Anglican Church, which had enjoyed a privileged position as the 'Established Church' in most of the Colonies outside New England, was disestablished and in almost all the states a clear separation between Church and State was written into the constitution. Other privileges, like quit rents, entails, primogeniture and tithes, regarded by Americans as feudal relics, were also swept away.

One institution in particular presented a problem to the reformers. That was slavery. When the war broke out there were about half a million slaves in the American colonies, the great majority concentrated in the south. Were they to share in the rights to 'life, liberty and the pursuit of happiness?' The first step was to check the importation of fresh slaves. Congress and the states collaborated over this, and by the year 1808 the slave trade was prohibited everywhere in the U.S.A., though a good deal of illegal smuggling of slaves still went on. But freeing the slaves was another matter. In the north, where their numbers were few, it was a relatively simple task and all the states north of that Mason and Dixon* line which separates Pennsylvania from Maryland put emancipation laws into effect. South of the line the position was different. Not that slavery in the south was less detestable, nor that all southerners upheld it. Patrick Henry and Jefferson, for example, fully recognized the harmfulness and sinfulness of slavery and worked for its gradual abolition. But the economic and social system of the South grew up on slavery. The staple crops of tobacco and cotton on which the South depended required mass labour for their cultivation, and slave labour seemed ideal for that purpose. Vast fortunes were invested in this human property: if the slaves were to be set free how, after an

* So called after the surveyors who charted it.

impoverishing war, could their owners be compensated? Again, hundreds of thousands of ignorant and semi-savage Negroes could not be given their immediate freedom without giving rise to problems almost as great as those of slavery itself. The fact that immediate abolition was not possible should, of course, have made the South all the more concerned to work out a plan for doing it by degrees, but in fact it came to be accepted as an excuse for not doing it at all. Meanwhile the southern economy, built on this slave foundation, flourished, the investment in this repulsive form of property increased, and the cost of emancipating it mounted ever higher. It has been well said, 'Except in South Carolina and Georgia, almost every southerner looked upon slavery as an evil, but a necessary one; in time it became so necessary that it ceased to appear evil'.*

It was not only in politics and in social customs that the war brought changes and questionings. It gave a new impulse to education. Even before the war America, in proportion to the size of its population and its wealth, was a remarkably well educated country, equipped not only with schools in considerable numbers, but also with universities of quality, such as Harvard, Yale, Princeton and William and Mary. To all this independence gave a new impetus. Old colleges were transformed (like King's College in New York, which was re-opened after the war as Columbia), new ones were started, and a great movement got under way for modernizing and liberalizing education in general. Scientific subjects and modern languages were recognized for the first time. The study of medicine and law was put on a serious footing. At the same time care was taken to extend facilities for education more widely, both at schools and at universities. The best brains in the young republic devoted themselves to this problem. Benjamin Franklin himself superintended the modernizing of the University of Pennsylvania and it was characteristic of Jefferson that he preferred to be remembered as the 'father of the

* Morison & Commager: *Growth of the American Republic*, Vol. I, p. 131.

University of Virginia' than as one of the fathers of the Constitution.

Thus in every aspect of the national life – political, social, cultural – independence and the war brought sweeping changes. If by revolutionary is meant a complete destructive break with what has gone before, then these changes should not be so described. And yet the American usage which speaks of the Revolutionary War has justice on its side. These changes were something more than the result of mere independence. They were the expression of a new spirit which was abroad elsewhere in the world, but was especially strong in America, a spirit compounded of nationalism, liberalism and democracy. These were ideas which had their roots, it is true, in America's Anglo-Saxon and European past, but their impact was so powerful that they changed the face of a whole continent's future.

The peace that began with the Treaty of Paris found an America that was independent, that was republican, that had its feet set on the path of democracy and the Rights of Man, but which was still an America of thirteen states, imperfectly united, a confederation headed, but not governed, by a Congress. Congress had not the powers of a government. It could deliberate and devise, but was able to act only when nine states out of the thirteen were in agreement and only when each was prepared to take the necessary trouble or expense to put the recommendation into action. Congress could not tax: it had to *ask* the states for money. It had not control over foreign or internal trade. It could not keep an army in being except in so far as states voluntarily permitted it to retain their contingents under arms. If any state refused to abide by the decisions of Congress or refused to treat another state equitably Congress had no powers to bring it to book. These weaknesses had hampered the conduct of the war, but war itself is a disciplinarian, and under the discipline of war the thirteen states had co-operated in Congress and somehow found the unity which was necessary for victory. When the war was over this unity, the product of danger and a common cause, began to break up.

Each state became more conscious of its own private needs and worries and more indifferent to the common welfare. There was a serious risk that the new nation would just break up into thirteen independent states. The Articles of Confederation had created 'a league of friendship', but how if the states, blindly following their selfish interests, should cease to be friends?

The facts of geography did not make unification easy. The 3,000,000 inhabitants of the United States in 1783 were strung along a sea coast over 1,000 miles long and were spread inland over an area so vast that they averaged less than five persons to the square mile. The natural lines of communication were not to and from any single focal point, but along the river valleys which formed independent, parallel arteries from the mountains to the sea. It was easier to get from New York to Canada along the Hudson Valley than from New York to Philadelphia by land. There were no really large centres of population which could speak for the country as a whole. Philadelphia, the largest city, still had less than 40,000 inhabitants and counted, even inside its own state, merely as one voice among many in the vast hinterland of Pennsylvania. How were all these voices of Philadelphia, of Boston, of Georgia, of New Jersey, of the sea coast and the frontier, to be brought even within hearing distance of each other, much less into the same harmonious chorus?

The first sphere in which the interests of these scattered 3,000,000 people seemed likely to clash was the West. In the old colonial days it had been one of the chief bones of contention with the mother country. The British had now been thrown out, but the West remained, a problem and an opportunity. Fortunately for the future history of the United States, the new republic had the wisdom to take advantage of the opportunity, while the Second Continental Congress was able, in this one case, to act in the interests of the nation as a whole. This was an immeasurable advantage because all the states that bordered on the West could, as a result of their original charters, make large and often conflicting claims to the ownership of the western lands which, if they had been persisted in, would have led to endless boundary disputes if not to wars. Fortunately the states, one by one, agreed to cede all their claims to the Congress, the most important, in area and population, being the territory north of the Ohio which Virginia, under Jefferson's governorship, ceded in 1781. Into Kentucky, throughout the years of the war, immigrants had been pouring under the leadership of Daniel Boone, trapper and explorer, who had opened up the route through the Cumberland Gap by which the settlers' wagons wound their way across the Alleghany Mountains.

Now that Congress had these territories, what was to be done with them? They were fertile and accessible: settlers were pouring in. They must have some government. It was for this that Congress in 1785 passed the Land Ordinance, which provided for a survey of the western lands, and instructed the surveyors how they were to mark it out for settlement. The unit was to be, as it had been in New England, the 'township', an area of six miles square, which was to consist of thirty-six equal holdings of one square mile each. Four sections were to be reserved as Government property and for public buildings, while another section was set aside for the use and support of the schools of the township. This Congress made provision not only for orderly settlement, but, what was more important, for civilized settlement. America was anxious, not merely to people the wilderness, but to redeem it.

And, since these areas were in a state of transition from trackless forest to settled communities, Congress provided an elastic form of government such as was suited to their needs. By the North-West Ordinance of 1787 the territory north of the Ohio River was given a governor and judges appointed by Congress, with a provision that when the area came to have 5,000 male inhabitants they might choose a legislative assembly, and when that 5,000 increased to 60,000 the Territory should be admitted to the Union as a State on an exactly equal footing with the original thirteen.

Lastly, a brief but forward-looking clause stated simply, 'There shall be neither slavery nor involuntary servitude in the said territory.' This Ordinance, adopted originally for the North-West Territory, became a model from which the government of the whole West was copied, a democratic, adaptable, and yet simple device which contributed enormously to the successful growth of the United States.

Unfortunately the Congress, so successful in coping with the early problems of the West, was unequal to the burden laid upon it by the internal problems of the still imperfectly United States. The end of the war had brought, as wars so often do, a business depression. Britain closed her ports at home and in the West Indies to the exports of her rebellious colonies, and France and Spain showed very little more regard for the commerce of their late ally. During the war, government and people had lived largely on credit. Congress, unable to induce the states to raise the necessary levies for it, had had recourse to loans on a large scale. Still without power to tax, Congress could not refill the Treasury to repay them: only a further loan from Dutch bankers staved off bankruptcy. The public credit sank lower and lower and the paper money, which Congress and states both issued to meet the obligations, became more and more worthless. As distress mounted, disorders broke out over the country. In Massachusetts they assumed the dimensions of a serious rising when an ex-captain of the army, Daniel Shays, led a force of two thousand men against the government. Although Shays' Rebellion was put down, the discontent remained.

In desperate efforts to protect themselves the states began to put up tariff walls against each other and those who had no ports or access to the sea were victimized in their trade by their more fortunate neighbours. The game of tit-for-tat was played regardless of the consequences. When New York farmers complained of the competition of vegetable growers in New Jersey, the New York legislature put a tax on every boat that crossed the Hudson from the New Jersey shore, while New Jersey retorted by placing a tax on the lighthouses which New York had built on New Jersey soil at Sandy Hook.

Trade disputes were succeeded by boundary quarrels. New York and New Hampshire came to blows about Vermont, while the Vermonters, rather than have their claims flouted, were prepared to secede to Canada. Further south Maryland and Virginia disagreed about their boundary along the Potomac – a disagreement which at last precipitated action elsewhere.

At Washington's invitation the two parties, Virginia and Maryland, sent their commissioners to discuss their boundary dispute at Mount Vernon, Washington's country seat. As they investigated the problem, they realized that the control of the Potomac, with which the boundary issue was closely bound up, was a matter of concern to *all* the states that lined its banks and those of its tributaries. This led Virginia to suggest that the opportunity should be seized to hold a general convention to discuss the trade between all the states other than merely those who used the Potomac as their waterway. Accordingly a convention met at Annapolis, Maryland, in 1786. Attendance, in fact, was disappointing, eight states omitting to send representatives, and the only action resulting was a report, largely written by a New York representative, Alexander Hamilton, which urged on Congress the need for a convention of all the states, with wide powers to consider the problems of disunity.

With Vermont and New Hampshire, Connecticut and Pennsylvania at each other's throats, with the embers of Shays' Rebellion still smouldering and liable to re-awaken new flames, Congress accepted the suggestion. On February 21st, 1787, invitations went out to the states to send delegates to a convention at Philadelphia on May 14th, 'for the sole and express purpose of revising the Articles of Confederation.' On the day appointed the convention duly met, each state having sent its delegation, except Rhode Island, always happy to be in a minority of one, and always suspicious of the designs of her more powerful neighbours. The

Convention met on May 25th in the room in which the Declaration of Independence had been signed. That Declaration had brought forth a new nation; the Convention was to bring forth what was scarcely less important, a new government.

CHAPTER XII

From Confederation to Union

THE Chairman of the Convention, by unanimous choice, was George Washington. He thought of himself as much more a general than a politician: since the war ended, his major interests had been farming and the development of the West. Nevertheless, he could not be indifferent to the future of the nation for whose birth he had been so largely responsible, and his very disinterestedness recommended him as the ideal chairman for a Convention in which almost every one of the other fifty-one delegates had strong ready-made views. He spoke seldom, but his experience, patience and, above all, his moderation, contributed very largely to the success of the Convention.

While Washington was the official chairman, the presiding genius was, in many respects, Benjamin Franklin. By the time the Convention opened in his own home town, Franklin was already an old man, but at eighty-one he still retained an extraordinary youthfulness of spirit, to which he added a long record of life spent in the service of his country. More than any other delegate, Franklin typified the average American of his day. His life was a 'success story' which embodied the ideals and ambitions of nine out of ten Americans. Born in Boston in poverty, the fifteenth of a family of seventeen, he learnt printing as his trade, ran away to Philadelphia at the age of seventeen to work as a journeyman printer and rose by the age of twenty-four to the position of a successful publisher, printer, postmaster and journalist in his own right. To these business interests

Franklin added an extraordinary gift for inquiry and discovery in half a dozen fields of knowledge – science, farming, exploration, engineering, economics. He was an inventor of remarkable talent. The first electric battery, the lightning rod, a new domestic stove (which, in the days before central heating, made all the difference between misery and comfort for the average American throughout his ice-cold winter) – all these are the products of Franklin's own experiments. But along with all these activities, Franklin found time for a political career. He was the earliest proponent of a plan for American Union, at the Congress of the Colonies at Albany in 1754, when they met to discuss defence against the Indians. He had represented Pennsylvania and other states in London and by his outstanding knowledge and ability became, in fact, the unofficial spokesman for the colonies in London during the years of wrangling that preceded the war. No man worked more patiently for compromise while it seemed possible, or more vigorously for independence when that seemed the only way.

When war broke out he went to France and it was largely his efforts and prestige, as philosopher and diplomat, that secured French assistance in the Revolutionary War. As one of the Commissioners for the peace he was largely responsible for securing such favourable terms for the United States and on his return was fittingly honoured with the office of President of Pennsylvania. To the admiring outside world, Franklin appeared as the symbol of the new republic, the philosopher king, the poor boy whose rise to fame and prosperity proved that in America at last the rights to life, liberty and the pursuit of happiness had found tangible realization. To his fellow-countrymen he was the beloved reflection of their own best selves whose homely wit and practical wisdom proved that there were no frontiers, whether of learning, society, race or geography, that the average American need regard as closed to him. With the example of Franklin before his eyes, the humblest apprentice of America could feel himself the equal – if not the superior – of any crowned head of Europe. It was his spirit which infused the Convention at Philadelphia with confidence in its power to make a new government with its own bare hands. It was his geniality, either in the council chamber of the Convention or when serving tea to the delegates under the mulberry tree in his garden, that sweetened their discussions with good temper and preserved their unanimity throughout their differences.

Of another complexion altogether was the principal instigator of the Convention, the delegate from New York, Alexander Hamilton. This remarkable man, to whom all Americans must always be grateful, even if to gratitude they cannot add the tribute of affection, was still only thirty years of age when the Convention met. He had been born poor and obscure, on the island of St Nevis in the West Indies and owed his education to the charity of discerning friends. Like Franklin, his ambition raised him to greatness, but, unlike Franklin, he despised his own small beginnings and developed the sympathies and prejudices of an aristocrat. Finding himself at college in New York when the quarrel with Britain was at its height, he ardently took up the cause of the colonists, organized a band of volunteers for Washington's army, and soon became military secretary and aide-de-camp to the commander. In this position he had ample opportunity to observe the weaknesses and defects of the Confederation, and, although still only twenty-four when the war ended, he had a wealth of practical experience which older men might envy. After the war he was elected to Congress, and saw from the inside that same drama of inadequate powers and divided purpose that he had observed from General Washington's tent. More than any other delegate to the Convention, he knew what he wanted – a strong, aristocratic central government, with ample powers.

Strongly sympathetic to Hamilton's mode of thinking was James Madison, of the Virginian delegation, who had had a large hand in drafting the Constitution of his own state, and who added to this practical experience a wide knowledge of political theory and constitutional history, both ancient and modern. In the same delegation was George Mason, author of the Virginian Bill of Rights, a document which was to have a big effect on the Convention's decisions. Other eminent delegates included James Wilson, a Pennsylvania Scotsman, one of the staunchest advocates of Independence, and a drafter of the Declaration; General Pinckney of South Carolina; Elbridge Gerry, a brilliant young man from Massachusetts; Gouverneur Morris, man of the world from Philadelphia, later to be the representative of the United States of America in the France of the Revolution; and John Dickinson, pamphleteer of Independence. There were fifty-five in all and their average age was only forty-two. Seldom has so rich a galaxy of political talent been assembled from so small a population. Their first step after their assembling was in some respects their boldest. It consisted in ignoring their instructions, which strictly limited them to drafting amendments to the original Confederation, and instead setting to work to plan a new national government. As a result they were able to make a new start and raise the structure of the United States on entirely new foundations. The crux of their problem was to reconcile the independence of the states with the need for national unity. Early in their deliberations, two schools of thought became distinct – those who wished to keep effective power in the hands of the states and those who wanted to transfer it to the central government. The first group consisted in the main of the small states – from a natural fear that in a central government the votes of the small states would be swamped by those of the large: they therefore wanted to keep the central government as weak as possible. Save for Alexander Hamilton, the New York delegation lined up with the small states on this issue, owing to New York's fear that her trade interests would suffer from a strong Congress. Heading the opposite group was Virginia, who from the outset advocated a strong government with powers to prevent a repetition of the weaknesses of the Confederacy. Between these two points of view agreement seemed impossible. Tempers ran so high that it was only Franklin's proposal that they should begin their meetings with prayer which cooled the atmosphere and paved the way for a compromise.

The compromise was principally embodied in the provisions laid down for election to the federal legislature. There were to be two Chambers – everyone agreed on that – but in the one the larger states would predominate and in the other all would stand on an equal footing. That was to say that in the House of Representatives, Virginia with 420,000 inhabitants would receive representation proportionate to its population, while Delaware with 37,000 would receive proportionately less. But in the Senate, Delaware would come into her own, for there each state would have two Senators irrespective of size or population. Once this was propounded and accepted, the back of the Convention's work was broken. There still had to be give and take on many delicate issues, involving the balancing of power and liberty, of the small unit and the large. But from then onwards the Convention throve on its own success and by September 17th, 1787, was able to present a brief, clear, beautifully-phrased document for the approval of the people of the United States. While the last members were signing it, Franklin, observing with characteristic felicity that Washington's chair bore as its decoration a gilded half-sun, remarked:

> I have often and often in the course of this session and the vicissitudes of my hopes and fears as to its issue, looked at that behind the president without being able to tell whether it was rising or setting. But now at length I have the happiness to know it is a rising and not a setting sun.

What kind of a brain child was born in those sessions at Philadelphia, those deliberations behind closed doors? 'I consent, Sir, to this Constitution', said Benjamin Franklin, 'because I expect no better, and because I am not sure that it is not the best.' The American people were to echo this verdict, and to make it their Constitution, not just for a trial period, but for their whole ensuing national history, down to the present day. Indeed, it is from the adoption of the Constitution that the United States dates its birth.

It was in the first place a federal constitution, not setting up one government in place of those of the thirteen states, but sharing out political power between the centre and the circumference. Neither element in the Constitution was superior to the other. With respect to certain spheres the federal government was sovereign, with respect to others the states continued to be masters in their own houses. Broadly speaking, the basis of division was that those matters which were of common concern should be administered from the centre while all the rest should remain in the charge of the states. Thus, to give a brief catalogue of the principal items, the federal government had control of the armed forces, with right to make war or peace, control over all foreign and inter-state affairs, from trade to immigration, the exclusive right to coin money, maintain a Post Office and administer the Western lands. Finally, what was most important of all, the new federal government had, what the Confederate government had lacked, the means of enforcing its will. It should not rest on a pyramid of states, but could go direct to the individual citizen. As he voted for it directly, so it could tax him directly, punish him directly, conscript him directly, and award him direct justice in its own courts.

This did not mean that the states were reduced to impotence. They were left with all the powers that had not been explicitly granted to the central government. Most criminal and much civil law was theirs to administer. They kept order within their own frontiers. They could levy taxes and were indeed until relatively recent times the principal agents of taxation. They continued to maintain the main responsibility for the general welfare and it would be true to say that the ordinary citizen of, say, Pennsylvania felt little personal change when the new Constitution came into force: where government affected him, nine times out of ten it continued to be the government of his own state.

The Constitution was very clear about the form of the new federal government which it created. Almost all the Convention members, whether they were 'big state' or 'little state' men, were obsessed by the prevailing eighteenth century notion that if a government was not to develop into a tyranny its powers must be 'divided'. That is to say, the executive must not control, or be controlled by the legislature, and neither must be mixed up in either sense with the judiciary. Only so could you prevent a centralization of power which would sooner or later make havoc of the liberties of the citizen. In line with this view, the Constitution set up a President who was not a member of Congress and who did not depend for his election or his tenure of office upon the support of Congress; a Congress whose members were expressly debarred from holding any office and whom the President could not appoint or remove; and lastly a judiciary who were indeed appointed by the President, since they had to be appointed by someone, but who, once appointed, were irremovable except by impeachment.

The safeguards against tyranny did not end there. To many Americans of that generation who had organized a rebellion against a tyrannical government, all government seemed to a greater or less degree tyrannical and they would have readily agreed with Jefferson that, if only it were possible, to have no government at all was best. However, since government there must be, let the wise legislator see to it that the power to harm is kept to the absolute minimum. For this, the eighteenth century had another device besides that of division of powers – 'checks and balances'. By this, each department of government was instituted watchdog over the others, and the action of each was made in some degree dependent on the acquiescence of the others. Thus the President could veto a bill passed by Congress, but Congress could re-pass it over his veto by a two-thirds majority. Or again, the President appoints officials and judges, but such appointments must be approved by the Senate. He can make treaties, but only if two-thirds of the Senators present concur – a very considerable limitation over his control of foreign affairs. Similarly both Houses of Congress must agree before a bill can go up for the President's signature, and, though the Senate has these special powers over appointments and treaties, the House of Representatives is the place where money bills must be initiated. The result of this 'government by safeguards' is that the federal government has been strong or weak, swift or slow, largely according as the President and Congress have been in agreement or at loggerheads.

The Convention had been much more concerned with protecting liberty than with promoting equality. It was a 'republic' they spoke of, not a 'democracy'. This was not merely because, as many modern critics have contended, they were concerned about protecting the rights of property, but also because in the America of the eighteenth century, democracy in the modern meaning of the term was patently impossible. Only a minority of the population could read or write, and in none of the states was universal suffrage the law. The Constitution did in fact go to the limits of what was feasible by saying that the qualifications for voting for federal Representatives should be the same as those for 'the most numerous branch' of each state's legislature. The Senators were, of course, regarded as ambassadors for their states rather than as spokesmen for the people: they were consequently to be appointed by the state legislatures. The President was viewed as a kind of republican substitute for a monarch. His four year term of office was thought to give him stability without the risk of making him too powerful. He was to be responsible to the people – but not directly responsible. They, or their representatives in the State legislatures, would vote for 'electors' who, as wise men exercising a dispassionate choice, would then select the best man in the land and make him President. In fact, this device broke down almost immediately and the presidential electors have never exercised their freedom of choice since 1792, but have merely registered the will of the voters in their states.

All this apparatus for 'filtering' the national will falls far short of democracy as the term is understood to-day, as a mechanism of representation for giving as direct effect as possible to the majority's will. The difference is due in part to the considerations listed above, but to them one other point must be added. The eighteenth century thought the essence of a 'free government' lay just as much, if not more, in what it could *not* do, as in how it did it, in its limitations as much as in its representativeness. Consequently the men who in 1787 were concerned to preserve in the new Constitution the sacred principles of the Declaration of Independence, about the equality of men, their inalienable rights and their consent to their own government, directed their gaze to certain clauses in the Constitution which were entirely negative in character. The most notable of these was Section 9 of Article I, which prohibited such acts as the suspension of *habeas corpus*, Bills of Attainder or *ex post facto* legislation. These were expressions of the same zeal for civil liberties as the Americans' own forebears had manifested in the Bill of Rights in 1689. In fact, to the liberals of 1787, eyeing the document offered them by the Convention, these clauses did not seem to go far enough, and a popular demand arose for the addition of a longer and more explicit Bill of Rights which would mark out in black and white those liberties which not even a federal government should infringe. The demand was successful, and at the same time as the Constitution was ratified ten amendments, amounting to nothing less than a charter of civil liberties, were also adopted. The first ten Amendments to the Constitution catalogue the traditional liberties of freedom of speech, press and assembly, the right to jury trial, etc., which the Americans had inherited from the British tradition of government under law. In grave and clear language, they stand as reminders that the Constitution, in the words of its own opening paragraph, was created, not only 'to form a more perfect union, establish justice, insure domestic tranquillity, provide for the common defence, promote the general welfare', but also 'to secure the blessings of liberty' to the citizens of the thirteen states and their posterity.

But the Constitution, even with the addition of the popular ten amendments, the Bill of Rights, did not recommend itself to everybody. On the contrary, keen opposition was evoked by the new scheme of union. All whose principal attachment, by sentiment or interest, was to the state governments looked askance at the enhanced power of the federal authority. Although men of property welcomed the stability and security which the new government promised, frontiersmen who had no need of money, and debtors who wanted it as cheap as possible, disliked the clauses which forbade the states to print paper dollars or cancel inconvenient contracts. Radicals protested because it was not democratic enough, and because one man, the President, would have more power, as they complained, than the king. Nothing in the Constitution pleased everyone and opponents could always find faults to criticize and alterations to demand. But its supporters did enjoy one advantage – they had a plan, something concrete and workable, thought out in all its parts and as a whole. Consequently, while the critics were divided, the advocates spoke as one. Two men in particular pamphleteered and campaigned with boundless energy, inexhaustible resource and remarkable debating skill. These were Hamilton and Madison. *The Federalist*, their series of articles published in certain New York journals between 1787 and 1788, constitutes one of the most closely reasoned and lucidly expressed volumes in the whole of political literature. It is not too much to say that as Paine's *Common Sense* projected America into the war, so *The Federalist* argued America into the Constitution.

One of the wisest provisions in the Constitution was the last Article, which stipulated that the Constitution should go into effect the moment it was ratified by nine of the states. The framers had well realized that to wait for the approval of all thirteen would be to postpone decision indefinitely. It was also sensibly decided that for this purpose it should not be the state governments who should do the ratifying, because they inevitably were biased in favour of the present system and their present powers, but popularly elected state conventions who would have no other functions than to pass judgment on the document presented to them. These two techniques, of accepting a majority agreement as a basis for ratification and of appealing direct to the people and not to the governments for their opinion, saved the day. One by one the leading states swung into line. In Massachusetts and Virginia in particular the arguments were long and keen, as one might expect from the states of Shays' Rebellion and Patrick Henry, but eventually, after the concession of the first ten Amendments, the supporters of ratification carried the day. The Constitution went into force with North Carolina and Rhode Island still uncooperative, but it was felt that their adherence would come with time, as indeed it did: North Carolina joined in 1789 and Rhode Island in the following year. So in July 1788 the old Congress notified the states that the new Constitution was adopted, and instructed them to set about choosing Representatives, Senators, a President and a Vice-President to enter on office in the following spring. The ratifying states complied, and duly returned the legislators by the day appointed. Fortunately for the new Constitution there could be no question as to which citizen should bear the honour of being the first President. In January and February, 1789, the electoral colleges cast their votes unanimously for George Washington. On April 30th, on the balcony of the Federal Hall in New York City, George Washington took the oath of office and solemnly swore to the best of his ability to 'preserve, protect and defend the Constitution of the United States'. The march towards 'a more perfect union' had begun.

CHAPTER XIII

Washington's Presidencies

WASHINGTON'S first task was to appoint the chief officers of government. His difficulty here was not any lack of talent, but the problem of securing an even balance between the contending elements in the Union, the Federalists and the anti-Federalists, the North and the South. His success was as much due to the confidence he himself inspired as to the selections he made. To look after the foreign affairs of the

Union, as Secretary of State, he needed someone with diplomatic experience, and so his choice very naturally fell on Thomas Jefferson, who at the moment of appointment was acting as Minister to France. For the Treasury there was obviously no one to compare with young Alexander Hamilton who had a natural genius for finance and whose appointment would also balance Jefferson's, setting off New York against Virginia and an extreme Federalist against an ardent States' Rights man. The other leading appointment was that of John Jay, who had made his reputation as Minister to Spain and negotiator of the Treaty of Paris, and who now became head of the third arm of the government, Chief Justice of the Supreme Court of the United States.

The most pressing problems facing the new government were financial and Alexander Hamilton, in consequence, had an immediate opportunity to prove his mettle. The federation began life encumbered in debt, inheriting this dismal legacy from the old Continental Congress. There were, first of all, the foreign debts – money borrowed overseas from France, Spain and Holland to finance the Revolutionary War. These amounted to over $10,000,000. Then there were debts which the Treasury had incurred to investors inside the country, complicated and various, and assessed by Hamilton at about $42,000,000. Merely to settle these debts required a lot of money, but Hamilton decided not to stop there. The constituent states also had their debts, $25,000,000 of them, for the most part incurred at the same time and for the same purpose as the federal debts – the Revolutionary War. Hamilton induced Congress to carry these too. His motives were complex. In the first place, though this total of $80,000,000 was a staggering figure for so small and poor a country to meet, Hamilton properly recognized that nothing would so much recommend the new government to its neighbours overseas and convince them that it was a power to be reckoned with as this demonstration of financial strength and probity. But the new government also had to recommend itself to neighbours at home. It had largely been instituted to put a stop to the hand-to-mouth financing, the endless cycle of borrowing in order to pay, set up by the weak Continental Congress. It had to prove itself to its supporters. And lastly, in assuming those debts of the states which were not properly the federal government's at all, Hamilton was being very astute and far-sighted. Not only was the federal government thus conferring a handsome gift upon its chief rivals, the states, but it was also transferring to itself the support and interest of all those investors, large and small, who looked for some return on the money they had lent years ago. A whole new class of citizens, whose interest in the new constitution had previously been only lukewarm, now became seriously concerned for its stability and prosperity, because it and it alone looked like keeping them solvent.

The assumption of these debts was not put through without opposition. The states with good balance sheets, like Virginia and New York, were naturally reluctant to pay off the debts of their less solvent neighbours, though it could plausibly be argued that the bulk of these debts had been incurred in a common cause, the struggle for independence. To carry the bill, more southern votes were required, and the southern states demanded some *quid pro quo*. The outcome of the bargaining was that they gained a shift of the capital from New York City to a spot on the banks of the River Potomac where, it was argued, the government would be more responsive to the wishes of the South. The site chosen was mostly on the Maryland side of the river, with a small facing strip in Virginia, but the territory was removed from the government of either of the states and put under the direct control of the federal government. Thus the nation would have a capital in its own right, and no state could claim an advantage over any other. The territory was named the District of Columbia and an ardent French town-planner, Charles L'Enfant, who had served in the Revolutionary Army, was given the task of laying out a city worthy to house the government of the United States. His plans were on a grandiose scale and it was a long time before anything took shape along the banks of the Potomac. But an important decision had been made – fraught with future significance – that the capital of the United States should border on the South, rise on a spot unencumbered with history, industry or commerce, and dowered with a climate which, if not unhealthy, is certainly uncomfortable. Meanwhile the temporary capital, after its short-lived residence at New York, reverted to Philadelphia.

Besides assuming the state debts, Hamilton, as a firm believer in the wisdom and desirability of giving the federal government as much power as possible, was the ardent advocate of a national bank, to be the American equivalent of the Bank of England. The plan was opposed on two grounds: one as unconstitutional, because nowhere did the Constitution say that the federal government could establish a national bank; and two, as an attempt by the urban and financial interests to dominate the economic life of the country. Jefferson in particular opposed the measure on both these grounds. But Hamilton argued that the Constitution gave the federal government all the powers 'necessary and proper' to carry out its duties and one of its duties was to keep stable finances. Thus went the first of many arguments over what the Constitution did and did not permit. In this case Hamilton had his way. Congress passed the bill by a narrow margin, Washington gave it his signature and a national bank came into being in 1791.

To meet the expenses of his policy Hamilton had recourse to a tariff on imported goods. But the success of this, like the commercial prosperity of the country as a whole, was dependent on the volume of overseas trade, and three-quarters of America's trade was with Britain. Although Britain's attitude to her recently rebellious colonists remained cool, it improved by degrees – in 1791 the first British Minister was appointed to the new government – as America gave signs of regaining stability and acquiring power. Hamilton well knew that for the sake of American trade good relations with Britain must be maintained, but many manufacturers thought that Britain could be bullied into trade concessions, while the ordinary American persisted in a post-war dislike of his late enemies. This was the position when events succeeding the French Revolution threw England into a blaze, the sparks of which were to fall on inflammable tinder in America.

Hamilton's policy of a strong central government, supported by adequate finances, fostering industry and controlling trade, obviously depended greatly upon the federal taxing power. One of the great differences between the new Constitution of the federation and that of the 'confederation' which had existed before was the authority given to the federal government to go direct to the citizens of the states and tax them in the interests of the national treasury. In 1791, acting under this authority, Hamilton secured the passage of an Excise Act, which levied a tax on the manufacture of spirits. It was an unpopular tax, especially along the western frontier where the mountaineers had long been accustomed to supplement their meagre farm income by distilling their corn into whisky for sale or barter. By 1794 opposition to the tax in western Pennsylvania reached the dimensions of outright rebellion and organized refusal to pay.

It was a test case of the powers of the new government. There were no federal police to enforce the law, but the Constitution gave the federal government the power to call forth the state militia to enforce its will. Washington decided to exercise the power thus granted him. Would it work? Would the states acknowledge the federal authority? They did. The militias of four states, even including Pennsylvania, where popular sympathies for the rebels were strongest, turned out at the President's command. Confronted with such a show of force, the 'rebellion' melted away without serious bloodshed. An important principle had been established – the right of the federal government to enforce its own laws and the duty of the states to assist it in so doing.

This was the last of Hamilton's Treasury triumphs. For private reasons, principally the difficulty of maintaining a large family on his official salary, he resigned in 1794 to resume a private practice. His interest in politics, however, remained and he continued to be consulted by Washington and to direct the Federalist Party until his death in 1804. Jefferson, who had no enthusiasm for Washington's foreign policy, had already resigned his Cabinet office, the Secretaryship of State, at the end of 1793, but continued privately to watch and shape public affairs from his home at Monticello, the beautiful house he designed and built for himself in the Virginian mountains.

Thus it came about that Washington concluded his second term as President with neither of his two most famous and rival lieutenants holding office in his Cabinet. Their withdrawal from his moderating influence inflamed the strife of parties and made him the target for an increasing volume of public criticism and even abuse. Thus when his second term drew to a close in 1796 it was with no regret that Washington prepared for retirement, and declined all invitations to stand again (so incidentally establishing a tradition against a third presidential term which lasted until 1940). But before withdrawing into private life Washington bequeathed to his countrymen a political testament which has become so famous in American history that it deserves separate consideration. It is his Farewell Address, which appeared in a Philadelphia newspaper on September 19th, 1796. In it the Father of His Country described the course he thought the United States should follow if she was to prosper and realize her own high ideals.

First he emphasized the importance of the Union and the extent to which the interests of the North and the South, the East and the West were interdependent. He warned against the danger that the selfish designs of any region should prevail against the common interest of the whole, a warning which the later history of the Union was to bear out. Speaking with the vehement rivalries of Federalists and Republicans fresh in his mind, he deplored 'the baneful effects of the spirit of party'. The history of the United States, as of Britain, is a proof that large democratic states cannot in fact get along without political parties, and this portion of his injunctions has not been heeded then or since.

But when he went on to speak of foreign policy he preached a doctrine far more potent. Recognizing that Americans, drawn from all the national stocks of the Old World, carried in their bones sympathies and animosities bred on the other side of the Atlantic, he warned his people that:

> Nothing is more essential than that permanent inveterate antipathies against particular nations, and passionate attachments for others, should be excluded; and that, in place of them, just and amicable feelings towards all should be cultivated ... Against the insidious wiles of foreign influence, I conjure you to believe me, fellow citizens, the jealousy of a free people ought to be *constantly* awake.

And the reason is that:

> Europe has a set of primary interests, which to us have none, or a very remote relation. Hence therefore it must be unwise in us to implicate ourselves, by artificial ties, in the ordinary vicissitudes of her politics, or the ordinary combinations and collisions of her friendships or enmities.

Instead, it is America's 'true policy to steer clear of permanent alliances with any portion of the foreign world', though, 'taking care always to keep ourselves, by suitable establishments, on a respectable defensive posture, we may safely trust to temporary alliances for extraordinary emergencies'.

This was the wise counsel to the young nation, whose primary interest and duty lay not in the complications of European international politics, but in the consolidation of the new union and expansion into the West. The United States of America has heeded Washington's advice and prospered. If the world of today is not the world of Washington, and if new circumstances call for new counsels, it is nevertheless a remarkable tribute to the first President's sagacity that his principles should have held good for so long. Indeed, Washington had already had an opportunity to put his principles of foreign policy to the test, for events in Europe, even before the end of his Presidency, had made their impact on the infant United States.

In 1789 the autocratic and incompetent government of Louis XVI had collapsed, giving the French people their long-awaited opportunity to throw off the control of a despotic monarchy and a feudal nobility. From the sack of the Bastille to the execution of the king and queen, events moved with breath-taking rapidity before the eyes of an astonished world. The effects were felt everywhere. As Thomas Paine said, 'From a small spark, kindled in America, a flame has arisen, not to be extinguished'. And since so much of the kindling had been American – Jefferson's Declaration of Independence, for example, having been a major stimulus to the French Declaration of the Rights of Man – it was not surprising that America felt the effects immediately. The Revolution was hailed with applause, and France was toasted as the first country to follow in the steps of the republican United States. But as the Revolution became more and more violent, with Jacobin extremists taking control, and the toll of executions mounting day by day, American opinion, like opinion in Britain, began to divide into those who still supported the Revolution, despite its excesses, and those who saw in it nothing more than a gigantic design to overthrow all established decencies and standards. It was scarcely surprising that Jefferson became identified with the first group and Hamilton with the second.

As the Revolution poured over the frontiers of France, European war developed. When French designs menaced the independence of the Low Countries, British security was threatened, and by April, 1793, France and Britain were at war. In America the debate on the merits of the Revolution took a new turn – should America take sides in the war? Washington insisted that absolute neutrality was the only course that the United States could pursue consistent with its national interests and accordingly issued a Proclamation enjoining neutrality upon all United States citizens. But France looked for something more from her late ally, and her newly-appointed ambassador, Genet, called 'Citizen Genet' as a symbol of his revolutionary origins, made it his object to turn the United States into an active ally. But he went too far. He raised recruits, tried to use American ports as bases for French privateers and even, finding Washington unsympathetic, so far intervened in domestic politics as to organize a movement to turn him out. Even Jefferson's sympathies would not tolerate this and in 1794 the French were requested to recall him. His name lives in the pages of American history as a classic warning against the perils of foreign intervention in internal American affairs.

But the war produced worse problems than Citizen Genet. As between Britain and France the struggle was mainly fought on the high seas, with the blockade one of the most potent instruments of war. Both sides employed privateers, both sides claimed the right to search neutral American vessels for contraband. But, as the British were the more powerful naval power, it was they who most often came up against the mercantile fleets of the United States. Moreover, one particular source of friction developed with Britain – the British-born sailors who worked on United States ships. Were they deserters? Could United States ships be searched and the British tars impressed? These issues touched the sensitive pride of both countries and linked up with the pro- and anti-revolutionary feeling in the United States of America.

In addition there were problems still outstanding since the Revolutionary War. Britain still held the North-West posts along the Canadian frontier which she promised by the Peace of Paris to give up 'with all convenient speed': the Americans were still in arrears on their war debts. When in 1793 Lord Grenville told the American Ambassador that Britain proposed to hold the posts indefinitely, American tempers began to rise, and even Hamilton, whose sheet-anchor was friendship with Britain, became exasperated, while Jefferson's anti-Federalists were regarding war as inevitable. To prevent such a war Washington sent John Jay to London, to present America's cause and negotiate an agreement.

He negotiated an agreement, the treaty which bears his name, and war was, at any rate temporarily, averted.

Britain evacuated the North-West posts and various frontier adjustments were arranged. The trade agreement which Hamilton so keenly wanted was secured, but in return Jay had to acquiesce in the British right of search at sea, for both men and contraband, and the United States government was made responsible for the debts which private citizens had contracted to Britain before the war. It was a hard bargain, and it took all Washington's and Hamilton's influence to get the treaty ratified by the necessary two-thirds majority of the Senate. Worse, it implanted in the American mind the firm belief that British diplomacy was not to be trusted where American interests were involved. Within America it sharpened the animosity between Republicans and Federalists still further.

CHAPTER XIV

Adams and Jefferson

WHEN Washington retired in 1797 to his beautiful estate at Mount Vernon (where you may still visit his house high on the banks of the Potomac, a few miles from the capital which bears his name), Americans had to face the problem of electing a new President. On the two previous occasions, in 1788 and 1792, when a presidential election fell due, Washington had been so obviously the only candidate, the one dominating figure, that no other contestant had even been thought of. But with his retirement there was no one else on whom everyone could automatically agree. Instead the two parties each chose their own candidate and fought it out. So began the first presidential campaign in American history.

The Republicans, the party of States' Rights, tinged with Radicalism, chose, as was natural, Thomas Jefferson. The Federalists selected John Adams, the Massachusetts leader who had been Vice-President under Washington. There was some vigorous campaigning, as a result of which John Adams, securing the backing of all the states north of Virginia, except Pennsylvania, was elected by a narrow majority. One important feature of the election was the behaviour of the 'electors'. The theory of the Constitution, drawn up a mere eight years before, was that the people at large or their state legislatures should vote for these 'electors' who would then, in joint deliberation, choose the President. In fact, the electors with one or two exceptions divided according to their political affiliations – the Federalists voted for Adams and the Republicans for Jefferson. In other words, the 'electors' abdicated all power of discretion and became, what they have since remained, mere figureheads who register the people's choice. The Constitution thus suddenly became one degree more democratic than its founders had ever intended it to be.

Having been Vice-President under Washington for eight years, and the first American Minister to Britain (from 1785 to 1788) as well as the representative of Congress on a variety of special diplomatic missions all over Europe, Adams was well versed in public and diplomatic affairs. He suffered unfortunately from a strong streak of personal vanity which made him a poor judge of men and a difficult man to work with. But he lacked neither courage nor integrity, as events were to show.

France's Revolutionary War continued to present acute problems to the United States of America. Jay's Treaty had bought agreement with Britain, but only at the price of aggravating feeling among the French, who resumed piratical attacks on United States shipping and refused to receive the new American minister, Thomas Pinckney. To find a peaceful settlement a commission was sent to Paris which included Elbridge Gerry of Massachusetts, a Jeffersonian who, as such, was judged acceptable to the revolutionary government. The three commissioners were curiously treated and were given to understand by French agents that a necessary preliminary to doing business with Marshal Talleyrand, the French foreign minister, was the payment of a large bribe and the granting of a ten million dollar loan to France on very doubtful security. The commissioners reported these facts to Congress, and the result was a spontaneous outburst of public indignation. 'Armed neutrality' became the popular watchword with the attendant slogan 'millions for defence, but not one cent for tribute'. American merchant ships were armed and a state of undeclared war came into existence at sea with American privateers holding their own in several engagements and protecting United States commerce with the West Indies from French depredations.

Hamilton would have liked to go further and would have welcomed an outright break with France. Adams was content to secure observance of America's rights and when signs of a more accommodating spirit began to appear in France he was prepared to meet it half-way. (From this difference, incidentally, there proceeded a split between Hamilton and Adams which, beginning as the personal rivalry of two leaders, ended with the break-up of the Federalist party.) Accordingly, acting on hints from Talleyrand that an American minister would now be received, Adams in 1799 asked Congress to support the appointment, if not of a minister, at any rate of a commission of three. Various delays – in particular vigorous obstruction from Hamilton's wing of the Federalist party – held up despatch of the commissioners until 1800. They found in Paris a powerful Napoleon, flushed with victory, and the terms they obtained were not generous. But at any rate they secured a cessation of the trade war and a relief of the political tension between the two countries. For the present war was averted.

During these years, when the country was trembling on the brink of war with the French Republic, men of property in the United States, like their counterparts in Britain, watched with increasing anxiety the spread of 'revolutionary doctrines' from France and sought to protect the existing order from threats at home as well as from overseas. They were worried in particular about the influx of refugees – although the same refugees contributed enormously to the country of their adoption – and about 'agitators' in speech or writing at home, although there was never any serious revolutionary movement in America comparable to that in France. The Federalists, as the party of property, lent a ready ear to these anxieties, the more so because they provided a good stick to beat their Republican rivals with. In 1798 they put through Congress a series of measures which constituted a serious threat to the civil liberties of the young Republic. The Aliens Act enabled the President to deport foreigners at his pleasure. The Sedition Act redefined sedition and treason in such wide terms as practically to make it an offence to criticize the government at all. With this weapon in their hands the Federalists went to work with a will and inflicted heavy prison sentences on a number of their Republican opponents.

This was not government: it was persecution. And it evoked vigorous protests, particularly from two states where the leading figures of the Republican party held sway. In Virginia Madison, and in Kentucky Jefferson, drafted a set of resolutions for their state legislatures which became famous as the Virginia and Kentucky Resolutions and which were supported all over the country by a flood of spoken and written criticism. The 'Resolutions' protested against the 1798 legislation on the ground that it was unconstitutional. The first Amendment to the Constitution had declared that 'Congress shall make no law ... abridging the freedom of speech or of the press'; consequently, the argument ran, any law which Congress may pass that attempts to do this should properly be regarded as null and void. But the Resolutions went further: charging that the Federalist government had attempted by this legislation to overstep the boundaries set upon it by the Constitution and to dictate to the separate states, the Resolutions maintained that by so doing the Federal Government had broken the 'compact' which was the Constitution and that consequently no obligation rested on the states to observe federal law. This was the theory of 'States' Rights' – that the states had given up none of their sovereignty when they made the Union: they had merely made a 'compact'; if the Federal Government broke its side of the 'compact' the states had a perfect right to ignore the legislation and if necessary to withdraw from the Union. This theory, first aired in 1798, is one which was to be heard enunciated in harsher and louder terms as the history of nineteenth-century America proceeded. Its principal importance at the moment was that it gave Adams's opponents an argument that sounded convincing. Jefferson played his hand well, the Federalists overplayed theirs. Hamilton's zeal for an open war with France split the party and discredited the Federalist cause. And the election of 1800 came at a moment when the Federalist ranks were in confusion.

For the election of 1800 the Democratic Republicans, as they were now tending to call themselves, chose Jefferson and Aaron Burr as their candidates; the Federalists stuck to Adams and Pinckney. The Federalists were defeated; in the electoral college the votes were seventy-three to sixty-five. But, under the system then prevailing, that still left open the question of which of the two Democratic Republicans should be President and which Vice-President, since the votes for both were equal. Jefferson was the real head of the party, but Burr was an influential politician; indeed, the reason that he had been nominated to run with Jefferson was the control he exercised in the important 'key' state of New York. The dispute went to Congress for decision and the voting was so close that one state could turn the scale. At this point a very remarkable thing happened. Hamilton, Jefferson's most serious rival, prevailed upon the Federalists of two states to abstain from voting and the election went to Jefferson. Hamilton's motives, no doubt, were mixed: his quarrel with the Adams wing of the Federalist party gave him a certain spite against his old allies. But also he had the wisdom to discern, beyond the welter of party rivalries, that Jefferson was a great man of Presidential stature, a statesman and patriot, whereas Burr, for all his ability, was lacking in integrity and unworthy of being entrusted with the destinies of his country. Events were to prove Hamilton abundantly right.

The man who thus, at the age of fifty-seven, succeeded to the Presidency of the United States was a very remarkable figure. Thomas Jefferson, who vies with Abraham Lincoln for the title of the great American democrat, sprang from a Virginian background which was markedly aristocratic. Jefferson was, in fact, in many respects a Whig – an American counterpart of Charles James Fox, who combined aristocratic ancestry and tastes, landed wealth and local influence with a genuine belief in the doctrine of the rights of man and the wickedness of governments. But Jefferson was also remarkable amongst his contemporaries for the extraordinary range of his interests and talents. (In this respect his only rival was his great contemporary Benjamin Franklin.) Like Washington, Jefferson regarded politics not as his principal profession but as a duty which a gentleman should discharge when required but from which he would gratefully return to the civilized occupations of rural life. What Mount Vernon was to Washington, Monticello was to Jefferson – indeed more, because Monticello was of Jefferson's own building, a house which incorporated not only his ideas of architectural beauty but also his bent for practical ingenuity. Beds that disappeared by folding, dumb-waiters that simplified service, an extraordinary clock with a series of weights and pulleys – these were all designed by Jefferson himself. In this he showed himself peculiarly American – a man who did not merely pursue happiness in abstract theory but who actively concerned himself with finding out practical devices to lighten the laborious chores which for the ordinary man in the pre-industrial era consumed so much time as to leave little leisure for civilized living. In a similar spirit Jefferson threw himself into the development of education. As Governor of Virginia he instituted a system of public education based on the principle that the able child, no matter how poor, should be enabled to pass from primary school to university. When he retired from political life it was to the establishing and the actual building – he was his own architect – of the University of Virginia that he devoted himself.

In politics Jefferson held certain very definite ideas. Unlike Hamilton, who spoke of the people as 'a great beast', Jefferson believed in the intelligence and decency of the average voter, confident that if left to himself he would, in the long run, do the wise thing. Men, in Jefferson's opinion, were 'naturally' good: it was only power that corrupted them. Hence the object of government was to check possible abuses of power. One method was to divide up the power as much as possible – separate executive, legislative and judiciary, separate State from Federal authority. Another was to set bounds to government by a written constitution which listed what government could and could not do. On the whole the safe rule, Jefferson thought, was for the government to do as little as possible, and since the tendency of people with power was to want more, Jefferson would even go so far as to say that 'a little rebellion now and then is a good thing ... as a medicine necessary for the sound health of government'.

But in addition to all these political devices for checking abuse of power – equal suffrage, the Constitution, etc. – Jefferson also counted on one social condition – a wide diffusion of property. The ideal society, in his view, was a society of small freeholders, citizens who each had a right to as much land as was needed to support his family. They would thus be sturdily independent, able to resist the blandishments of wealth or the pressure of a tyrannical government. In line with this, Jefferson was always trying to keep the American economy on an agricultural basis, resisting the development of large industries such as Hamilton favoured, and encouraging the opening up of the frontier where there was always abundant free land. 'I think we shall remain (virtuous) as long as agriculture is our principal object, which will be the case while there remain vacant lands in any part of America. When we get piled upon one another in huge cities, as in Europe, we shall become corrupt as in Europe, and go to eating one another as they do there.'

Whether or not it be true, as Jefferson supposed, that political virtue goes out when industrialism comes in, one thing is certain, that the growth and preservation of American democracy were intimately connected with the fact that, throughout the first hundred years of the Republic, there was always free land for the taking on the frontier. Men could always escape from a government they did not like by moving West. Oppressive landlords, stingy employers, tyrannically-minded politicians – a man of independent spirit could always escape from these by moving West where he could be his own master on his own land. So it happens that the tradition of Jeffersonian democracy becomes a Western tradition; it concerns itself with the problems of the public lands, of the settler on the frontier, of the small farmer. Andrew Jackson, Lincoln, Bryan – the great leaders of popular feeling – these, in their turn, came from the frontier, from the West. They carry on, each in his different way, this principle of Jefferson's – that democracy in America is closely dependent on the maintenance of the yeoman farmer and the right of access to the free lands of the West.

'Our first and fundamental maxim should be never to entangle ourselves in the broils of Europe.' It is one of the paradoxes of history that the statesman who had reiterated this maxim should as President have to devote a greater part of his time and energies to 'the broils of Europe' than anyone of his successors before Woodrow Wilson. Jefferson found the rôle distasteful – he would have liked to devote his Presidency to the quiet prosecution of domestic affairs – but he was not ill-prepared to cope with the problems which the European situation presented. From 1785 to 1789 he had represented the Confederacy as Minister at Paris and from 1790 to 1793 he had been Secretary of State under Washington. It was therefore no novice in diplomacy who faced the problems of a Europe and an Atlantic, which were menaced by the ambition of Napoleon.

It was not, however, Napoleon who first entangled Jefferson in 'the broils of Europe', but a much less famous individual, the Pasha of Tripoli, whose Barbary corsairs exacted from all the seagoing powers an annual tribute in return for leaving their merchant marine unmolested. This tribute had been paid since Washington's time, but in 1801 the Pasha decided to increase his price, bolstering his demands with a declaration of war. Congress accepted the challenge and for four years an intermittent naval war raged along the North African coast. It was not a great war, by any standards, but it had its own significance. In the first place it proved that, even under the 'continental-minded' Jefferson, America had certain vital interests for whose defence she would make war even in Europe – the interests of her trade and her merchant marine. Secondly, the success which attended American arms – the pirates were worsted and the tribute cancelled – proved that the American nation, though new and tiny, could not be trifled with. Thirdly, it gave great confidence to the United States Navy whose ships and men covered themselves with distinction: in particular a young captain, Stephen Decatur, who was soon to be heard of again.

But while these almost story-book exploits were taking place, as the song had it, 'on the shores of Tripol-ee', the impact of far greater European developments was being felt on America's own doorstep. At the moment of his greatest success in Europe, after the victory of Marengo and with the Emperor soon going to be forced to sue for peace, Napoleon was elaborating grandiose schemes for world domination. In the Americas the French flag already flew over the island of Haiti; in 1800 Napoleon took steps to secure a foothold on the mainland itself. Since 1763, when France had been compelled by the Peace of Paris to cede the territory to Spain, the territory of Louisiana had remained in Spanish hands. It was an area of vast and uncharted extent, ranging from the Mississippi to the Rocky Mountains; the area covered by the modern state of Louisiana was merely the core of this, the colony centring around New Orleans and the Mississippi delta, where some 40,000 settlers of French extraction lived on the labour of Negro slaves and the trade of the river mouth. Even as early as 1800 this trade was quite important. As the outlet for the Mississippi valley New Orleans received the produce of all the settled territories west of the Alleghanies. From Tennessee, Kentucky and Ohio came tobacco, flour, hemp, whisky, in fact all the produce which was too bulky for transport over the mountains to the east. To these states, fast filling with settlers, it was a vital matter who controlled New Orleans. So long as the Spaniards were there the settlers were happy because from them they enjoyed the rights of transhipment free of customs duty. But the French might easily exercise a stranglehold, for France was a rising power with ambitions and strength.

These fears were not unfounded. In 1802 Spain ceded Louisiana to Napoleon and along with the transfer went a stoppage of the customs immunity which the Americans had enjoyed. The present and the future of the West were imperilled. Jefferson recognized the danger and sent Monroe to Europe to see what could be done to avert it, short of war. But in fact events elsewhere were already turning the tide. In Haiti the French had won not a rich sugar island but a hotbed of Negro unrest in which the Negro chieftain, Toussaint L'Ouverture, organized a rebellion which, along with malaria, robbed the French army of 24,000 men. And, at this very moment, the threat of war between Britain and France revived in Europe. Napoleon decided to cut his losses. Suddenly, without warning, France offered the American envoys the sale of Louisiana. Scarcely believing their own good fortune, the Americans closed the deal without delay. For twelve million dollars they purchased Louisiana. So it came about that Jefferson, who believed in States' Rights and economy, spent a huge sum – as it then was – and gave the Union a new power – the right to purchase and own territory – which was not explicitly mentioned in the Constitution. But Congress endorsed his action, quick to see that the purchase opened up prospects for the future of the West so vast that they could only be guessed at, but compared with which the expenditure of twelve million dollars was a mere bagatelle.

But America's entanglements in the 'broils of Europe' did not end with the extrusion of European powers from the territory of Louisiana. In Europe and on the Atlantic the Napoleonic war, after the short-lived Peace of Amiens, was in furious spate again. From this conflict it was Jefferson's sincere wish to remain aloof, but the course of the war soon involved American interests and security. The British decided to employ against Napoleon the one weapon which gave them mastery and which he soon learnt to fear – the blockade. In 1807 a new turn was given to the screw when British Orders in Council debarred all neutrals from trading with any European port under French control. Napoleon retaliated in kind, by forbidding trade with Britain. Each country began to seize American ships and to confiscate their cargoes.

In another way, too, the naval war of France and Britain affected the United States of America. Both navies, but particularly the British, manned their ships by sailors captured by the press gang. To evade this, and to escape the foul living conditions prevalent in the British Navy, many a sailor deserted to American ships. There, if he could only assume the right accent, he could easily pass himself off as an American. The British not merely claimed the right to stop United States ships and recover their deserters, but often, in so doing, took off American citizens as well. This practice provoked in 1807 the incident of the *Chesapeake* and the *Leopard*, in which the British frigate fired on the *Chesapeake*, which refused to halt for inspection, killed three of her crew and removed four deserters, three of whom were in fact Americans who had been impressed into British service. American pride was stung. The country would readily have gone to war.

But Jefferson was determined to resist any such clamour. Harking back to the old days before the Revolution when the colonies had brought effective pressure to bear on Britain merely by refusing to trade with her, he induced Congress to pass an Embargo Act, forbidding any vessels to leave United States ports for foreign destinations and excluding from America any goods which came from France or England. But circumstances had changed since the days of 1766 and the 'non-importation association'. Britain could now get along better without American goods than American exporters and manufacturers could get along without the British market. It was the Yankee merchants who most resented the Act, not the British government. They were making such profits out of running the blockade that they were prepared not merely to flout Jefferson's Act but even to risk capture by Napoleon, who now extravagantly claimed that since any American vessel which put to sea violated its own country's Embargo Act it was a legitimate prize for French arms. As a device for coercing Britain or France the Embargo Act thus failed miserably. Its main effect was to increase, especially in New England, the resentment, which on other grounds was already strong, against the Jefferson administration. In 1809, just before going out of office, Jefferson was obliged to sign its substantial repeal.

CHAPTER XV

War with Britain

DELIGHTED at being able to resume the life of a Virginian philosopher-farmer, Jefferson gladly handed over the Presidency in 1809 to his fellow-Virginian and warm supporter, James Madison. The Federalists had not been able to prevent Madison's election, but dissident Republicans were soon busy venting on him the resentment which Jefferson's policy had aroused. It was Madison's intention to pursue a policy of conciliation with Britain, but from two quarters his policy met opposition: within his own party and from Britain.

More and more, the Republicans were drawing their strength, especially in the Senate, from the new population of the West. 'Free land' had been one of the cardinal principles of 'Jeffersonism', and those Republicans who were not restrained, as Jefferson was, by a deep love of peace, were prepared to go to any lengths to get it. The leader of this group was a young and eloquent lawyer from Kentucky – itself a frontier state – Henry Clay, who in 1810 was chosen as the Speaker of the House of Representatives. He employed this position in the interests of an aggressive policy, appointing to the important committees of the House, such as the Committee on Foreign Relations, those members of his party who could be counted on to advocate an expansion of American territory and control.

These young Republicans, the 'War Hawks' as they came to be called, wanted more land for settlement and a greater control of the profitable fur trade. Two groups stood between them and their ambitions, first the Indians who, in order to resist further encroachments on their territory, had banded themselves in an alliance under an able chieftain, Tecumseh, and secondly the British in Canada who had a big interest in the fur trade and also, the Westerners erroneously believed, bolstered Tecumseh's Confederacy. The issues at stake bore a remarkable resemblance to the issues of 1776. Then the disputed frontier had been along the Alleghanies; now it was the Mississippi Valley. But the War Hawks felt, with some justice, that they were continuing the struggle for control of the West which the Treaty of Paris of 1783 had left unsettled.

But though the Westerners of 1812 took their stand where the Westerners of 1783 had left off, that was not true of the business men and industrialists of the East. The War of Independence had done for them what its name implied – they were, economically, free of British control. All they wanted was as much trade with Britain as possible. This was what Madison's policy of conciliation tried to bring them. In 1809 he negotiated an agreement with Erskine, the British ambassador, which conceded most of the points at issue; in return for exemption from Britain's Orders in Council, the United States of America would lift all its bans on trade with Britain, while at the same time forbidding

United States ships to trade with France. Canning foolishly and arrogantly refused to ratify the agreement. Nevertheless Congress legalized trade with Britain, and promised to whichever belligerent first recognized neutral rights that it would forbid American trade with the other. Napoleon took advantage of this opportunity to promise in 1810 that he would withdraw his Decrees if the British would revoke their Orders in Council. Madison, not recognizing this as a trap of Napoleon's to involve him in war with Britain, demanded that the British should revoke their Orders. When the British pointed out that Napoleon's word was not to be relied on and that they could not change their policy merely on his promises, Madison forbade trade with Britain.

In Britain and America 'non-intercourse' was unpopular. Each side needed the other's trade. The true interests of each country stood on the side of peace. But an Anglo-American war meant different things in Britain and America. To Britain, locked in a life and death struggle with Napoleon, a struggle which in the winter of 1811–12 was more intense than ever before, differences over neutral rights seemed a small thing and even the prospect of a war with the United States, at a moment when Britain was already at war with almost every other great power, seemed a trifling addition to her already great burdens. But in America the war evoked echoes of 1776 and in the West in particular it seemed like a final bid to make real the claims to Independence which had been staked out then. The war meant land, the prestige of a young nation, the chance to take advantage of the quarrels of old Europe to establish the destiny of young America. On this basis, popular enthusiasm was whipped up and on June 18th, 1812, Congress declared war. There was no wireless and no telegraph to tell them that two days before, on June 16th, Lord Castlereagh had announced in the House of Commons that the British Orders in Council would be suspended immediately. The war, in fact, had been begun two days after the alleged cause had been removed.

America entered the war divided. The 'War Hawks' succeeded in winning a majority in Congress, but it was a narrow majority with which to wage war. In the House the voting was 70 to 49, in the Senate 19 to 13: the figures reflected the fact that New England, New Jersey and New York opposed the war. It wrecked their trade, endangered their territory, and violated the principles of all of their citizens who believed in friendship with Britain and deplored the military dictatorship of Napoleon. Their opposition did not wane, but rather increased, the longer the war went on. They discouraged volunteering and refused to place their militia at the disposal of the Union. In the winter of 1812 they ran a peace candidate, De Witt Clinton, a Federalist of New York, to oppose Madison's re-election to the Presidency. The voting in the election proved more clearly than anything else the sectional nature of the war. The Federalists carried every state north of the Potomac except Pennsylvania and Vermont: only the South and West voted for Madison and the war. So continuous and bitter was New England's opposition to 'the Republican War' that in 1814 the New England States met in convention at Hartford, Conn., to discuss the revision of the Constitution with a view to the greater protection of their interests – and even the possibility of secession. It was a bad moment for the United States. True, New England had never wanted the war. True, her trade and her shipping were seriously threatened, her coastline was endangered by British landings while her back country was being invaded from Canada, her taxes were heavy and the numbers of her unemployed were mounting. Even so, had the Hartford Convention come out for secession or a separate peace the days of America as the *United* States would have been numbered, and the great experiment of the Union would have been wrecked by that very party, the Federalists, who had done most to promote it. Fortunately, wiser counsels prevailed, and the Convention contented itself with criticizing Madison's conduct of the war and demanding a larger voice for the states in the control of defence and taxes. And by the time the Convention's emissaries had arrived in Washington with their protestations, peace had been signed and the war was over.

The details of the conduct of the war need not long concern us. Both sides fought with one hand behind their back – the British because their major enemy was Napoleon, the Americans because of New England's antipathy. The principal battlefield was the American-Canadian border, the shores of the Great Lakes and the three great 'bottlenecks' represented by Niagara, Detroit and Mackinac Island, while on the lakes themselves the British and American fleets struggled for control of the land approaches. At sea British and American naval vessels and privateers fought a series of isolated and bitter actions, while the British utilized their superior numbers to enforce a blockade of the New England coastline. Despite the relatively small numbers of the forces engaged the war was fought with considerable ferocity, partly attributable to the employment by both sides of Indian allies, who introduced the tactics of the forest in place of the military ethics of the Anglo-Saxon. Thus, when the Americans raided the capital of Upper Canada, the village of York (later to become the city of Toronto), their indiscipline resulted in the burning of the bulk of the government buildings. The British replied in no better style when in 1814 the navy landed a force in Maryland which marched on Washington, routed its defenders and burnt all the public buildings, including the Capitol and the White House.

To Britain the war was a sideshow to the great Napoleonic struggle, a tiresome diversion which promised neither power nor glory. They fought it out in routine style, without enthusiasm or concentration. But to those Americans who supported it, the war was a very serious business. It was, after all, fought on their doorstep and for them it was not a sideshow, but the first – and most vital – trial by battle which the young nation had had to undergo. On the water in particular the American Republic felt that her prestige and her pride were involved in the contest with the greatest maritime power in history. The Republic acquitted herself well; the result has been that the War of 1812 is principally remembered as a repository of naval traditions. The exploits of Stephen Decatur in the Atlantic and Commodore Perry on Lake Erie gave the American navy the same kind of self-confidence and pride that the British sailor draws from the memories of Drake and Nelson.

For over two years the war inclined, haphazardly, now to one side, now to the other, with America winning most of the victories and Britain feeling least of the hurts. When statesmanship eventually brought the war to an end it was not as a result of any clear-cut military decision. On the contrary, the principal military engagement of the war was not fought until after the peace was signed – once again owing to the absence of a transatlantic cable to speed the news – when General Jackson defeated a British force that was trying to close the Mississippi by the seizure of New Orleans. The negotiation of peace was due to a sensible recognition on both sides that nothing was to be gained by prolonging the war. With the defeat of Napoleon in 1814 most of the points of dispute ceased to be live issues. Both sides wanted the resumption of trade and the cessation of hostilities. The delegates met on neutral soil, at Ghent, the American delegation including both John Quincy Adams, of the New England family, and Henry Clay, the young 'War Hawk'. The treaty was signed on Christmas Eve, 1814. Critics made play with the fact that on the points about which Britain and the U.S.A. went to war, the practice of impressment and the rights of neutrals, the Treaty was totally silent. It concerned itself merely with boundary questions and fishing rights – and even on these it decided nothing beyond the appointment of commissions to decide them later. But, looking back from the distance of 130 years of unbroken peace between Britain and the U.S.A., we can assess the Treaty of Ghent somewhat differently. We can now see that its great achievement was to terminate a stupid war which should never have been begun and whose continuance could breed only increasing ill-feeling. In place of such meaningless bloodshed the Treaty established a precedent of settlement by negotiation which both American and British statesmen have recognized and acted upon ever since.

CHAPTER XVI

The Presidency of Monroe

ONE major result of the War of 1812 was to intensify nationalist sentiment in the United States. The young country was naturally proud of having been able to preserve the independence it had so recently won. It felt a new confidence in itself, a new ability to stand on its own feet and carve out its own destiny. Characteristically, it was the young 'War Hawk', Henry Clay, who translated this new national sentiment into a programme. He called it 'The American System' and embodied in it many of the ideas which Alexander Hamilton had advocated in his 'Report on Manufactures' in 1791. 'The American System' rested on two policies – protection and internal improvements. By protecting American manufactures behind a tariff high enough to keep out competing imports Clay, like Hamilton, hoped to build up the industry of the country. By spending federal funds on the construction of much-needed roads and waterways, he hoped to improve internal communications and so counteract the tendency of the young Republic to outgrow itself—to spread westward so fast that the frontier would get out of touch with the seaboard.

Clay found a warm welcome for his schemes of protection. The War of 1812 had given a big fillip to manufactures; the return of peace threatened a revival of British competition and the loss of the domestic market. The Westerners who were growing wool for the mills of New England gave their support to the proposal and the result was that in 1816 a duty of 25 per cent. was laid on imported textile goods. Linked with the tariff was a second Bank of the United States. Hamilton's original creation had been allowed to lapse in 1811, owing to doubts about its constitutionality. This time it was a Southerner, John C. Calhoun, an ardent supporter of Clay's, who succeeded in putting it through

Congress in 1816. This gave the federal government a valuable control over credit and bound the commercial interests of the country ever more closely to the Union.

Clay and Calhoun were less successful with their schemes for 'internal improvements'. Monroe, who succeeded Madison in the Presidency in 1817 with scarcely any serious opposition from the Federalists, because the viewpoints of Republicans and Federalists were by now almost indistinguishable, was prepared to go a long way in company with the new nationalist tendencies and their consequent federalizing influence, but he was doubtful whether the Constitution gave Congress the power to use federal funds for *inter-state* roads and canals. He favoured a constitutional amendment, to remove all risk of unconstitutionality. But a constitutional amendment takes time and infinite effort to put through, and the practical effect of Monroe's opposition was to cripple most of Clay's projects. Clay did induce Congress to spend money on one route, though only on condition that each section, on completion, should be made over to its appropriate State; that was the famous 'Cumberland turnpike', a road which linked the Potomac with the Ohio and so provided a route across the Alleghanies which linked up at each end with a navigable river. Until 1840 it remained the principal route for western emigration. Further north New York State, when it became apparent that Monroe would do nothing out of federal funds, began work in 1817 on the Erie Canal. This canal, which was completed in 1825, ran from Albany to Buffalo and so linked the Hudson with the Great Lakes above the level of Niagara Falls. Its great value lay in the fact that at a time when roads were still bad and railways unknown, it united the north-east and north-west by a cheap system of water transport. It linked New York with the expanding west and did a great deal to give that city its commanding position as a centre of trade, finance and transport.

This concern with communications reflected the rapid growth of the west. The War of 1812 had been largely provoked by the expansionist tendencies of the west: now that the war was over and the Western settler was guaranteed against the risk of having his territory annexed by Britain, and also was promised federal defence against the Indian, that expansionist movement was speeded up. In the ten years from 1810 to 1820 the population west of the Alleghanies grew from 1,080,000 to 2,234,000, and by 1820 more than a quarter of the population of the Union was living across the mountains. In quick succession the new 'territories' thus populated were admitted to statehood – Indiana in 1816, Mississippi in 1817, Illinois in 1818 and Alabama in 1819, with the result that within four years of the end of the war all America up to the Mississippi had been carved up into the same pattern of states that one sees on a modern map of the U.S.A. – Michigan and Florida alone excepted, representing the extremes of north and south which lay outside the main channels of immigration.

The West in fact grew *too* fast—as it always had done and always would do. Quite early in its history, in 1796, the United States had tried to establish an orderly procedure for the settlement of the West. By this Act the Union took over the principles which the Confederation had laid down in its Ordinance of 1785, providing for the surveying of land into units six miles square and their sale at low prices to settlers. By this the government hoped to control the rate of settlement and prevent the frontier being either too thinly or too thickly populated. But the frontiersman took little notice of this scheme. He tended to squat where the land seemed good, to stay as long as the game was abundant and his neighbours not too numerous, and then, if either condition changed, to move on, without bothering too much about the title to his property. Nor was settlement much tidier at the next stage, that of the farmer. He mostly bought the title to his land not directly from the government, but from land speculators, who bought up large territories at a cheap rate and sold them piecemeal for what they would fetch. The years after the 1812 War were, as often happens after wars, boom years. The prices of cotton, cattle and grain soared and the prices of land soared with them. The hordes of settlers who spread into the new states paid fancy prices for their lands and were almost all in debt to the land companies from whom they bought them. Men incurred debts far beyond their capacity to pay, and after the boom came the inevitable slump. Farmers defaulted, speculators went bankrupt, the hundred and one 'wild-cat' banks which had sprung up went smash and almost the only financial institution to survive in the West was the Bank of the United States, which acquired title to millions of acres of Western lands.

The result was to produce one of those cleavages between East and West – between the East which owned the money and the West which lived off the land – which repeats itself in the history of the frontier. The East insisted on payment in full, the West wanted to meet its debts by printing paper money and so lowering the value of the dollar. The immediate effect of the Land Panic of 1819 was two-fold – to turn the West against the Bank of the United States, which was regarded henceforth as the 'money monster'; and to cause a swift drop in the price of land. It did nothing, however, to slow up the rate of Western settlement.

This settlement proceeded very much on East-West lines. That is to say it was mostly New Englanders who settled in Ohio and Indiana, Virginians who moved into Kentucky, Carolinians who crossed into Alabama and Mississippi. The result was to reproduce across the Alleghanies something of the sectional differences which existed along the seaboard. In nothing was this so pronounced as in the question of slavery. Since the earliest colonial days the South had known and practised Negro slavery. Three factors had made it possible. The first was the system of land tenure which had given the South so many large plantations in contrast to the small freehold farms of the North. The second was the type of settler and the form of government which, except perhaps in the case of Virginia, was less conducive to the establishment of democratic principles than in the Northern colonies. The third and most important was the agricultural economy of the South. The South, partly because of the soil and climate, partly because of its European markets, concentrated on three great crops – cotton, tobacco and sugar – but, above all, on cotton. These lent themselves very easily to cultivation by unskilled slave labour. Savage Africans who could never have been trained to work on the small, mixed, all-purpose type of farm common in New England, could easily be mobilized, under overseers, to work in unskilled groups of cotton pickers or rice planters on the plantations of Georgia or South Carolina. Thus the cheapness of these staple crops, on which the South relied for its prosperity, depended on the employment of a mass of unpaid Negro labour.

For all these reasons nothing was said in the Constitution about slavery. It was regarded as being a matter for the states, not the Union, to settle, although one clause dealt with the slave *trade* in a manner which clearly indicated what the general expectation on the subject was. The clause prohibited Congress from passing legislation curtailing the slave trade until a period of twenty years had elapsed. As soon as the period was up Congress passed the legislation and abolished the slave trade on January 1st, 1808. By that date all except three southern states had already passed similar legislation. *Slavery* itself, as apart from the *trade* in slaves, was abolished in all the northern states by 1805, and, since the Ordinance of 1787, which set up the North-West Territory, had prohibited slavery throughout that area, all the new states carved out of the Territory – Ohio, Indiana, etc. – were free states, too.

This liberal movement might have attained similar success in the South had it not been for an event that occurred in 1793. In that year Eli Whitney, a New Englander visiting the South, invented his 'cotton gin'. By the use of this machine an ignorant slave could clean cotton of its seeds at a rate 100 to 1,000 times faster than by hand. The result was to make raw cotton available at a greatly reduced price; this coincided with the mechanization of the whole cotton industry in Britain and New England. In consequence vast new markets were opened up for cotton,* which thus became

* The export of cotton from the South jumped from 192,000 lb. in 1791 to 6,000,000 lb. in 1795.

the staple crop throughout the South, which in turn depended more and more on slave labour for its production. Thus at the moment when humanitarian considerations were eliminating slavery everywhere else, economic changes were fastening it on the South. There were Southerners who saw where this must lead. 'I tremble for my country', Jefferson wrote, 'when I reflect that God is just: that his justice cannot sleep for ever.' But there was no one who seemed able to control the drive of these economic forces. As the cotton trade grew, new lands were put under cultivation by slave labour – across the Alleghanies, south of the Ohio, and even across the Mississippi in Louisiana. Then, in 1819, a crisis was reached.

Up to 1818 the South had held her own – and indeed more than held her own – in the balance of power within the Union. New states were admitted, but the balance was preserved. If the North had a new state, Indiana, in 1816, the South had Mississippi in 1817. Illinois in 1818 was balanced by Alabama in the next year. Thus the South kept an exact balance in voting strength in the Senate. This was particularly important because in the House of Representatives, where seats were allotted not by states but by population, the South was gradually losing to the more populous North. Then, in 1819, Missouri, the new Territory across the Mississippi, applied for admission to the Union. Missouri fell within the 'Louisiana Territory' which Jefferson had purchased in 1803. In ratifying that purchase Congress had said nothing about slavery within the area and the South therefore expected that Missouri, like Louisiana itself, would enter as a slave state. But a New Yorker in Congress introduced an amendment to prohibit slavery in the new state and the bill passed the House in that form, though it was defeated in the Senate.

When Congress adjourned in March, the issue was taken up and debated in the country at large. Passions ran high and there was some talk of 'secession' if the South did not get its way. However, by January, 1820, when Congress reassembled, a compromise had been arranged. Missouri was

WASHINGTON
Astoria
OREGON COUNTRY
Portland
OREGON
acquired
IDAHO
1846
MONTANA
Butte
NORTH DAKOT
Bismarc
LOUISIANA
SOUTH DAKOT
purchase
WYOMING
NEBRASKA
1803
Cheyenne
NEVADA
Salt Lake City
CALIFORNIA
Sacramento
San Francisco
UTAH
THE MEXICAN CESSION
Denver
COLORADO
Kansa
KANS
Los Angeles
ARIZONA
1848
Santa Fé
NEW MEXICO
OKLA
GADSDEN PURCHASE 1853
TEXAS
annexed
1845
El Paso
TEXAS

U.S.A.

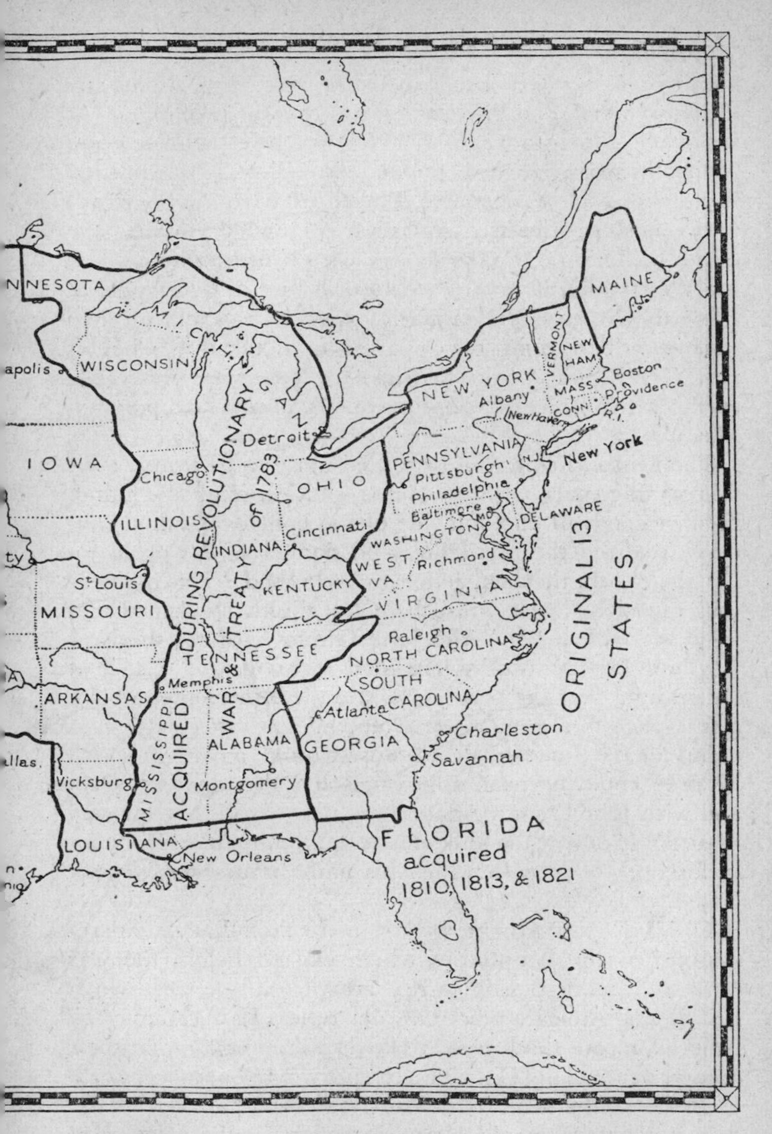

NNESOTA
MAINE
VERMONT
NEW HAM
MICHIGAN
apolis
WISCONSIN
NEW YORK
Albany
Boston
MASS
Providence
CONN
R.I.
New Haven
Detroit
PENNSYLVANIA
N.J.
New York
IOWA
Chicago
Pittsburgh
OHIO
Philadelphia
Baltimore
MD
DELAWARE
ILLINOIS
Cincinnati
WASHINGTON
INDIANA
WEST VA
Richmond
ORIGINAL 13 STATES
St Louis
KENTUCKY
VIRGINIA
MISSOURI
ACQUIRED DURING REVOLUTIONARY WAR & TREATY of 1783
Raleigh
NORTH CAROLINA
TENNESSEE
Memphis
SOUTH CAROLINA
ARKANSAS
Atlanta
Charleston
ALABAMA
GEORGIA
Savannah
llas.
Vicksburg
Montgomery
MISSISSIPPI
FLORIDA acquired 1810, 1813, & 1821
LOUISIANA
New Orleans

POLITICAL

admitted as a slave state, but in the rest of the Louisiana Territory north of a line 36° 30′ slavery was prohibited. At the same time, to keep the North-South balance even, Maine, hitherto a scantily populated territory, was admitted to statehood – free, of course. Thus the horizontal boundary between slave and free states was extended, so that the South could hope to take slavery with it into those parts of the West which lay along its natural line of development, while the North could similarly expect to expand into free territory. The right of Congress to determine whether new Territories should be slave or free was preserved; at the same time the South won its immediate point in Missouri.

The Missouri compromise settled nothing. It simply gave a breathing space within which a solution might be found. Men of goodwill on each side of the controversy had suddenly realized the immensity and danger of the problem. For the South, the aged Jefferson exclaimed, 'This momentous question, like a fire-bell in the night, awakened and filled me with terror.' And John Quincy Adams, the New England President-to-be, confided to his diary, 'I take it for granted that the present question is a mere preamble – a title-page to a great tragic volume.'

But for the time being calm was restored, a calm in which Monroe could be peaceably re-elected President in 1820, and with John Quincy Adams once more as his Secretary of State could devote the bulk of his attention to those problems of foreign policy with which his name is deservedly associated.

The Treaty of Ghent, by the mere fact that it had re-established the boundaries which existed before the war broke out, made possible a real advance in the trust which Britain and America placed in each other. Its acceptance by America meant that the War Hawks were abandoning their dreams of annexing Canadian territory, while its acceptance by Britain put an end to the American fear that their Canadian neighbours would try to encroach on the Mississippi Valley. Men of good sense and good will on each side of the Atlantic, recognizing these facts, went on to ask themselves the question – if the grounds for conflict are removed, why keep up the means for making war? Now that the frontier was no longer in dispute, why not demilitarize it?

In a surprisingly short time both sides arrived at the same sensible conclusion. In 1817 Richard Rush, the American Acting Secretary of State, and Charles Bagot, the British Minister at Washington, representing Lord Liverpool's administration in London, signed the famous Rush-Bagot Agreement, which is the first example of limitation of armaments by international agreement. Under its terms both Britain and the U.S.A. undertook not to maintain any armed naval forces on the Great Lakes where so recently their rival navies had come to such bitter blows. Out of this grew a tacit agreement not to keep armed forces anywhere along the U.S.-Canadian frontier, so that from then until now the boundary line between the two countries has been a tangible proof of their determination to settle their disputes by peaceful processes.

The details of the boundary line thus demilitarized were settled by the Convention of 1818, which met to work out the implications of the Treaty of Ghent. From the point where the natural boundary of the Great Lakes left off, a purely artificial boundary was established along the 49th degree of latitude, as far west as the Rocky Mountains. This was so far ahead of the existing frontier of settlement that the question of determining the boundary beyond the Rockies was unfortunately left open, and had to be thrashed out again with some acrimony in 1846.

The United States had thus succeeded by 1818 in settling her northern boundaries. There remained the minor problem of the south. The Louisiana Purchase brought under the American flag a vast area west of the Mississippi, but how far it affected Spain's holdings east of the Mississippi, in Florida, was a matter of dispute. Jefferson had been very anxious to remove this last European foothold along the southern boundaries of the U.S.A. and put strong pressure on Spain to yield up the territory. The controversy dragged on, while more and more American settlers filtered into the disputed territory and the strength and manhood of Spain were drained away in the long and terrible Peninsular War.

Out of Spain's weakness the U.S.A. gathered strength. Madison took advantage of disturbances in West Florida to bring the area by degrees under American control, so that the end of the 1812 War saw only East Florida (the area covered by the present State of Florida) still under the Spanish flag, and even in this area Spain was too weak to preserve order and check hostile Indian forays, which were a continual source of disturbance to the neighbouring state of Georgia. Eventually, in 1819, Adams concluded a very lengthy series of negotiations with the Spaniards, which settled boundary lines both west and south. In return for five million dollars Spain ceded all her lands east of the Mississippi and also gave up all her vague claims to lands in the west, the so-called 'Oregon Country'. A boundary line between the U.S.A. and the Spanish colony of Mexico was established which, for the time being at least, defined, very satisfactorily for the U.S.A., just what it was that Jefferson had obtained when he purchased 'Louisiana'.

It was the weakness of Spain which enabled the United States thus cheaply, and without war, to expand to the 'natural' limits dictated by geography and her own ambitions. It was the same Spanish weakness which now began to pose an issue of supreme importance for the future of the whole American hemisphere. At the end of the eighteenth century Spain still controlled, under a very rigid administration operated from Madrid, the whole of Latin America, the Portuguese colony, Brazil, alone excepted. The overthrow by Napoleon of the Spanish dynasty in 1808 was the signal for the revolt of all these colonies from Spanish control. Restoration of the 'legitimate' Spanish monarchy in 1814, on the defeat of Napoleon, gave Spain a chance to recover her control, but she was too weak to re-establish herself unaided. Revolution throughout Latin America flared up again in 1817 more fiercely than ever. In the face of it the Spanish king turned to the Holy Alliance, the league of anti-revolutionary European monarchs, in the hope that they would help him to recover his lost possessions.

There were two countries to whom a restoration of Spanish control in Latin America was a displeasing prospect: Britain and the U.S.A. Britain had always resented the way in which Spain debarred her colonies from trading with other countries; the revolt of the colonies opened them up for British commerce for the first time in history. American traders welcomed it for the same reason. In addition, American public opinion in general liked to think of the South American revolutions in the same terms as the North American revolt of 1776 and was flattered when one South American country after another adopted constitutions that outwardly were copies of the American model.

Nevertheless, the U.S.A. was cautious. The government's first step in 1815 was to issue a proclamation of neutrality, and it was not until 1822 – after the conclusion of the Florida negotiations – that President Monroe and Congress recognized the rebellious colonies as independent republics. It was at this stage that Spain appealed to the Holy Alliance. The dominant power in the Holy Alliance was Russia, with whom, on another issue, the United States was already at odds. In the eighteenth century Russian fur traders and fishermen had established themselves in Alaska; ever since they had been edging southwards along the Pacific coast. In so doing they entered an area, the somewhat vague and ill-defined 'Oregon', in which both the U.S.A. and Canada were developing a keen interest.

As early as 1811 John Jacob Astor of New York had established the trading post of Astoria at the mouth of the Columbia River. When, therefore, in 1821 the Tsar issued an edict by which he assumed ownership of the Pacific coast as far south as the fifty-first parallel, he was in effect encroaching on a territory which the Americans and the British had agreed to reserve as an area for joint exploitation. To Adams this seemed like a bid by the most reactionary member of the Holy Alliance to spread its dynamic principles on the very soil of free North America. He informed the

Russians that the U.S.A. did not recognize such a claim and took the view that 'the American continents are no longer subjects for *any* new European colonial establishments'.

At this stage, and while Adams's rebuke to Russia still awaited further action to enforce it, Britain stepped in. Her foreign minister, Canning, proposed to Rush, the United States minister in London, that Britain and the U.S.A., since their interests in respect of Latin America were parallel, should make a joint declaration to the Holy Alliance warning its members that they would not permit any European power to re-subjugate the independent republics. Jefferson and Madison were in favour of accepting this proposal outright, but Adams persuaded President Monroe against precipitately and openly associating the U.S.A. with a European power. In line with this policy Monroe agreed to suspend action for a month or two. Impatiently Canning went ahead. He informed the French Minister, in what came to be known as 'the Polignac Memorandum', that Britain would not tolerate any French intervention aimed at the newly liberated states of Latin America. Britain's position was thus clear beyond dispute, and there stood behind it the power of the British navy upon which any such policy must depend, since it alone could control the Atlantic, and decide whether in fact the Holy Alliance would or would not be able to put its plans for reconquest into effect. Monroe now felt that with Britain's might so firmly pledged to a 'hands-off' policy he could now safely make public the convictions of the U.S.A. He waited for Congress to meet and then, on December 2nd, 1823, delivered the Message ever since associated with his name.

The Message announced that 'amicable negotiations' had been begun between the U.S.A. and Russia over the Alaska boundary, and went on to assert the principle 'that the American continents, by the free and independent condition which they have assumed and maintained, are henceforth not to be considered as subjects for future colonization by any European powers.' In a word, no new European colonies in North or South America. Nor, it added, would the U.S.A. tolerate any European attempt to interfere with the political systems of countries in the Americas.

Equally, the Message asserted, the United States would abstain from taking part 'in the wars of the European powers in matters relating to themselves'. They would follow Washington's advice and not embroil themselves unless their own rights were 'invaded or seriously menaced'. In return, Europe could rest assured that 'with the existing colonies or dependencies of any European power we have not interfered and shall not interfere'.

The wording of the Message annoyed Canning, and he suspected (erroneously) that the remarks on 'colonization' were designed to keep the British out of Oregon. Consequently there was no British endorsement of the 'hands-off' principle, and the agreements with Russia, by which she confined her Alaskan boundary to 54° 40′, were made separately at St Petersburg by the U.S.A. and Britain. Nevertheless the two main principles of the Message – of preventing further European aggrandisement, territorial or political, in the Americas – chimed in with his earlier Polignac Memorandum. For Americans the importance of the Monroe Doctrine was not that it kept the Holy Alliance out of Latin America – it was Canning and the British navy that had done that – but that it laid down the principles of U.S. foreign policy for generations to come. The clarity and cogency of its arguments led Americans to set Monroe's Message side by side with Washington's Farewell Address as a cardinal text of national policy. Only in one respect has the phrasing of the Message proved somewhat misleading. Monroe's preference for an independent statement, parallel to Canning's but making no explicit reference to it, obscures the fact that the Monroe Doctrine reposed upon the tacit support of Great Britain. Had any European state challenged it in the days of the U.S.A.'s infancy as a great power, only the British navy could have saved Latin America from that 'colonization' and 'interference' which the Doctrine forbade, and indeed it is not to much too say that it was the knowledge that the British navy would, if necessary, be so employed that really served to check any such aggressive designs. In that sense the Monroe Doctrine rested upon what was almost an unwritten Anglo-American alliance, and derived its force from that very fact. Unfortunately the absence of any mention of such a fact in Monroe's Message itself meant that later generations of Americans sometimes overlooked it, and formed the mistaken impression that the width of the ocean plus the unaided strength of the U.S.A. were themselves sufficient to keep all foes away from the American continent.

CHAPTER XVII

Marshall and Jackson

WITH the end of Monroe's second Presidency in 1825 there also ended what had been called 'the era of good feelings', the eight years after 1816 during which the strife of parties was at a lower ebb than at any other time between the founding of the Union and the Civil War. The rivalry between Federalists and Republicans had ceased. The Federalists suffered a fate which often befalls political parties, of seeing their doctrines generally accepted just as they themselves are going into liquidation. The behaviour of the New England Federalists at the Hartford Convention in 1814 gave the party a bad name from which it never recovered. But just at that moment Federalist doctrines began to find a far more powerful advocacy in the Supreme Court through the judgments of Chief Justice Marshall.

There have been other Chief Justices whose learning and character have left their marks on the history of the United States, but none of them who compares in importance with the great Marshall — the Chief Justice who, in private life, was one of the most unassuming of men, but on the bench was one of the strongest personalities of his age. The Constitution had set up three branches of government for the federal union. The first of these, the executive, immediately attained prestige and power, from the day when Washington assumed the responsibilities of the Presidency. The second, Congress, similarly established itself as a body whose membership and powers commanded public respect. But the third branch of the federal government, the federal judiciary, had lagged behind in importance and popular estimation. Right away, in 1789, Congress had utilized its powers under the Constitution to set up, by a Judiciary Act, a system of Federal Courts – District Courts, one for each state or territory, and a high court of appeal, the Supreme Court of the United States. But the first Chief Justice, John Jay, famous for his diplomatic triumphs, was not a great force on the bench. His term was cut short by his assignment, in 1794, as envoy extraordinary to London to negotiate the treaty which bears his name, and his successor, Oliver Ellsworth, was a figure of little importance. Then in 1800, Jefferson's election to the Presidency swept the Federalists from the seats of power in White House and in Congress. Adams, the outgoing President, had one shot left to fire before he withdrew. In November, 1800, Ellsworth resigned; without delay, in the brief period that remained before his own retirement, Adams appointed his Secretary of State, John Marshall, to be Chief Justice. It became immediately apparent that a figure of no small importance had come on to the legal scene.

In addition to appointing Marshall, the outgoing Adams had persuaded Congress to pass an Act increasing the number of federal judgeships, vacancies which Adams had then filled with persons of his own party. One of these 'midnight appointments' made by Adams just before leaving was of a certain Marbury, a Justice of the Peace in the District of Columbia. Madison, Jefferson's Secretary of State, refused to give Marbury his commission. The case was taken to the courts and tried before Marshall. Marshall sternly rebuked Madison for his behaviour, asking, 'Is it to be contended that the heads of departments are not amenable to the laws of their country?' in tones which made it clear that the court regarded itself as on a par with other agencies of government. But the case involved a still more important point. Marbury invoked clause 13 of the Judiciary Act of 1789 to prove that the Supreme Court could and should give him a writ against Madison and so provide him with a remedy. On looking into the Constitution, Marshall could find no clause which conferred any such power or duty on the courts. In other words, an Act of Congress and the Constitution were found to be in conflict. What was the court to do? The question of the issuance of a writ was not of great importance; the question of a clash between Congress and the Constitution was.

The object of the Constitution is to set down certain general principles according to which the government of the United States is to be conducted, but surprisingly enough it does not say in so many words who is to have the deciding voice when the meaning of any of those principles is in dispute or when any part of the government seems to be violating them. In Britain the problem does not arise. Parliament is a sovereign body which is not bound to any written constitution. The laws which it passes are the highest law of the land; if they conflict with earlier legislation that legislation has to give way; if they override the bye-laws of a county or borough those bye-laws are automatically superseded. Consequently the job of the courts is never to question the laws of Parliament, but only to expound them. In the U.S.A., however, Congress is not the only law-making body: the states make laws as well. The spheres of each are limited by the Constitution. If they come into conflict with each other or with the Constitution someone must adjudicate. Who? Marshall, the first figure who had to decide such a question, did not hesitate to reply, 'the courts'.

'(In the United States) the powers of the legislature', said Marshall in his famous decision, 'are defined and limited; and to what purpose is that limitation committed to writing if these limits may at any time be passed by those intended to be restrained? ... It is a proposition too plain to be contested that the Constitution controls any legislative act repugnant to it ... A legislative act contrary to the Constitution is not law ... It is emphatically the province and duty of the judicial department to say what the law is.' So, although the Constitution nowhere explicitly says that the courts can pass on the constitutionality of laws, Marshall arrived at the conclusion that the Constitution clearly implies as much and would be meaningless if it did not.

To many of his contemporaries Marshall's decision came as a great shock, but the force of his reasoning soon carried conviction. Some body had to decide these disputes. The President and Congress were scarcely fitted to do so, since they would almost always be interested parties, whose acts or whose laws were the points at issue. Alternatively, if the conflict were between federal and state legislation neither Congress nor a state government could claim to be impartial judges. The charge would often be made that the Supreme Court was not impartial either – indeed Marshall's decisions were repeatedly attacked as being too friendly to the federal power – but no one ever suspected a Supreme Court of justice of being corruptible and no one, to this day, has been able to devise a better tribunal for settling constitutional disputes. Consequently, since the days of *Marbury v. Madison* the Supreme Court has exercised a power comparable with that of Congress itself, in the capacity to decide the constitutionality of legislation, the power of 'judicial review'.

As might be expected, the years succeeding *Marbury v. Madison* saw a number of cases of the greatest constitutional importance come before the court. On all of them Marshall pronounced with a clarity and firmness which powerfully influenced the course of constitutional development during the early and formative years of the Union. Perhaps the most important case of all was the famous *McCulloch v. Maryland* which dealt with problems arising out of the re-establishment by the federal government of the Bank of the United States. A branch of the bank was opened at Baltimore and the state of Maryland in 1819 claimed the right to tax it, as property situated within the state's territory. But this claim raised an earlier question – had the U.S.A. in the first place the right to establish a federal bank? Its enemies had contended that among the powers enumerated in the Constitution as belonging to the federal government the establishment of a bank was not listed. To this Marshall replied by drawing attention to the clause which entitles Congress 'to make all laws which shall be *necessary and proper*' for executing the various powers it enumerates. This clause, Marshall said, meant that the national government should enjoy a wide range of choice in the selection of means for carrying out its enumerated powers. 'Let the end be legitimate, let it be within the scope of the Constitution, and all means which are appropriate, which are plainly adapted to that end, which are not prohibited, but consist with the letter and spirit of the Constitution, are constitutional.' This 'loose construction' of the terms 'necessary and proper' thus enabled Congress to do a number of things which a strict interpretation would have prevented.

Congress has the right to establish a bank, but cannot Maryland tax it? Marshall decided no, because such taxation would 'impede' the operation of the bank, might even be used by a State as a weapon to defeat Congress's purpose, since, as Marshall pointed out, 'the power to tax is a power to destroy' – so the bank might be taxed out of existence.

As these rulings suggest, Marshall was a believer in a strong Union, and an opponent of those who would interpret the Constitution in a way which favoured States Rights. His opinion in *McCulloch v. Maryland* is the classic statement of his general position. The powers which the Constitution gives to the federal government are not delegated by the states. Just as the Constitution begins with the words, 'We, the people of the United States ...' so 'the government of the Union is emphatically and truly a government of the people. ... Its powers are granted by them and are to be exercised directly on them and for their benefit'. A state cannot interfere with, or oppose, what the whole people of the United States have thus decided.

In line with this 'federalist' or 'national sovereignty' interpretation Marshall defined many other ambiguous phrases of the Constitution. The Constitution gives Congress power over 'inter-state commerce'. Does commerce merely mean 'trade', or 'intercourse' in general? The difference is obviously immense and Marshall's decision in *Gibbons v. Ogden* in favour of 'intercourse' gave Congress great powers over all forms of transport, as well as trade. Again the Constitution forbids a state to interfere with contracts. In the famous *Dartmouth College* case Marshall defined a charter to a corporation as a contract. This had the excellent effect of protecting institutions of learning from interference by state legislatures and the less beneficial effect of making it very difficult for states to control the behaviour of business companies within their borders.

For thirty-four years, during the most formative period of the Constitution, Marshall sat as Chief Justice, outlasting Presidents and Congresses, employing his massive intellect always to drive home a few simple principles, of which these three may be regarded as the most essential :

1. The Constitution emanates from the whole people of the United States and is not a compact of states.
2. Consequently, it is to be interpreted with a view to securing the general welfare of the people as a whole and not with the purpose of safeguarding state sovereignty.
3. The Constitution was further designed, as near as may be, 'for immortality' and was meant to be 'adapted to the various crises of human affairs'. It should, therefore, not be interpreted with a narrow literalness, but with a due regard to the needs of the times.

These principles have lasted to become part and parcel of the accepted thinking of American jurists and statesmen and Marshall must always have an honoured place among the nation's founders for his foresight and courage in their enunciation. But they were by no means accepted by the mass of his contemporaries and even as he was formulating them an opposite theory was in the making, which later was to find forceful expression through a Southerner, John C. Calhoun.

In 1825, when John Quincy Adams, Monroe's Secretary of State, succeeded to the Presidency, such constitutional issues formed no part of the four-cornered contest. The issues,indeed, were more personal than political. Adams had the appeal of long and meritorious public service. William Crawford, previously Secretary of the Treasury, could claim that as a Virginian he was in the long line of descent that went back to George Washington. Henry Clay had charm, parliamentary virtuosity and the backing of the settlers who were based upon the Ohio and Mississippi valleys. Andrew Jackson of Tennessee had a military record and a frontiersman's egalitarianism to display before the country. Faced by such a bewildering choice, the electors failed to give any candidate the overwhelming majority that the Constitution demands. The election was accordingly settled by the votes of the House of Representatives. Adams won, less by his own appeal than by the decision of Clay to switch over to Adams the votes which, he knew, would never be sufficient to obtain a majority for himself.

In office Adams enjoyed to the full the frustrations and disappointments that a democracy so often heaps on the heads of devoted, deserving but humourless and self-righteous politicians. Fortunately no great crises at home or abroad marked the four years of his Presidency, but on such matters as did arise he found himself thwarted by House and Senate and misunderstood by the country he was unimaginatively trying to serve. The campaign of 1828 that followed his administration was direct and bitter. Adams was opposed by Andrew Jackson of Tennessee and the campaign was largely conducted with open appeals on each side to class interest – Jackson, champion of the poor, and Adams, guardian of the rich – while the private lives of the candidates were vilified by each other's supporters. In such a contest numbers and vehemence were on the side of Jackson and in 1829 John Adams quietly vacated the White House to the victor from the West.

Every earlier President had had some first-hand and notable experience in foreign affairs before he came to the White House, and it was perhaps significant that they had, each of them, come from states which fringed the Atlantic seaboard and looked towards Europe. Andrew Jackson's experience, by contrast, had been almost exclusively military: he was the victor of the Battle of New Orleans against the British in 1814 and the hero of Florida campaigns against Indians and Spaniards. He had been born on the Carolina frontier, had lived on the frontier, and now in 1829 came to Washington from Tennessee. His election was a victory for the frontier, the southern and western states, aided by Pennsylvania and New York. It represented the new interests of the hinterland, the pioneer, the backwoods farmer, the prospector, the people who pinned their faith on opening up the interior rather than on commerce or shipping on the seven seas. The major preoccupation of the new President was to be the development of the West and the problems which that development posed for the balance of interests inside the United States itself.

One notable feature of Jackson's frontier constituents was their rough and ready democracy. Socially, it expressed itself in a dislike and contempt for all formality and distinction: the scene in the White House on the day of Jackson's inauguration, when the entire street crowd flooded the premises, made free with the refreshments and played havoc with the furniture, reflected the rough equality of frontier society which recognized no distinction of birth or race. Politically it was based on the conviction that not only was every man's vote as good as his neighbour's, but also that the day-to-day business of government required no special knowledge or training, but could be done as well by one citizen as by another. 'The duties of all public office', Jackson observed, 'are so plain and simple that men of intelligence may readily qualify themselves for their performance; and I cannot but believe that more is lost by the long continuance of men in office than is generally to be gained by their experience'. Since most of the existing offices in

1828 were filled by Easterners of one kind or another, it was a natural corollary of this doctrine that Jackson's victory should be the signal for a purge of government officials and their replacement by proven friends of the new administration. Thus the doctrine became respectable that 'to the victors belong the spoils' and, in place of a civil service that should be politically impartial, the United States nourished the practice of changing officials with each change of government, while politicians used government posts as patronage with which to reward friends and punish foes. The practice had its justifications. It was true, as Jackson claimed, that a great many of these offices did not require much expert knowledge for their discharge. Government was a simpler business in 1828. The system also served as a kind of political cement, to hold parties together and to prevent Congress and the President from becoming too independent of each other. In a country so vast, where parties are not usually built around a particular doctrine, but are generally a coalition of interests, something was needed to give continuity and keep the coalition united. Patronage contributed something to that. Also the separation of powers imposed by the Constitution made it very easy for President and Congress to get out of step and even get at loggerheads with each other. The President's control over appointments imposed some check on that. As in eighteenth-century England, Congressmen were anxious to get jobs for their constituents; the President's power to confer or withhold jobs gave him some means of controlling votes. But although it served these purposes, the practice of political patronage which Jackson's regime so stimulated was of very doubtful benefit to the Republic. It delayed the growth of an efficient and expert Civil Service, it encouraged Congressmen to think too much about the local electorate and too little about their national duties, and it gave excessive openings for corruption and incompetence in national and local government.

But Jackson's own worries came from another source than this. The South, and especially the Carolinas, had supported Jackson largely out of discontent with the economic policies of the North-East. The War of 1812 gave a great fillip to American manufactures and after the war was over manufacturers sought to protect themselves by building ever higher tariff walls. But the South, whose prosperity rested not upon the sale of manufactured goods within America, but on the export of their agricultural products, notably cotton and tobacco, to England, found the tariff ruining their British markets, because it kept out the manufactures by which alone British merchants could pay for their American imports. Thus when in 1828 an even higher tariff was raised, the so-called 'tariff of abominations', the South began to think of more extreme measures of self-defence. Their leader in this movement was John C. Calhoun, the Vice-President.

Like a great many Southerners, Calhoun came of Scottish ancestors who, after originally settling in Pennsylvania in the early eighteenth century, moved into up-country South Carolina. His parents were yeoman farmers, of moderate means, but Calhoun married into the wealthy aristocracy of Charleston, thus uniting the interests of the smallholders of the Piedmont with those of the planters of the sea coast. He was a striking figure, tall, slender and emaciated, with an incisive, logical mind and a rigid integrity of character. He had started off, like Clay, as an ardent nationalist, but as his own section of the country came more and more to develop a set of interests separate from the rest, Calhoun moved into the States' Rights camp and emerged as the spokesman for the cotton South.

Personal considerations also entered into Calhoun's change of front. As Vice-President Calhoun had nursed the expectation that after Jackson's retirement he would be the Democrats' next choice for the Presidency. But it soon became apparent that he had a rival in Van Buren, the astute New York politician whom Jackson made his Secretary of State. Van Buren played up to Jackson's foibles, as Calhoun did not, most notably in the matter of entertaining 'Peggy' Eaton, the wife of the Secretary of War (some time the daughter of a Washington innkeeper at whose house Jackson used to stay in his Senatorial days). Jackson contended that any friend of his and any wife of Eaton's was entitled to the full honours of Washington society, but the aristocratic Mrs Calhoun led the 'petticoat revolt' of Washington ladies who refused to have anything to do with anyone so lowly as the daughter of an innkeeper. These were parlour quarrels, but when Van Buren disclosed to Jackson that Calhoun had been responsible, as Secretary of War in 1818, for having Jackson censured for exceeding his orders in the Florida campaign, the breach between the two men was complete and to their political differences were added personal resentments.

The march of events hastened the break between the two leaders. The Senate was the natural battle-ground for opposing political opinions, but Calhoun, as Vice-President of the U.S., was also President of the Senate and, as such, debarred from taking part in debates. Thus when in 1830 the Senate devoted itself to a full-dress debate on the pros and cons of the Southern case, it was not Calhoun who voiced the Southern point of view, but the Senator for South Carolina, Hayne. In the great oratorical contest that ensued, with speeches lasting, as was then the habit, for days on end, Hayne, the voice of Calhoun, was met by Daniel Webster, a massive New England intellect and the greatest orator of his time, who opposed to Hayne's philosophy of States' Rights the Marshall theory of the paramount claims of the Union. The Hayne-Webster duel became famous and although the details of their wordy battle are no longer of interest the peroration of Webster's big speech, by its eloquence and prophetic insight, left an enduring impression. As the favourite subject for 'penny readings' and school elocution contests it left its mark on generations of young Americans long after the author was silent:

> It is to the Union that we owe our safety at home and our consideration and dignity abroad. ... While the Union lasts, we have high, exciting, gratifying prospects spread out before us, for us and our children. Beyond that I seek not to penetrate the

veil. God grant that in my day, at least, that curtain may not rise. ... When my eyes shall be turned to behold for the last time the sun in heaven, may I not see him shining on the broken and dishonoured fragments of a once glorious Union; on States dissevered, discordant, belligerent; on a land rent with civil feuds, or drenched, it may be, in fraternal blood! Let their last feeble and lingering glance, rather, behold the gorgeous ensign of the Republic ... bearing for its motto spread all over in characters of living light, blazing on all its ample folds, as they float over the sea and over the land, and in every wind under the whole heavens, that other sentiment, dear to every American heart – 'Liberty *and* Union now and for ever, one and inseparable!'

A few months later another scene even more strikingly dramatized the clash of opinion. At a banquet held to celebrate Jefferson's birthday, Calhoun's followers seized the opportunity to make a series of speeches extolling States' Rights. But when it came to the toasts, Jackson, the guest of honour, met them squarely. Looking straight at Calhoun, he proposed 'Our Union! It must be preserved!' Calhoun drank with the rest, but then amid silence offered his own rejoinder, 'The Union! Next to our Liberty most dear!' Thus two opposing philosophies crystallized each in a phrase.

Soon they clashed in deeds as well as words. In 1832 Clay, supported by most of Jackson's party, brought in a new tariff bill, which, although it did not raise the tariff to any serious degree, did imply, as the South complained, that 'protection must now be regarded as the settled policy of the country'. To meet the challenge, Calhoun elaborated his celebrated doctrine of *nullification*. The Union, he argued, is not a union of the whole people; it is a union of *States*. The states united under a compact, which is the Constitution. If the federal government exceeds its constitutional powers or if any combination of states, using the federal government, passes legislation crippling to another state, then the offended state has the right to ignore the act or the law in question and to declare it *null* and void. This view, of course, ran completely counter to the whole Hamilton-Marshall-Jackson theory of the Union, that states must abide by the decision of a majority in Congress, provided the action of that majority was constitutional, and that disputes over constitutionality could not be settled by separate and aggrieved parties, but only by the Supreme Court. Calhoun's course, they contended, made each state judge in its own case and must necessarily lead to a break-up of the Union. Calhoun did not admit such a conclusion, regarding 'nullification' merely as a form of passive resistance, but since he contended that any attempt on the part of the federal government to enforce its law by force would and should provoke resistance and secession, he was in fact threatening as much.

This theory in its entirety was accepted in 1832 by the South Carolina legislature and embodied in a Nullification Ordinance, as a reply to the tariff of that year. What was Jackson to do? Allow South Carolina to ignore the federal tariff, or enforce it with troops? An issue imperilling the peace and the future of the Union had been joined.

It was in face of this problem that Jackson showed himself a great President. He met the challenge squarely, issued a proclamation that 'Disunion by armed force is treason' and asked Congress for a 'Force Act' to give him the necessary powers. At the same time he refrained from overt action likely to give rise to bloodshed and was content to rally national feeling without fomenting passion. This gave Clay, 'the great pacificator', time to work out a compromise – a lowering of the tariff by two-year stages. Congress passed Clay's tariff and Jackson's Force Act. South Carolina accepted the tariff and 'nullified' the Force Act – an empty gesture, since it would not now be put into operation. So the clash subsided. But a pistol had been held to the head of the federal government and by a refusal to obey a state had had its way. Worst of all, Calhoun's doctrines had sunk deep into the minds of a large section of the nation. Persisting thirty years later, they were to justify not merely nullification but secession. More than a generation afterwards Walt Whitman, poet of the Civil War, heard a soldier say that Calhoun's real monument was the ruined South, a generation of young men destroyed, society torn up by the roots and slaves become masters.

While Jackson showed himself a 'Unionist' when presented with the threat of nullification there was another issue of federal *v.* state power on which he harked back to Jeffersonian principles. That was the federal Bank. The West had always disliked the Bank, as representing the money power of the East, and in this respect Jackson was a true westerner. He intended, indeed, to leave the question over until 1836, when the Bank's charter came up for renewal. His opponents, however, injected it into the Presidential campaign of 1832, when Jackson ran against Clay, representing the National Republicans. Jackson vetoed a bill for renewing the Bank's charter, beat Clay in the ensuing campaign and rightly interpreted that as a national endorsement of his policy. So the Bank petered out, the West recovered its financial independence and Hamilton's dream of a Bank of the United States analogous to the Bank of England was defeated. But Jackson's victory was won at the expense of greatly souring his relations with Congress and most of his second term was taken up with acrimonious disputes with a hostile House and Senate.

Such a setting of confused politics was ideal ground for the rise of a figure like Van Buren. When 1835 came round he was Jackson's obvious choice as his successor. The National Republicans put up four sectional candidates, in the hope of splitting the vote and so throwing the final choice into the House of Representatives. The best candidate, Webster, received the fewest votes, but all together they could not defeat Van Buren. He secured a clear majority and left 'Old Hickory' free to retire to his Tennessee 'Hermitage' happy in the conviction of his own and his successor's popularity.

CHAPTER XVIII

Western Expansion

IN the 1820's, when British colonists were pouring into Canada, Australia, the Cape of Good Hope (and the U.S.A.), Americans with a similar enthusiasm and for very similar reasons were migrating into Texas. The Texas of 1821, into which Stephen Austin, a Connecticut Yankee, led his American colonists, was just in process of becoming Mexican territory, as Mexico, along with other New World territories, won her independence from Spain. The young Mexican Republic welcomed the settlers and gave generous land grants in the fertile, vast plains of the South-West; at the same time it undoubtedly expected the settlers eventually to abandon their American allegiance and become good Mexicans. It insisted on immigrants being Roman Catholics – though the regulation was frequently violated – encouraged inter-marriage and retained Spanish as the official language. But as the numbers of American immigrants increased, and added to Stephen Austin's peaceful farmers boisterous adventurers, like the Bowie brothers from Louisiana, who invented the knife that bears their name, a change came over the relations between the Americans and their Mexican landlords. There was much talk in Washington and in Texas to the effect that all the land up to the Rio Grande properly belonged to the United States, that it really formed part of the Louisiana Purchase, and that Mexico was an anarchical state which could not be trusted to keep law and order even within her own boundaries. Such talk alarmed the Mexicans, who revised their original and generous policy, restricted immigration, militarized the frontier and clamped high tariffs on American imports. The colonists in turn chafed under these restrictions and began to feel towards Mexico as their ancestors before 1776 had felt towards Britain – that they were victims of discriminating taxation – without representation, threatened with military rule, and unable to develop their own institutions in accord with their own principles. They were in very similar plight to the Uitlanders in the Transvaal fifty years later, settlers in a foreign country, retaining their own speech and customs, and feeling themselves oppressed by the practices and legislation of their hosts. At first, like the American colonists of the 1770's, the Texans wanted only 'home rule'. They held a Convention and asked for Texas a position inside the Mexican Republic which should be equivalent to statehood in the U.S.A. But the Mexican Republic soon gave way to the personal despotism of a revolutionary, Santa Ana, and his growing tyranny provoked, in 1835, armed Texan resistance. In San Antonio less than two hundred Texans gathered in the Alamo, a fortified mission building, and resisted Santa Ana's force of three thousand until every Texan was dead. 'Thermopylae', the saying went, 'had its messenger of defeat; the Alamo had none', and to the cry of 'Remember the Alamo', the colonists declared Texas an independent republic and elected Sam Houston, who had learnt to fight under Andrew Jackson's command, to be its first President. From the southern states came volunteers for the Texan army, but Washington was slow in according formal recognition to the new republic, and it was not until March, 1837, the day before he retired from the Presidency, that Jackson put his hand to the document of recognition.

For the next ten years Texas was a complicating element in every American political problem. This was due to the fact that the constitution of Houston's republic legalized Negro slavery from the River Sabine to the Rio Grande. For this reason the slave South was passionately eager for annexation. Out of the huge area of Texas, Calhoun calculated, four or five states might be carved, which would give the slave-holding interests eight or ten Senators to counterbalance the Northern recruits from Michigan, Wisconsin and Iowa and thus prevent the passage of any national legislation prejudicial to slavery. In the North a feeling was rising which was as passionate in the opposite direction. In

1831 a new voice had made itself heard in America, when William Lloyd Garrison issued at Boston the first number of his paper, the *Liberator*, in which he stated his determination to stick at nothing until slavery was abolished. 'I am in earnest – I will not equivocate – I will not excuse – I will not retreat a single inch – AND I WILL BE HEARD.' He gathered round him a team of fellow New Englanders and set to work with fanatical zeal and courage to rouse the country to the evils of slavery. The year in which Texas annexation first became a matter of national concern was also a year in which abolitionist sentiment was blazing most fiercely, because in November, 1837, the abolitionist Lovejoy was murdered by a mob in Alton, Illinois, and so furnished the first martyr to the cause. To those outraged by this crime the annexation of Texas seemed merely a slaveholders' move to be resisted at all costs. Outside the opposing ranks of slave-owners and abolitionists, opinion about Texas fell into two groups – those who wished to see new territory added to the Republic and pioneer Americans readmitted to their homeland, and those who feared the war with Mexico which annexation might involve and feared still more the introduction of a new element which would upset the delicate North-South balance established by the Missouri Compromise.

Van Buren, as President, was principally concerned to keep the peace, both internally and externally. 1837 was a year when his hands were full enough with other troubles. The speculation in Western lands, fed by worthless paper money and large investments from England, and now deprived of the salutary control of the Bank of the United States, ended in one of those periodic financial panics which accompanied the 'winning of the West'. In the crash both American and British investors lost their fortunes. (Charles Dickens was one of these: it was his losses in the 'Cairo City and Canal Co.' which provoked his visit to the U.S.A. in 1842 and the sharp satire of *Martin Chuzzlewit*.) By degrees, as always happened in those days of free land and continuing expansion, the ensuing chaos sorted itself out, though not without much distress and impoverishment. But while it lasted Van Buren was anxious, above all, to avoid further complications with Mexico, and he kept the debate on Texas annexation going without any decision until in 1838 John Quincy Adams smothered it with a speech that took three weeks of the time of the House.

It was not only the south-western frontier that embarrassed Van Buren. Canada had long been restive under a British rule which still resembled what the thirteen American colonies had rebelled against in 1775. In 1837 this led to outbreaks of disorder in what are now the Provinces of Ontario and Quebec. People across the border in the United States hailed these as heralding a new American Revolution and there was a good deal of surreptitious assistance across the border. Fortunately, Van Buren was determined to maintain neutrality and Lord Durham, the British High Commissioner who reported to London on the disturbances, had the courage to recommend Canada for a large dose of self-government, which allayed the growing ferment. With the grant of responsible government in 1841 the Canadian problem was solved, but Anglo-American relations had trodden a delicate path during the previous years, with touchy tempers on both sides. Even in '41, one intricate problem connected with Canadian affairs remained to be solved. Ever since the Treaty of Ghent, Britain and the United States had been bickering about the precise boundary of the state of Maine. Maine was not willing to yield, Palmerston was in no mood for surrender. But with Palmerston and Melbourne's parliamentary defeat of 1841, Aberdeen was able to try calmer counsels. Lord Ashburton, who knew the U.S.A. and was married to an American, was sent across to settle the dispute. He and Daniel Webster, then Secretary of State, hammered out a compromise in the Webster-Ashburton Treaty of 1842. Another source of Anglo-American friction was thus at last eliminated.

Such complications distracted the public's mind from the question of Texas, and when Van Buren had to stand for re-election in 1840 Texas did not loom large in the campaign.

Indeed, no clear issues were presented to the electorate. The Whigs, who had succeeded to the inheritance of the National Republicans, chose as their candidate old General Harrison, who defeated the Cherokee Indians in 1811 in a not very glorious battle at Tippecanoe, Indiana. Their Vice-Presidential candidate was a 'nullificationist' Virginian, John Tyler – a sop to Calhoun's followers. Inevitably therefore the Whig campaign slogan was 'Tippecanoe and Tyler too'. The Democrats had no very definite policy and the Whigs, by skilful electioneering, swept the board. Within a month of his inauguration Harrison died and left Tyler to succeed to the Presidency. Clay and Webster both hoped that the inexperienced President would accept their advice and control, but Tyler soon made it evident that his notions of States' Rights would not be subordinated to their Federalism. The result was party warfare. In Congress Tyler had to face continuous opposition: his cabinet broke up and he was expelled from the Whig Party. By 1843 the inevitable had happened: Tyler went over to the Democrats and appointed Calhoun as his Secretary of State.

It was in these circumstances that the Texas question flared up again. Hostilities broke out once more between Mexico and the rebellious republic and when the British Minister, Lord Aberdeen, recognized Texas in 1843 and tried to mediate with Mexico, Calhoun had no difficulty in persuading the anti-British elements in the North that if the U.S.A. did not annexe Texas Great Britain would. The idea was preposterous, but with the Canadian boundary disputes still fresh in their minds many Americans were found to believe it. And those Southerners who might have been sceptical noted with alarm Aberdeen's interest in the anti-slavery movement and his desire to see Texas a free cotton republic. But in the moment of victory Calhoun overreached himself. In 1844 he urged an annexation treaty on the Senate on the grounds that it would remove all risk of Texas adopting abolition. This was too much: the treaty failed to pass.

This was the position in the summer of 1844 when

politicians of both parties turned their thoughts to the presidential election of the autumn.

The election of '44 was largely fought around questions of territory. By the '40's the line of settlement in the West had reached the Mississippi and beyond – into Minnesota, Iowa and Missouri. And where regular settlement left off prospecting and pioneering began. From Independence on the Missouri River prairie wagons set out to explore the fabulous riches of the West. At what is now Kansas City the trail forked, the northern route continuing along the Platte River into Wyoming, across the Rockies, and down the Columbia River to the Oregon coast (this was the Oregon Trail), the southern dipping down to the Arkansas River and New Mexico, where the old Spanish settlement of Santa Fe gave it the name of the Santa Fe Trail, beyond which it crossed the western deserts and eventually reached California at Los Angeles. Along these two trails intrepid prospectors travelled for almost forty years. The story of their hardships and persistence, in the face of hostile Indians and extremes of climate and terrain, is one of the great epics of American history. In the year 1844 both the Oregon and the Santa Fé Trails were still thinly trod and perilous paths, but they were bringing American settlers to two territories, Oregon and California, which were the subject of international dispute.

California in '44 was Mexican territory, unaffected by the Texan rebellion, and harbouring only about seven hundred American immigrants. But already voices in the East were to be heard saying that it ought to form part of the U.S.A. Oregon had a larger population of Americans – some six thousand in all, mostly fur traders – and here the problem was the competition in the fur trade with the Hudson's Bay Company and the defining of a precise boundary with the British in Western Canada. The Treaty of 1818 had left undecided the question of the U.S.-Canadian boundary west of the Rocky Mountains. By '44 both sides had hard and fast ideas: the British wanted the Columbia River as the boundary, while the U.S.A. insisted that the 49th Parallel should be the dividing line, west as well as east of the Rockies.

On all sides then – in Texas, in California, and in Oregon – the U.S.A. was in expansionist mood when it faced the election of '44. The Whigs, under the leadership of Clay, were hesitant in the face of this popular temper. First Clay said he opposed Texan annexation; then, frightened at losing Southern votes, he said he would support it if it could be obtained without war or dishonour. This alienated the Northern abolitionists, who ran an obscure candidate of their own: James G. Birney. The Democrats were deadlocked between the claims of Van Buren and Calhoun; at last, in despair they chose an unknown young man, 'a dark horse', James Polk of Tennessee, who would arouse the jealousy of neither the New York nor the Southern wings of the party. Polk decided to come all out for annexation and expansion. In Oregon he pushed the U.S. claim to extravagant lengths and did not hesitate to speak in purely jingoistic terms during his campaign. His chief slogan was '54° 40′ or fight'. Thanks to the votes which Birney's defection took from Clay, Polk and the Democrats won. In the face of his opponent's success Tyler did not delay; in the interval between the election and his leaving the White House Tyler offered Texas annexation. Polk arrived in time to face the consequences.

Polk first of all tried negotiation, but it was negotiation buttressed by force. At the same time as he sent his Minister, Slidell, to Mexico City, he sent General Zachary Taylor with an army into Texas and a naval force to stand off the Californian coast ready for any disorders that might break out on shore. The Mexicans refused to accept his envoy, who returned to Washington in May, 1846. Within a few days the Mexicans provided the sort of provocation which Polk was not sorry to meet and which indeed was certain to occur sooner or later with hostile armies facing each other across the Rio Grande. A detachment of Mexican soldiers crossed the river and 'shed American blood on American soil'. Congress declared war and Taylor marched.

The war did not yield the quick and glorious successes that were hoped for. Polk helped to reinstate Santa Ana, the revolutionary dictator who in turn had been overthrown by a fresh *coup d'état* in the '30's, but Santa Ana, once back in Mexico, played him false and refused to arrange the peace Polk expected. Taylor had a lot of hard fighting to do and although in 1847 he won a remarkable victory with depleted forces at Buena Vista, it was not until General Winfield Scott, working inland from Vera Cruz, succeeded, after a series of spectacular victories, in capturing Mexico City that the war could be counted as won.

Meanwhile along the Santa Fe Trail another force had worked its way through New Mexico into California, where Frémont, an explorer of the West, had already, in advance of the news that war had been declared, organized a revolt of American settlers.

So by the end of 1847 the war had ended in victories everywhere. Nevertheless, it was not a popular war. The North regarded it as a war of sectional aggression, promoted by the slave interest of the South. The conduct of the war was marred by friction between Polk and the two generals, Taylor and Scott, both Whigs, whose behaviour he distrusted and whose success he disliked. Peace negotiations were prolonged and complicated, but eventually in 1848 the Treaty of Guadeloupe Hidalgo secured the Rio Grande as the Texas-Mexico boundary and added New Mexico and California to the territory of the U.S.A. in return for some eighteen million dollars in settlement of claims.

In the North-West Polk's ambitions had not seen quite such successful fulfilment. With so many Mexican worries on his hands, Polk was not in fact prepared to carry out his 'Fifty-four-Forty or fight' boast, and both sides instead wisely decided to make compromises. The result was a settlement based on continuing the 49th Parallel across the Rockies to the Oregon coast.

While this was going on along the borders of the U.S.A. a scarcely less important expansion was occurring in the centre of the continent, which recalled the seventeenth century in its combination of religious and colonizing zeal. In the 1820's a young man in upper New York State (always a breeding ground for religious movements), Joseph Smith by name, announced the discovery of a new faith, which he called Mormonism, according to which the lost tribes of Israel had in fact migrated to America and were due to be led and organized by Joseph Smith. He collected about 1,200 converts, enthusiastic and industrious souls, and established them in a settlement at Independence, Missouri. But their peculiarities and indeed their industry (which led them to succeed where others failed) led them to be distrusted and shamefully persecuted. They were accused of converting and freeing slaves and forced to flee into Illinois, where, however, they fared no better. In 1844 Joseph Smith and his brother were killed by a mob and it was under the leadership of Brigham Young that the Mormons in 1846 decided to seek safety and independence in the West. 12,000 of them trekked to the Great Salt Lake and there, in the face of considerable difficulties, they succeeded, by pertinacity, polygamy and a skilfully planned economy, in making the desert yield them a living and a home. In 1849 they were numerous and settled enough to give themselves a constitution, to appoint Brigham Young governor and apply to Washington for admission to statehood.

CHAPTER XIX

North and South

THUS by conquest and colonization the United States by the end of Polk's term of office had come into possession of tracts of Western lands, huge in extent, rich in resources and ripe for settlement. But over all this territory there hung, like a great question mark, the issue – should slavery be permitted in this area? (The Missouri Compromise, which fixed 36° 30′ as the boundary line for slavery, only applied to the territory within the Louisiana Purchase.) As early as 1846 an anti-slavery Congressman, David Wilmot, proposed that slavery should be banned throughout any newly-acquired territories. The 'Wilmot Proviso', as it was soon called, failed of passage, but it was still a burning issue in 1849 when events in California introduced a new element into the situation. In that year the discovery of gold in California was announced, and the great 'gold rush' of the 'forty-niners' brought thousands of immigrants into California – by sail round the Horn, by covered wagon on the overland trails, singing to the tune of 'Oh: Susanna' –

> Oh! California!
> That's the land for me;
> I'm off to Sacramento
> With my washbowl on my knee.

California was flooded by a huge, hectic migration which overnight gave the territory enough population to qualify for statehood and at the same time made the organization of some form of government an urgent necessity.

The election of 1848 had put Zachary Taylor in the White House. He was a Whig, but he came from the South and believed very strongly in the validity of States' Rights. Consequently his solution to the problem was far removed from the spirit of the Wilmot Proviso. It was simply to let the people of the prospective states (California and New Mexico) organize State governments and decide for themselves whether to be slave or free. But although Taylor was President, Clay was the real leader of the Whig party and to meet the clashing demands of Northern abolitionists and Southern slavery expansionists it was Clay who produced in the Senate a compromise proposal around which the debate centred. Clay proposed to admit California as a free state, to organize New Mexico and Utah as territories free to enter the Union with or without slavery when sufficiently populous, to prohibit the slave *trade* in the District of Columbia (Northerners had long complained of this relic of barbarism under the very shadow of Congress) and to pass a stronger fugitive slave law (which would oblige Northern states to return runaway slaves to their owners in the South). In addition there were clauses defining the boundary of Texas and authorizing the Federal Government to take over the Texas national debt. The Compromise gave something to each side: the North did not get the Wilmot Proviso but in fact the new West was given every chance to remain free; the South did not get an expansion of slave territory but slavery was given additional safeguards where it already existed.

The debate on Clay's proposals was in the classic style – in particular, the three great figures of the last thirty years in Congress argued out the issue in oratorical tournament across the Senate floor, each of them conscious that he had not long to live, each anxious to strike a last blow for the cause he most believed in. Clay pleaded for compromise, Calhoun insisted that the South be granted every tittle of her demands, Webster adjured his audience to set the preservation of the Union above everything else. Clay succeeded in securing a majority for his Compromise; President Taylor, who might have persisted in his opposition, was taken suddenly ill and died in the summer of 1850 and the Vice-President, Fillmore, who succeeded him, was readily disposed to listen to Clay's persuasions. The Compromise thus became law before the year was out. The South, though still uneasy, because the admission of California now gave the free states a majority, abandoned its talk of secession and decided to accept the scheme. The North too accepted it, but the Fugitive Slave Act stuck in the throats of honest and humane men from Massachusetts to Illinois. Of the debaters in the Senate, Calhoun did not even live to see the Compromise become law. Bitter and extreme to the last, he died in the spring of 1850. Clay and Webster saw their immediate wishes realized, but when they died in 1852, the last great statesmen of their generation, the clouds were already beginning to gather again. In that year a lady by the name of Harriet Beecher Stowe published a book called *Uncle Tom's Cabin*. The book was fiction but its author claimed that it was based on fact. Before the end of the year 300,000 copies had been sold. Throughout the North it made converts to the anti-slavery cause; throughout the South it was denounced as lying propaganda. To-day, removed from the passion of the period, we can assess with some degree of fairness the facts about the South and slavery. What were they?

There were about three and a half million slaves in the South in 1860 in an area where there were only five and a half million whites. But only about one in four of the whites was of the slaveholding class and the majority of the slaves were in fact concentrated on the great plantations of the plains, not distributed among the small farmers of the hill-country. Southerners argued that the slave's lot was a happy one, that the Negro was in any case fitted only for menial work and that the slave was better off on a plantation where he was fed and clothed and housed than he had been as a savage in Africa or than he would be if emancipated and obliged to fend for himself. But Southerners who spoke thus were forgetting that not all masters were good masters, that on the big plantations the Negro was often regarded as a machine, to be used while he lasted and then thrown aside, that discipline was hard and often brutal, that the slave had no rights at law, and that over every slave's head there hung the horror of the slave trade – the risk of being separated from wife or children and sold off, like cattle, to an unknown master. Nor was there any adequate answer to the fact that year after year runaway slaves faced fearful perils and cruel punishments in the hope of escaping to Canada merely in order to be free.

Nevertheless there was a sense in which the South was enslaved to slavery. It was the abundant supply of slave labour which had made possible the huge expansion of the cotton crop on which the South based its prosperity, but 'King Cotton', as the Southerners proudly called it, soon showed himself to be a tyrant, not a constitutional monarch. Lured on by the huge prices that cotton fetched, planters sank more and more capital into the purchase of land and slaves. They went in for bigger and bigger plantations devoted exclusively to the one royal crop, cotton. But cotton, like tobacco, is a crop which exhausts the soil in which it grows, unless the soil is given a rest by the cultivation of other crops instead. And since the unskilled slave labourer was little use for mixed farming the Southern planter who had invested so much money in buying slaves had no alternative but to go on buying up fresh land for his cotton crop, as fast as he exhausted the old. The result was that the South by the time of the Civil War was on the road to agricultural decay, with huge plantations, like the *latifundia* of the Roman Empire, driving the small independent farmer off the soil by buying up his land, and then exhausting its fertility by concentrating on a single crop. And the system had its victims in an ever-tightening grip. The more money he invested in slaves, the more anxious the planter was for some immediate return on his capital. The only crop that could give him this immediate return was cotton. But cotton used up his soil so fast that he soon had to be spending the profits of this year's crop to buy fresh land for the next. The result of this policy was largely concealed before the Civil War by the fact that there was always fresh land in the West, to which the poor or dispossessed could emigrate, but the basis was none the less being laid for that tragic impoverishment which has persisted in the South right down to the present day.

Few Southerners perceived this. Instead they gloried in 'King Cotton', and frankly accepted slavery as the South's 'peculiar institution' which was indispensable to the maintenance of Southern civilization. That civilization was a very real thing. At a time when most of the world was moving towards industrialism and democracy, the South still based its way of life on agriculture and an aristocracy. It was a rural, almost feudal, society and it was marked by the virtues and faults characteristic of such a society. It set great store by its code of 'chivalry': the typical Southerner was a courteous squire of dames and a practised and courageous soldier. It despised trade and industry, and so the South never developed a middle class worthy of the name. It prized the arts and learning, and despised the dollar and the stock market: at the same time the South's achievements in literature and science never rose above the level of genteel mediocrity, while many a Southern gentleman had to turn to Northern creditors to meet the expense of his hospitality and his tastes. It was a society of real grace and charm resting on a basis of equally real inhumanity and ignorance. At its best it realized the ideal of *noblesse oblige*; at its worst it found expression in lynching and the lash.

By contrast the North was advancing fast along the nineteenth century road of urban industrialism. New England in particular was emulating old England in the speed with which it seized and exploited the inventions of the Industrial Revolution, herded its increasing population into towns, and financed its industrial expansion through the machinery of the joint-stock company. Thus already in 1850 one-eighth of the population of the Northern states lived in cities; by 1860 this had increased to one-sixth. The population itself grew hugely during those years, from fourteen million to nineteen million, an increase very largely due to the great influx of European immigrants (who, incidentally, settled almost exclusively in the north and west – the south remained almost entirely Anglo-Saxon and Negro).

The factory system, which Lancashire and Yorkshire had created and developed, found a natural soil in such a society. In Massachusetts the textile factories of the city of Lowell were the American counterpart of Lancashire's Rochdale, while the woollen mills of Lawrence attempted to rival the products of Leeds. Just as the conjunction of iron ore and coal, found in the Pennines, led to the development of Sheffield, so a similar coincidence in the mountains of Eastern Pennsylvania made Pittsburgh the Sheffield of America. On the basis of these staple products 'Yankee ingenuity', financed by New York, Boston – and also London – bankers, developed a host of new industries, forerunners of the great industrial enterprises which are the economic life-blood of modern America. By 1860 the Eastern states had developed an industrial society and civilization which, in its main outlines, was similar to that of the present day.

It was a democratic society, in which every adult male (including, in some Northern states, Negroes) enjoyed the franchise and in which a serious effort was being made to educate the masses. The decades before the Civil War were especially famous for the work of Horace Mann, the educational reformer, who was put in charge of the educational system of Massachusetts in 1837 and had a great influence on education throughout the Northern states. New England set the standards but the West was no less enthusiastic. By 1860 most states were providing free education for young children, while colleges and universities, for both men and women, were springing up right across the continent. At the same time there was some truth in the Southerner's criticisms that the urban poor in the North were no better off than the slaves in the South. Conditions in the factories were often bad, wages and hours being entirely uncontrolled, with children working at an age when they ought to have been in school, and overcrowding, bad sanitation and ventilation being the rule rather than the exception. When slumps came, as they did in 1837, there was unemployment, lower wages and longer hours. Fresh and cheap labour was always pouring in from Europe and the attempts of the workingmen to form unions which would protect their standard of living were even less successful than similar attempts in Britain during the '40's and '50's.

But the man who failed in the cities had another course open to him. 'Go West, young man' was the famous advice given by Horace Greeley, editor of the great *New York Tribune*, and thousands followed it, seeking the fertile plains and prairies beyond the Ohio and Mississippi. And just as Eli Whitney's cotton gin gave a fillip to settlement and expansion south of the Mason and Dixon Line, so Cyrus McCormick's mechanical reaper patented in 1834 speeded the westward movement in the north; and in 1837 John Deere, by inventing a steel plough which could cope with the matted clods of the prairie, made it possible to farm territory which had previously provided only a scanty living for hunters or herdsmen.

More important still as an agent in westward expansion was the railway. The '50's were the great decade of railway building, comparable to the '40's in Britain. The mileage of track leapt from 9,000 to 30,000 (a great deal of it, incidentally, financed by British capital), with the result that by 1860 the railway map of the northern states as far west as the Mississippi had already taken the shape it maintains to-day, with New York and Chicago the two greatest centres of radiation, for the west and mid-west respectively. The main lines of communication for the American continent began to run west to east, not, as geography would have dictated, north to south along the valley of the Mississippi. Thus New York, Philadelphia and Baltimore began to supplant New Orleans as the great outlets for the riches of the Middle West. At the same time Boston reached the heyday of her glory, as the home port of the great clippers, those sailing vessels of huge length and vast spread of sail which broke all existing records for sea travel. Devised originally to link the Atlantic seaboard with the new-found riches of California, these beautiful ships, such as the *Sea Witch*, the *Flying Cloud* and the *Lightning*, enjoyed a wonderful short-lived maritime supremacy before vessels of steam and iron, cheap and dependable, took their place.

Boston was the home of other things besides the clipper. Without being the biggest city, or even the capital, it was nevertheless, like Edinburgh in the eighteenth century, in many ways the intellectual centre of the nation. America continued to accept the intellectual and cultural leadership of Britain, long after it had cast off political allegiance, but in the '40's and '50's a group of New Englanders, centring around Harvard University and the village of Concord (the American counterpart, as it were, of Edinburgh and the Lake District in the British Romantic Movement), developed a literature and taught a philosophy which had their roots in America itself. Emerson was the philosopher of the movement, who preached the perfectibility of man, the importance of democratic self-reliance, the great prospects that lay before America if only Americans would clear their minds of prejudice and self-seeking. Thoreau was the prose Wordsworth of the group, who found peace and satisfaction in such living alone with nature as he described in his

Walden. Longfellow, Lowell and Whittier were the poets, who found for the first time in American themes, like *Hiawatha* and *Evangeline*, or in American causes, like abolitionism, subjects for American poetry. A school of New England historians – Bancroft, Parkman and Prescott – developed at the same time, American counterparts to Hallam and Macaulay. Fenimore Cooper had already begun to write American novels, lineal descendants in the New World of Walter Scott's in the Old. Now Louisa Alcott struck a domestic vein in *Little Women*, Edgar Allan Poe explored crime and the macabre, and Hawthorne reached back into the New England past to express his sense of the haunting power of sin and the victorious capabilities of goodness.

But more and more this literary and intellectual society which made Boston of the '40's and '50's seem the Athens of America found its attention focusing on one theme. It was Boston that William Lloyd Garrison had selected as the headquarters of his abolitionist movement and by and by the issue of slavery touched each thinker and poet. Whittier and Longfellow lent their verse to describing the wrongs of the American Negro, while Lowell in his *Biglow Papers* satirized both the Southern politicians and the Northern compromisers. Emerson wrote of the Fugitive Slave Act: 'This filthy enactment was made in the nineteenth century by people who could read and write. I will not obey it, by God!' From Boston pulpits, in Boston drawing-rooms, in pamphlets, verses, novels, the issue continually presented itself, ever sharper, ever more insistent.

CHAPTER XX

Prelude to War

In 1853, when Fillmore gave up the Presidency, his place was taken by a colourless Democrat, Franklin Pierce. Both the major parties, Democrats and Whigs, were dodging the burning issue of slavery in the South, and it was Pierce's deliberate policy, by concentrating on schemes for expansion in the West and overseas, to distract public attention from dissensions at home. The policy resulted in quarrels with Spain over Cuba and with Britain over Nicaragua, where British territory in Honduras was felt to constitute a possible threat to American schemes for an Atlantic-Pacific canal. Fortunately both governments had the good sense to compromise; the British flag remained over British Honduras and the U.S.A. was still able to go ahead with its canal, whenever it should decide to face the gigantic engineering problems involved. In the Pacific itself a new chapter was opened when Commodore Perry in 1853 headed the first American mission to Tokyo, and so impressed the Japanese by his display of naval force that they permitted Americans to trade and to establish the first foreign consulate. Japan, whose government and ways of life were still in many respects mediæval, was thus 'opened up' to those western influences which were soon to make her a modern 'great power'.

But to the America of the '50's none of these overseas developments compared in importance with the winning of the West. And the weapon principally used in that great enterprise was the railway. One project in particular fascinated the public mind, the proposal to build a trans-continental railroad which would 'bind the continent with hoops of steel', as one enthusiast put it, and provide even faster communication from coast to coast than the record-breaking clipper ships. Many rival routes were proposed and debated. The South, anxious to strengthen its hold on the West, favoured a line which would run from New Orleans across Texas to San Diego, and, to make the route as direct as possible, Jefferson Davis, the Southerner who was Pierce's Secretary of War, persuaded Pierce to buy from Mexico the strip of southern Arizona and New Mexico which later bore the name of 'the Gadsden Purchase' after the South Carolina railroad owner who negotiated for it.

But Northern interests were equally keen. Many of the existing wagon trails had their starting points in Illinois.

Why should not the railway? So reasoned Stephen A. Douglas, the Democratic Senator from Illinois. He realized that just as the Southern route required acquisition of territory from Mexico, so his route would need assistance by the planting of settlers along the line whose traffic would make it a paying proposition. He therefore proposed to 'organize' the area immediately to the west of Iowa and Missouri into the two territories of Kansas and Nebraska. The South, he knew, would oppose the creation of any states which would give the North more votes and more senators. He therefore proposed that for the new territories Congress should not prohibit slavery but should leave the inhabitants free to settle the issue for themselves. But this Kansas-Nebraska Bill of Douglas's was in flat contradiction of the Missouri Compromise of 1820, which prohibited slavery from all western territory north of 36° 30″, and the moment it was introduced, in 1854, all the old passions were revived in a heightened form. All roads, it seemed, led back to the slavery issue; what began by being a discussion about a railway ended by being a national debate on the South's 'peculiar institution.'

As the debate on the Kansas-Nebraska Bill developed it became apparent that there were three possible attitudes to the slavery problem.

The first was the attitude of the South – that slavery was a legal institution and that Congress should extend positive protection to it everywhere, i.e. that as new territories were carved out of the West, Congress should insist that their constitutions should safeguard slavery. Opposed sharply to this was the view which had found expression in the unsuccessful Wilmot Proviso, that Congress should prohibit slavery in any new territory which it organized. Supporters of this position called themselves 'Free-soilers'. Stephen Douglas advanced a compromise theory, that it was not for Congress to prohibit or enforce, but for each new territory to determine for itself: this he called 'popular sovereignty'.

On the immediate point at issue Douglas won the day. Democratic votes carried the Kansas-Nebraska Bill into law in May, 1854. But it was a victory dearly bought. The Senator who remarked, 'If the Nebraska Bill should be passed, the Fugitive Slave Law is dead throughout New England,' was a shrewder prophet than most of his fellow-Southerners. Extreme abolitionists were furious and moderate men felt that by going back on the Missouri Compromise the slaveholders had broken faith with the rest of the nation. Compromise and peaceful adjustment seemed less and less feasible and the political parties who had tried to dodge the issue now found themselves broken on it. Northern and Southern Democrats split, while the Whigs, already weakened by the loss of their great leader, Clay, simply dissolved. It was not long before the events immediately following the Bill stimulated the birth of a new party which would fill their place.

Since the Kansas-Nebraska Bill left the new territory free to make its own slavery regulations, it was now the aim of each side to secure a majority of votes there. Abolitionists from New England financed the settlement of farmers who could be relied upon to vote for a free Kansas; southern planters similarly sponsored an inrush of pro-slavery men. Chaos resulted. Each side set up its own government, one establishing a strict slave code as harsh as any in the South, the other prohibiting slavery altogether. Meanwhile rival settlers poured in, determined if necessary to enforce their claims by arms. A Northern abolitionist, John Brown, with the single-minded zeal of a fanatic, led a midnight raid on a pro-slavery settlement at Pottawatomie; the resulting slaughter of five settlers was soon dubbed a 'massacre' and in no time the spark of passion was fanned into the flames of civil war.

The blood which flowed in Kansas had its counterpart in the United States Senate. Sumner, the abolitionist Senator from Massachusetts, delivered a crushing speech, 'The Crime Against Kansas', of which half a million copies were circulated to outside readers. One afternoon not long afterwards as he sat alone at his desk in the Senate chamber Sumner was attacked by Brooks, a young southern Congressman who, swearing that the South should be revenged for

Sumner's slanders, set upon him with his cane and inflicted injuries so severe that they left Sumner crippled for years.

It was against this background of guerrilla warfare in Kansas and open violence on the floor of the Senate that the nation, in the autumn of 1856, set about the task of electing a new president. Out of the turmoil of the last two years a new party had been born, which borrowed a Jeffersonian label, though it had no lineal descent from him or his disciples. The Republicans, as they called themselves, were an alliance of 'Free-soilers', northern Whigs and Democrats from the Border States who described themselves as 'the heirs of Jackson'. It was a middle-class, Northern party, consisting principally of the farmers of the west and the small business and labour elements of the east. In 1856 it was hard put to it to find a suitable candidate, and settled rather unwisely upon the glamorous and unsubstantial figure of Frémont, 'the Pathfinder of the Rockies' and the filibusterer of California. The party was a genuinely crusading movement, determinedly anti-slavery in sentiment: at their rallies, to the tune of the *Marseillaise*, they would sing

> Free speech, free press, free soil, free men,
> Frémont and victory.

Against them the Democrats, still straddling on the slavery issue, put up Buchanan, a Pennsylvanian who had been Secretary of State under Polk, a good Union man, but sympathetic by training and disposition to Southern aspirations. There was a third party, united only by dislike of the foreign-born immigrants who were now more and more frequent figures in the American scene; they called themselves the Know-Nothings and found a cloak for their stupidity and intolerance in the adoption of the respectable but unimpressive ex-President Fillmore as their candidate.

Buchanan won, but the new Republican Party made a very creditable showing particularly throughout the North. Despite their failure at the polls it was apparent that the Republicans had a strength which came of internal unity.

By comparison, the numbers of Buchanan's victorious Democrats were a deceptive index of their strength.

Buchanan had only been in the White House two days when the Supreme Court handed down one of those decisions which, like *Marbury v. Madison*, mark a turning point in United States history. A slave named Dred Scott had been taken by his master first into Illinois, then into the territory north of 36° 30″ where the Missouri Compromise had disallowed slavery, and then back into Missouri. He sued his master for his freedom on the ground that he had twice been resident on free soil. The Court by a vote of five to four, disallowed his claim in a decision which in the first place denied that Negro slaves could ever become United States citizens and secondly asserted that Congress had no right to forbid slavery in the territories – in fact making the Missouri Compromise unconstitutional and void.

Americans had come by 1857 to have a great deal of respect for the wisdom and impartiality of their Supreme Court, but the Dred Scott decision fell with a crash upon the ears of the ordinary citizen north of the Mason and Dixon Line. He realized that if the decision stood, nothing could stop the spread of slavery into all the new territories of the West, and that the sort of compromise preached by Douglas was impossible – there could be no 'popular sovereignty' when the Supreme Court insisted that slave property be respected whether the State be 'free' or not. When further he observed the narrow margin of the Court's majority and the fact that four out of the ruling five were Southerners, the average Northern voter soon began to agree with the Republican Party that the Dred Scott decision was bad law and undeserving of his respect.

In Kansas, meanwhile, the struggle between the two rival governments had come to a head. The pro-slavery element secured Buchanan's backing for their 'Lecompton Constitution',* but Stephen Douglas, faithful to his principles of popular sovereignty, convinced the Senate that it should be referred back to the citizens of Kansas for ratification before

* Named after the Kansas town where their convention met.

Kansas was admitted to statehood. The Kansans rejected it emphatically – but the Dred Scott decision remained, obliging Kansas, like all other western territories, to respect slave-holdings which had their origins in other states. To ardent abolitionists in the North the outlook was still gloomy and hopeless; the Anti-Slavery Convention which met in Massachusetts in 1857 saw such little hope of winning the Union for abolition that it openly advocated secession. No one but a handful of extremists supported this, but their numbers grew with every day that passed.

This was the position when in 1858 Stephen Douglas as Senator for Illinois came up for re-election, to be opposed by a Republican candidate, Abraham Lincoln. To most Americans, in 1858, Lincoln was an entirely new name; they knew little of his past and never imagined that he would have a great future. This was scarcely surprising in view of Lincoln's previous history. In 1858 he was a man of forty-nine years of age who had never held any position more important than that of Congressman for one term in the days of the Polk Administration. Nevertheless, during these years of comparative obscurity Lincoln had been growing into a man whose strength of character and nobility of purpose were to make him unique in his nation's history.

He came of poor, frontier parentage. In Hodgenville, Kentucky, you may still see preserved the one-room log-cabin with the dirt floor in which he was born. His mother died when he was only a child of eight, and it was to his step-mother that he owed the elementary schooling – the study of the Bible, *Pilgrim's Progress* and *Robinson Crusoe* – which took the place of a more formal education. He grew up with the frontier; his father, a typical frontier type, shiftless and restless, was always on the move and by the time young Lincoln settled down in New Salem, Illinois, at the age of twenty-two, he had already, in various places and in various odd jobs, acquired experience of most of the frontier West. In New Salem he managed the village store, kept the village post office, taught himself law and, in 1834, at the age of twenty-five, got himself elected to the Illinois State

Legislature as a Whig. From 1834 to 1842, as a member of the Legislature, he lived in Springfield, practising law in between sessions, and steeping himself in the problems and the thinking of the West. In 1842 he married Mary Todd, a well-to-do, ambitious woman who brought him, if not a deep affection, certainly a strong belief in his powers. In 1847 he was elected to Congress as a Whig and an opponent of the Mexican War. But there was nothing remarkable about his term in Congress, and in 1848 he failed of re-election, despite the widespread successes of the Whigs.

It has often been noticed that there is a point in great men's careers when they withdraw from public activity and enjoy a period of what outwardly seems to be a mere marking of time, but is in fact a recharging of their energies and a deepening of their resolve. Lincoln went through such a period from 1848 to 1854, remaining in retirement in Illinois while the great issues of North and South, slavery and abolitionism, sharpened themselves in debates in Congress, in newspapers and in market places and log cabins. From 1854 to 1858 Lincoln was translating the conclusions he had privately arrived at into the practical terms of party politics. He aligned himself with the new Republican party and rose high enough in their counsels in Illinois to be the obvious candidate in 1858 to oppose the practised and able Douglas.

The Lincoln-Douglas Debates, as they have come to be called, because the opponents conducted their campaign by public argument, appearing on the same platforms to debate face-to-face, became famous not by virtue of the election which they preceded (it was Douglas, in fact, who won the election), but because they thrashed out for all the nation to see the great question of how far honest Northerners could go in compromising on the slavery issue. Lincoln's achievement in the debates was in showing how the Dred Scott decision knocked the last grain of sense out of Douglas's theory that 'popular sovereignty' could provide a middle way between the claims of North and South. Rejecting Douglas's arguments, Lincoln insisted instead that, though slavery should be left alone in the states where it already existed, it should by Congressional action be excluded from the territories and also from the District of Columbia. This, he contended, respected the existing rights of the South and also conformed to the facts of the Constitution.

Meanwhile, however, tempers were mounting. The 'underground railroad'* carried its human freight from the slave South across the border to the free soil of Canada in ever greater numbers. More and more abolitionists openly defied the Fugitive Slave Law, while Northern legislatures made mockery of it by passing what they called 'personal liberty laws' which made legal in the name of the state what the Fugitive Slave Law prohibited in the name of Congress. Southerners complained that the Union of which they formed a part was being flouted and that such Northern behaviour was treachery to the Constitution. Then in 1859 John Brown, as he had done in Kansas in 1856, cast all considerations of law and order to the winds and engineered a scheme to achieve by violence the liberty which was being denied by the established organs of justice. With a small band of fellow zealots he planned to establish an abolitionist republic in the Appalachian Mountains, from which to organize slave revolts throughout the South. As the first step towards this he organized a raid on the federal arsenal at Harpers Ferry, Virginia. The militia succeeded in cornering John Brown and his band of eighteen; they resisted fanatically, and it was not until fifteen of the party had been killed or wounded that their stronghold was captured. John Brown, grievously wounded, was condemned to death for criminal conspiracy and murder, but nevertheless by his blind, zealot, Old Testament courage he suddenly became a symbol and a martyr to thousands who had never heard of him when alive. 'John Brown's Body' soon became the anthem of a crusade.

This was the atmosphere of inflamed public passions in which the parties in 1860 set about the task of selecting their candidates for the Presidency. The first to meet were the Democrats at Charleston, South Carolina. The Con-

* A chain of secret refuges along the route to Canada where fugitive slaves could find shelter and aid.

vention immediately revealed the dissensions within the party – between the extremists who demanded that the Federal government should actively protect slavery throughout the territories and the Northern moderates, under Douglas, who clung to the tattered remnants of 'popular sovereignty'. The two wings split and eventually held separate conventions of their own; the Northern Democrats nominated Douglas, the Southerners Breckinridge, the existing Vice-President, from the border state of Kentucky.

An odd group, consisting of the relics of the old Whigs and the Know-Nothings, calling themselves the National Constitutional Union, met at Baltimore, turned a blind eye to the whole slavery question and nominated a colourless Senator Bell of Tennessee.

The Republicans met without any obvious candidate commanding general support. The most distinguished Republican was Seward of New York, and his strongest rival was Chase, Governor of Ohio. It is one of the strange ironies of history that it was the rivalry of these two candidates and the difficulty of securing a strong majority for either that led to the choice of Lincoln – not, the Convention thought, the best man, but merely a compromise candidate whom no one could seriously object to. The Republican platform undertook to respect the rights of the States to regulate their own institutions, i.e. slavery, but reaffirmed the Wilmot Proviso, insisting that the Constitution forbade the introduction of slavery into the territories. It also advocated a higher tariff* and a Western policy of cheap land and 'internal improvements' reminiscent of Clay.

The election was a victory for Lincoln, with Douglas as runner-up and Bell bottom of the poll. Lincoln did not get a clear majority of the votes cast, but he easily topped the poll. It was significant for the impending struggle that it was in the free states of the North that Lincoln received all

* Since some writers have made much of the tariff as a source of dissension between North and South, it is worth pointing out that as recently as 1857 the tariff had been reduced and that the Morrill Tariff of February, 1861, the first serious increase since 1832, was passed only after Southern Senators had withdrawn from Congress.

his majorities, while Breckinridge carried all the cotton states plus North Carolina, Delaware and Maryland. The remaining border states, Virginia, Kentucky and Tennessee, went for Bell.

Immediately the result was announced the Southern extremists remembered their resolve to secede if that 'black Republican, Lincoln' were elected. The months between the election in November and Lincoln's assumption of office in March were months of growing strain, with the South moving towards separation, but each side anxiously trying to escape blame for the break. South Carolina was the first state to summon a Convention and announce its secession. The infection spread: by February Georgia, Alabama, Mississippi, Florida, Louisiana and Texas had followed suit. In Congress the border states tried to effect a compromise, but the basis of agreement was lacking. One by one the Southerners resigned from Buchanan's Cabinet and withdrew from Congress. Buchanan made it plain that secession was contrary to the Constitution and that the Federal government could not recognize it; at the same time he abstained from any suggestion of federal coercion. The South continued on the road to separation: the seceded states met and drew up a Constitution for a new Confederacy and chose as their President a Mississippian, Jefferson Davis, Pierce's Secretary of War. Within a fortnight of Jefferson Davis's inauguration at Montgomery, Abraham Lincoln made his way to Washington to assume the most onerous presidency in the history of the nation.

CHAPTER XXI

The Civil War: First Phase

LINCOLN set out his policy clearly and simply in the speech he delivered on the occasion of his inauguration. It was, in essence, to carry out all the duties of the federal government without attempting to coerce the seceding South. 'The power confided to me will be used to hold, occupy, and possess the property and places belonging to the Government, and to collect the duties on imports; but beyond what may be necessary for these obligations there will be no invasion, no using of force against or among the people anywhere.' He implored the South to think again before breaking up the Union. 'In your hands, my dissatisfied fellow-countrymen, and not in mine, is the momentous issue of Civil War. The Government will not assail you. You can have no conflict without being yourselves the aggressors.'

Such a policy, though unaggressive, was firm, and Lincoln soon showed that for all his respect for the feelings of the South he would not fail to carry out his duties as President of the Union. The Federal Government, as the only authority in the Union charged with external defence, had a fort in Charleston Harbour, on South Carolina soil, which was garrisoned with federal troops. The provisions in Fort Sumter had run so low that its commander warned the President that he could only hold out a few weeks longer unless supplies were sent. Lincoln decided that to evacuate Fort Sumter would be tantamount to conceding the South's claim to secession: at the same time he settled on the least provocative form of relief. He sent food only, not munitions, and informed the Confederacy of his action. The South, however, decided to regard this, mild as it was, as an act of war. The Charleston batteries opened fire even before the relief ships appeared; their shots were immediately recognized, in both North and South, as the signal of war. Partisans on each side felt this was the moment they had been waiting for, while everywhere men of moderate opinions who had hitherto hoped for a peaceful settlement remembered Lincoln's conviction, 'A house divided against itself cannot stand', and made their final, painful choice.

The American Civil War was in essence a family quarrel, and, like all family quarrels, has proved baffling to the outsider. The Englishmen of the period found it difficult to understand, even statesmen of the calibre of Gladstone committing wild errors of judgment about it, and their descendants have often been puzzled to know what each side was fighting for and why. It is, however, so much the central event in the history of the United States of America, to which so much leads up, and from which so much follows, that without some comprehension of its meaning the rest of American history becomes unintelligible.

The South thought of their cause in language derived principally from Calhoun. The Union was a mere alliance of states, who retained their sovereignty, free to ignore the laws and acts of the Union and to withdraw from it whenever their interests so dictated. According to this theory the failure of the Union to protect their property by enforcing the Fugitive Slave Law and to allow the expansion of their 'peculiar institution', slavery, into the territories of the West was so detrimental to their interest that they were perfectly entitled to break away and form a separate Confederacy among themselves. This Southern view of the Constitution was backed, as might be expected, by a peculiar emotional attachment. General Cass, a Michigan representative in Buchanan's Cabinet, summed it up when he told two of his colleagues, 'I see how it is; you are a Virginian and you are a South Carolinian; I am not a Michigander, I am an American'. This distinction between Northern and Southern feeling had not always existed. In the first generation of the Union no Northerner had exceeded the patriotic Union zeal of the statesmen of Virginia or South Carolina. Calhoun himself had once been an ardent Unionist. What had caused the change? In one word the answer was Slavery. Southern economy, Southern culture, white supremacy in the South had come to be so dependent upon the South's peculiar institution that Southerners found a new bond of union in it. To uphold slavery became an article of Southern faith. And as Northern feeling hardened more and more against a custom so abhorrent, the South felt the gulf of dissension broadening and the bonds of its own state patriotism tightening.

Alexander Stephens, the Vice-president of the Southern Confederacy, put the matter with brutal clarity when he said, 'The prevailing ideas entertained by Jefferson and most of the leading statesmen at the time of the old Constitution were that the enslaving of the African was wrong in principle socially, morally, and politically. Our new government is founded upon exactly the opposite idea; its foundations are laid, its corner stone rests, upon the great truth that the Negro is not the equal of the white man; that slavery – subordination to the white man – is his natural and normal condition. This, our new government, is the first in the history of the world based upon this great physical, philosophical and moral truth.'

At the other extreme were the abolitionists and their sympathizers, the Radical wing of the Republican Party. Slavery in their eyes was such a crying evil that all means could legitimately be used against it – from the open flouting of the Fugitive Slave Law to the murder practised by John Brown. They, too, were prepared to accept a version of the States' Rights theory which would enable them to deal with slavery in their own way – either by ignoring States' Rights in the South and forcing the Southern states to abolish slavery, or by invoking them in the North and withdrawing from a Union which they felt slavery had befouled. Either way they were prepared to destroy the existing basis of the Union in order to put an end to slavery.

Lincoln, too, hated slavery with a deep passion. But more than he hated slavery he loved the Union. Like his great forerunner, Webster, he realized that it was the Union which had made America. Not only had it devised a means by which the states of the new continent could live together in peace and amity: it also enabled them to undertake the great enterprise of Western expansion in co-operation for their common benefit – it was a key which opened the portals of the West. But most important of all, the Union enshrined the principles of democracy. Built on the ideas of the Declaration of Independence, the Union went on to embody all those great concepts of the Rights of Man which are set out in the Constitution and its amendments and which constitute the political faith of the American people. Lincoln viewed the Union as the organ by which these principles could be combined with the rights of the states, recognizing their differences but welding them into a democratic whole. He recognized that the Union had given to the states the right to legalize slavery or not, as they preferred. He believed that if slavery were kept within the bounds of the states in which it already existed it would, as the founders of the Constitution believed, die a natural death. The prime need therefore was, in his opinion, to keep it from spreading and on his view of the Constitution Congress was charged with the power to prevent such growth, either in the territories or in new states. But when the South, defeated at the polls in its effort to secure a President who could countenance slavery extension, wanted to contract out of the Union, Lincoln realized that America was faced with a threat even more serious than slavery itself. The States' Rights theory which sought to justify secession struck at the binding principle of the American nation. As the South wanted to apply it it meant that whenever a state disliked a decision of the majority it was at liberty to ignore it; such behaviour substituted lawlessness for democracy. If such secession were tolerated each state would follow in the steps of the South, as and when its own convenience dictated, and the United States would revert to the condition of the colonies after they had won their independence, but before the making of the Constitution – disorganized, wrangling, ready to settle their disputes by force, a kind of American Balkans, achieving sovereignty only at the price of peace. As the Civil War went on events in the South showed how right Lincoln was in this belief. The Southern Confederacy was an attempt at a Union based on States' Rights – a contradiction in terms – in which the states combined only at their own pleasure. The Southern states had their own coinage, raised their own armies, paid Confederate taxes or not as they pleased, while the poor Confederate government had to coax and cajole them into unity, like a captain whose team want to play the game each according to his own rules. Had war and the threat of defeat not imposed an external discipline on the Confederacy, it would have fallen apart of its own inner weakness. Had the South won and established secession as a principle the United States of America to-day would be a collection of small factious states, frequently at war between themselves and a prey to the rapacity of powerful neighbours.

This was the threat which Lincoln saw in Southern secession and which he felt to be so disastrous to his country's future that he was entitled to make war upon his fellow-countrymen in order to avert it. Although slavery was at the heart of the conditions which had produced this threat, slavery itself was not the point at issue. The issue was the Union: if the Union was not preserved, democracy in America would die, trampled in the conflicts of a score of sovereign states, and the death knell of freedom on American soil would have been sounded for Lincoln's generation. If the Union was preserved, democracy, Lincoln was confident, would find its way to deal with the problem of slavery. Hence, as Lincoln said of himself, 'My paramount object in this struggle is to save the Union and not either to save or to destroy slavery. If I could save the Union without freeing any slave, I would do it; if I could save it by freeing all the slaves, I would do it; and if I could save it by freeing some and leaving others alone, I would also do that.'

This was the faith in which Lincoln accepted the challenge of the South. It seems so reasonable and so little dangerous to the South that it is hard, even now, to understand why the South should have provoked war, by firing the first aggressive shots at Fort Sumter. The answer is, in part, that the more hot-headed Southern leaders had ceased to act from cool, realistic motives. They had begun to think of slavery not as an economic necessity (which was their forefathers' view of it), but as a positive good, and of the Southern way of life, which was built around slavery, as a civilization threatened by the barbarous Yankees. So they were not merely defenders; they were crusaders. These in turn were supported by cooler spirits who saw in the industrial growth of the North and the rising strength of the Republican party factors which would prevent the South ever again holding its old position of pre-eminence (or at the very least of equality) in the councils of the Union. To such men the election of Lincoln was the danger signal which meant that the South had passed the peak of its power and, proportionate to the North, was on the downgrade. Now, before it was for ever too late, was the moment to strike. If the South had had a little better luck, or if the North had had any leader but Lincoln such calculations might have been correct. As it was, when the guns fired at Fort Sumter it was already too late.

When the war began it was the general assumption of both sides that victory would come quickly. The North was convinced that its numbers alone would immediately prove decisive – twenty-three states against the eleven of the South (in addition to the Deep South the Confederates had Virginia and Tennessee; Missouri, Kentucky, Maryland and West Virginia, formed by secession from Confederate Virginia, declared for the North). In population the North had twenty-two million against the South's nine (of whom three and a half million were slaves). Lastly, the great preponderance of industrial and mineral wealth lay with the North. Against this, optimistic Southerners pointed out that the North had only a handful of trained soldiers at its disposal; the bulk of the regular army, particularly of the officers, was Southern, for soldiering in the South was every gentleman's calling and habit. Moreover, the South had the easier task: it had merely to defend its independence, while the North, to execute its avowed purpose, had to effect a subjugation. It was the very reasonable hope of the South that if only it could inflict one serious defeat on the North, or, at worst, protract its resistance long enough, the North would become war-weary and agree to an armistice. Perhaps, if Lincoln's leadership had been lacking, the South's hope would have been realized.

The South shaped its strategy in conformity with its

policy. The aim of the Southern generals was to capture Washington, the capital, and so convince the North that the war was lost and the rest of the world that the Confederacy should be recognized as a sovereign state. The North similarly, but much less sensibly, was obsessed with the aim of capturing the enemy's capital, Richmond. The fault of such a strategy lay in the fact that, in relation to the North's objective of subjugation, Richmond, though it had some prestige value, was not otherwise important. To break the South it was first necessary to cripple its communications – the great river system of the Mississippi valley, and the railway network centred on Atlanta.

But these were lessons the North was slow to learn. Its early inexperience cost it dear. When in July of 1861 General McDowell, with 20,000 Union men, was routed at Bull Run, only twenty miles from Washington, the North suddenly discovered that zeal, unaided by training, is not enough to win wars. Lincoln, who had to learn his military strategy by dint of trial and error, replaced McDowell by McClellan, called every hand to improving the defences of the capital, and concentrated on the double task of improving the blockade of the South and organizing throughout the winter an army which would be really adequate for its task. McClellan, who a few years previously had watched the British in the Crimea undertaking a similar task, achieved what he set out to do, and by the spring of 1862 the North had a well-equipped army of 150,000 men.

The strategy of 1862 envisaged Northern offensives in both the west and the east. In the west, despite initial successes in Tennessee, Grant found himself held and heavily mauled in Shiloh, and the Confederate grip on the Mississippi was not seriously affected. McClellan's plans in the east envisaged a sea-borne landing on the Virginia coast as part of a pincer movement aimed at Richmond. The landing of 112,000 men was successfully effected when politics intervened. McClellan's dictatorial manner had made him many enemies at home and while he was getting ready to march on Richmond Lincoln, under pressure from Congress, overruled his strategy and reduced him from being General-in-Chief to being mere head of the Army of the Potomac. For fear that the Confederates would march on Washington while McClellan's army was held on the Virginia Peninsula, McDowell, the other half of McClellan's pincer, was ordered to remain near the capital. Lee and Stonewall Jackson, the brilliant Southern commanders, took advantage of this timidity to strike at each army in turn. Despite a 'Seven Days' battle, McClellan failed to breach the Richmond lines, and sustained a loss of over 23,000 men, while at the battle of Manassas (twenty-five miles from Washington) the other Union army was flung back in disorder.

McClellan was called back to Washington to meet the crisis and his men were withdrawn from the Peninsula. Lee advanced into Maryland and was met by McClellan at Antietam. A bitter battle, costly for both sides, was fairly described as 'A defeat for both armies'. McClellan, perhaps unfairly since he had certainly checked the advance on Washington, was accused of letting Lee escape: he was dismissed from command of the Army of the Potomac and replaced by Burnside. Burnside caught Lee at Fredericksburg, but the result was only another of those brave, costly and forlorn Northern attacks which wedded bloodshed to failure. Inconclusive battles in the west brought no better prospects of future success and by the Christmas of 1862, after almost two years of war, victory seemed further from the North than ever.

Yet in fact, though there were few in the North and still fewer in the South who could see it, the basis had been laid for eventual Northern success. Not only had the North survived the first dangerous months of unpreparedness, preserving its capital, its communications and its industries intact. It had also, on one element at least, established conclusive supremacy. The Navy, unlike the Army, was in Union hands from the start and the blockade, which Lincoln proclaimed in April, 1861, became so fully effective that the South's cotton exports, which had been two million bales in 1860–1, were reduced to thirteen thousand for the year following. For the South, whose cotton exports went to buy all those munitions of war which it could not make for itself, this was crucial.

Out of the naval struggle developed the two great diplomatic crises of the war. In an early attempt to run the blockade, the Confederacy sent two of its diplomatic representatives, James Mason and John Slidell, as passengers to Europe on the British mail steamer, *Trent.* A Union warship stopped the *Trent* and removed the Confederates. Immediately Northerners were jubilant and Britons were furious. There was no doubt that in thus forcibly seizing passengers on a neutral ship on the high seas the North had violated international law; for months relations between London and Washington were seriously strained. But calmer counsels prevailed on both sides, Lincoln and the Prince Consort, Seward (Lincoln's Secretary of State) and Cobden (the great British spokesman for the North) working hard and successfully for an amicable settlement.

But barely had the *Trent* case been settled, when another dispute occurred. Unable to build in her own yards vessels that could compete with the new ironclads of the North, the Confederacy placed orders in Britain. In the spring of 1862 the *Alabama,* a powerful ironclad constructed to Southern specifications, was completed at Liverpool, and despite the protests of Lincoln's ambassador, Charles Francis Adams, she was allowed to leave port. In thus according aid to a rebellious government, Great Britain was certainly behaving improperly, but public opinion supported the policy, firstly because it had only a vague comprehension of the issues of the war and saw the South as an oppressed minority manfully struggling for independence, and secondly because there was a general conviction that the South was winning and would very soon have to be recognized as a legitimate government. But while the *Alabama* dispute was still raging, events occurred in the U.S.A. which profoundly modified British feeling towards the North.

Lincoln had always wanted to end slavery, despite his strong adherence to the view that the Constitution debarred

Congress or the President from dictating to the slave states what they should do about it within their own borders. When war broke out he advanced a scheme of compensated emancipation for the benefit of the border states who supported the North, by which Congress would recompense owners for the loss they sustained by having their slaves freed. (It was on just such a basis that the British Parliament had ended slavery throughout the Empire in 1833.) Unfortunately the border states rejected his scheme. Meanwhile slaves were deserting from the South to join the Union cause, pressure from the radicals in Lincoln's own party was increasing daily, and the need for weakening the domestic economy of the South mounted with every Southern military success. So finally, in September, 1862, as a military measure aimed at shortening the war, Lincoln, by virtue of his powers as Commander-in-Chief, issued an Emancipation Proclamation decreeing that on and after January 1st, 1863, all slaves in Confederate territory should be free.

In Britain the effect was marked. Cobden and Bright, who had always recognized the essential justice of the Northern cause, now had clinching arguments for their contention that the future of democracy in North America was bound up with the victory of the Union. The risk that the Confederate Government would obtain recognition receded and in 1863, when Adams protested to Lord Russell, the British Foreign Minister, about the building in Laird's yards of two ironclads as companions to the *Alabama*, he secured the detention of both ships.

But although these foundations for future victory had been laid both at home and overseas, the year 1863 did not open auspiciously for the Union armies. Lincoln was still having difficulties with his generals. After Fredericksburg he replaced Burnside by Hooker. To meet the need for soldiers a Conscription Act, the first in United States history, was passed.* At Chancellorsville, no great distance

* It was an unsatisfactory Act, since it allowed men to buy exemption from service by paying $300.00 or by furnishing an acceptable substitute. Draft riots resulted in New York and elsewhere.

from Fredericksburg, a fine Union army was rolled up by a much smaller Confederate force, though it was a dear victory for the South which cost the life of their brilliant general, 'Stonewall' Jackson. Lee followed up this success, by-passed Washington, and met the main Union army at Gettysburg in Pennsylvania. Each side fought magnificently, and the casualties in each army were enormous. Lee was halted and Washington was saved, but the North could not follow up its gains and prevent Lee retiring to Virginia with the remnants of his army. Nevertheless, Lincoln's choice of the field of Gettysburg for his great Memorial Address, summing up his democratic beliefs and the noblest aspirations of the North, was not misplaced. Judged by the stakes involved, the numbers of the participants, the heroism and the slaughter, Gettysburg was the greatest battle of the war.

Almost simultaneously in the West, Grant had been developing the strategy which was eventually to defeat the South. By besieging and capturing the stronghold of Vicksburg he cut the Mississippi as a north-south line of communication and threatened the South from the west. Grant followed this with a campaign in Tennessee, resulting in November in the great victory of Chattanooga which robbed the Confederates of control of a vital rail centre and of an important border state. After these successes it was not surprising that Lincoln appointed Grant to be Commander-in-Chief. At last, after three years of trial and error, he had found the architect of victory.

In 1864 the war entered on its last phase. The North had now mobilized its manpower and its machine power; superior in both, it could not fail to defeat a foe whose strength was by now fully extended. But to overcome the brilliant husbandry of Lee and to check the mounting war-weariness of the Northern voters, strong leadership was required. It was provided militarily by Grant, politically by Lincoln.

CHAPTER XXII

The Civil War: Second Phase

THE American Constitution, for all the checks and restraints which it imposes on the federal government, recognizes that in time of war governments must be in a position to act swiftly and firmly. Lincoln from the first grasped this fact, recognized that as President he had sworn to 'preserve, protect and defend' the Union and proceeded to exercise to the full the powers which the President, as Commander-in-Chief, possessed for that purpose. When war broke out Congress was not in session and eighty days elapsed before it assembled. Lincoln did not hesitate to act alone. He announced that a national emergency existed and called out the militia. He proclaimed a blockade of the South and gave orders for the federal army to be rapidly expanded. In normal times these were actions which could only be taken with prior Congressional sanction, but Lincoln was right in thinking that war could not wait for that, and Congress endorsed his judgment when, on assembling, it passed a bill ratifying his acts.

Wars are always testing times for democracies, civil wars most of all. 'It has long been a grave question,' said Lincoln, 'whether any government not too strong for the liberties of its people can be strong enough to maintain its existence in great emergencies. On this point,' he added, 'the present rebellion brought our Republic to a severe test.' Lincoln proved that the test could be passed, but his methods surprised, and even shocked, some of his contemporaries. The American Constitution, like the British Bill of Rights, forbids the suspension of Habeas Corpus, 'unless when in cases of rebellion or invasion the public safety may require it', yet Lincoln often suspended it and held persons without trial even in areas where the civil courts were functioning, in a manner closely resembling the British Home Secretary's wartime detentions under Clause 18B. Similarly he declared martial law in many areas behind the lines. But these inroads on the liberties of the citizens were made with no dictatorial intent, but only in response to the desperate needs of the time. Lincoln clearly distinguished between the minor and the major points at issue. 'Are all the laws but *one* to go unexecuted and the government itself go to pieces lest that one be violated?'

Though Congress, in the main, supported Lincoln on this issue and gave his acts a subsequent legalization, their relations with the President throughout most of the war were not good. The American separation of powers between legislature and executive always creates a certain strain between the two, but in war-time when the executive gathers such great powers into its hands the frustration of Congress and its consequent resentment are especially marked. Unable to share much in the conduct of the war, Congress developed a tendency to interfere for interference' sake. A committee of both houses, the famous Joint Committee on the Conduct of the War, was set up with wide powers of inquisition. The members visited the fighting front, undermined army discipline, intimidated the commanders and continually confused politics with strategy.

As far as politics were concerned, Lincoln's constant effort was to steer a middle course. There was a tendency for his own Republican Party to be dominated by the Radical wing, led by Senator Sumner of Massachusetts. It was this group which, after Fredericksburg, went to the unprecedented length of demanding that Lincoln dismiss his Secretary of State, Seward, hoping to surround the President with a Radical cabinet. But Lincoln combined diplomacy with firmness. 'The President said with a good deal of firmness that he was master, and that they should not do that.' He won; Seward remained, and the Radicals were discomfited. The differences, however, persisted. They were the differences between a party to whom the war was primarily a crusade against the South, and a President to whom it was primarily a defence of the Union.

But there were also Democrats in Congress – indeed they increased their numbers after the mid-term election of 1862. Many of them were loyal supporters of the North and the war, but they numbered in their midst many Southern sympathizers – 'Copperheads', to give them their opprobrious title derived from the poisonous snake so common in the South. These presented Lincoln with one of his most serious problems. Their leader was Vallandigham, an Ohio congressman who began, in 1863, to trade upon the war-weariness of the nation to propose a negotiated peace. Burnside, the commander in Ohio, had him court-martialled and imprisoned. Lincoln, who realized that Burnside's action was illegal, but also that Vallandigham's behaviour was unprincipled and dangerous, released him from prison, but handed him over to the Confederates whose cause he was pleading. To those who protested at this banishing of a Congressman, Lincoln, who was often accused of being too free with his exercise of the presidential power of pardon, had his answer ready: 'Must I shoot a simple-minded soldier boy who deserts, while I must not touch a hair of a wily agitator who induces him to desert?'

But in spite of the division and maladministration which existed behind the lines, it is a measure of the strength of the North that it was able, at the same time as it fought the war, to proceed with the development of most of its peace-time interests as well. The Republican Party rested on an alliance, above all, of Western farmers and Eastern business, and the domestic legislation of Lincoln's first four years reflects both these interests. The farmers wanted easy access to the great spaces of the West: the Republicans, true to their descent from the 'Free-soilers' of the '50's, effected the passage in 1862 of the Homestead Act. This was, in effect, a disposition of the western lands in the form of a public largesse: every citizen was given the offer of 160 acres, provided only that he would undertake to settle on it. Drawn on by this, by the fabled riches of the Gold Coast and by a desire to escape conscription, over 300,000 migrants moved west during the four years of the war. The railways failed to keep pace with them: the war held up labour and materials. But legislation in 1862 and 1864 prepared the way for immediate post-war resumption by making huge land grants to the Union Pacific Railroad with which to meet the cost of construction. Nor was this expansion conceived in exclusively material terms. A nation which at its very inception in 1785 had provided, in the North-West Land Ordinance, public land for the support of public schools, had since developed, principally through the stimulus of New England, the conviction that higher education, too, was essential to the proper development of the West. Consequently, contemporaneously with the Homestead Act, Congress in 1862 passed the Morrill Act, which assigned to each state, in proportion to its representation in Congress, a share of the public lands to serve as an endowment for a college of 'agricultural and mechanical arts'. At the least, this made possible the application of technical knowledge to the otherwise indiscriminate land-grabbing of the '60's, '70's and '80's; at best, it was the soil from which sprang the great State Universities of the West.

Business and industry formed the other leg of Northern Republicanism. They had long wanted a tariff which would 'protect' them against foreign competition, but Southern opposition had hitherto prevented the passage of other than revenue-raising tariffs. But now, first in 1862 and then in 1864, successive increases in the tariff were authorized by Congress which were definitely protective in intention. Northern industry, stimulated by war orders, supplied with an ample force of cheap, immigrant labour, now set out on its conquest of the domestic market, a market expanding with every Westward surge and every shipload of European immigrants. On the Western plains it might seem as if the Jeffersonian dream of a rural, freehold democracy was being realized; in the factories of New York and the steel mills of Pittsburgh a Hamiltonian America of self-sufficient industry seemed to be on its way. And meanwhile, fed by the wheat of the plains and the munitions of the factories, the war against the slave and cotton economy of the South mounted to its climax.

When 1864 opened there were two Southern armies in the field – Johnston's in the west and Lee's in the east. Grant appointed Sherman with 100,000 men to look after Johnston while he himself took on Lee. Sherman set out from Chattanooga along the line of the railway and slowly forced Johnston back to Atlanta. Sherman entered Atlanta, the great railway centre of the South, on September 2nd, and proceeded to march onwards to the sea, cutting a corridor of devastation sixty miles wide right across the heart of the Confederacy. By Christmas Day he had captured Savannah, dealt a crippling blow at the economic strength of the South and proved that no part of its territory could now escape the impact of Northern armies. But by this time events on Grant's front had inflicted their own lessons, too.

Grant crossed the Rapidan, in Virginia, on the same day as Sherman left Chattanooga, but he had a harder task and a more formidable rival. With an army of 150,000 he was faced by Lee's 90,000, but Lee's men were protected by the river valleys of Virginia and a strong system of artificial defences. Grant's object was twofold – to bring Lee to battle and to capture Richmond. To this end he despatched one army up the Shenandoah, to block Southern manœuvrings on that flank, while he led his main force into an area of dense thickets aptly named the Wilderness. In the confused battles fought there Grant lost 18,000, Lee 10,000. Then followed the trench warfare at Spotsylvania, at the end of which Grant's losses totalled 31,000 men. Earlier in the war this would have been the signal for the federal army to retire on Washington and re-form, but a different spirit animated them now. 'I propose,' said Grant, 'to fight it out on this line if it takes all summer.' Then came the costliest engagement of the war – Cold Harbour – where the Northern troops, knowing the strength of the enemy's defences, pinned their names to their tunics, so that at least they might be identified when their bodies were found. Frustrated in a frontal attack, Grant led his army across the river mouths between Richmond and the sea, a very remarkable transport and engineering achievement, and attempted to force a back-door entry, approaching Richmond from the south. Lee, however, was once again too quick for him: the Union army was held at Petersburg and badly mauled, while a bold, far-ranging Confederate force under Early not merely repulsed its enemies in the Shenandoah Valley, but actually crossed into Maryland and got in sight of the city of Washington. These were the circumstances in which Lincoln faced the Presidential campaign of '64 with strong forebodings of electoral defeat.

Most unprejudiced observers would have echoed Lincoln's fears. The dissensions within the Republican Party and the rivalry between it and the Democrats had increased under the strain of war to a most serious degree. In the spring of 1864 the Radicals of Lincoln's own party hatched a plot to build up Chase, the Secretary of the Treasury, as the Republican candidate for the Presidency. The 'Chase boom' collapsed, owing to clumsy management, only to be succeded by an attempt to advance the claims of Frémont, who was nominated at a breakaway convention in May. The main body of the party, however, recognized Lincoln as the best candidate and he was belatedly given the Republican nomination. The Democrats met a couple of months later against a background of heavy Union casualties and war-weariness. Vallandigham, who had escaped back into Ohio, was leading a peace agitation and several unofficial Southern 'peace missions' were dickering with interested public men in the North. Lincoln's own position was clear: he would welcome any peace which 'embraced the restoration of Union and the abandonment of slavery'. These were just the terms, of course, which the South would not agree to, but despite the proved failure of repeated peace negotiations, the Democrats allowed Vallandigham a free hand to draft most of their platform, which referred to 'four years of failure to restore the Union by the experiment of war' and demanded 'immediate efforts for a cessation of hostilities'. For candidate they chose McClellan, the general whom Lincoln had dismissed in 1862. McClellan repudiated the 'peace platform', but no one could deny that its wording still represented the predominant sentiments of the Democrat party, and it is hard to see how McClellan could have escaped the obligation to carry some of it out in the event of his being elected. So at least, it seemed to Lincoln, and, at the moment when his own party managers were warning him that the chances of a Republican victory were dangerously remote, he wrote a memorandum, sealed it and asked his cabinet colleagues to append their signatures without reading it. The memorandum read: 'This morning, as for some days past, it seems exceedingly probable that this Administration will not be re-elected. Then it will be my duty to so co-operate with the President-elect as to save the Union between the election and the inauguration (i.e. between November and March), as he will have secured his election on such ground that he cannot possibly save it afterwards.' In other words, Lincoln meant to use what moral authority would still remain to him to enlist McClellan's support in finishing the war off quickly before McClellan himself entered office committed to the restoration of slavery and a negotiated peace. As Emerson very truly remarked, 'Seldom in history was so much staked upon a popular vote. I suppose never in history'.

In fact, the corner was soon turned. Early had shot his bolt and the Confederacy's threat to Washington had not time to materialize before Sheridan's cavalry came to the capital's rescue and chivvied Early back into the Shenandoah Valley and the Virginia foothills. In the South Sherman's capture of Atlanta and his subsequent devastating 'march to the sea' brightened Union prospects just when the earliest Northern voters were going to the polls. Democratic prospects clouded over, the Frémont bubble burst and he withdrew his candidacy, while the Republican dissidents decided to forget their fears and grievances and rally behind the President. The President himself abstained from any campaigning, but silhouetted, as it were, against the dawn of victory, his gaunt figure took on the aspect of a visible symbol of all that the North had been fighting for these last four years.

The election itself did not differ from other American elections in the quality of the campaign oratory, the tactics of the party managers or the complexity and frequent irrelevance of the issues debated. Nevertheless the election of 1864 is entitled to be considered one of the brightest hours in the history of American democracy. No more than other elections did it escape the usual contamination of politics – the pledges impossible of fulfilment, the false accusations and the irrelevant rebuttals, the graft and the occasional bribery, the astute operations of party machines keeping just the right side of the law – this aspect of 'the strife of the election' was, as Lincoln observed, only 'human nature practically applied to the facts of the case'. But over and above this one fact stands out – that, at a moment when it was fighting for its very life within its own borders, American democracy was able to employ its own democratic methods to determine, by a free vote, its own future leaders and line of action – to pause, make assessment of the cost of its great struggle and decide by the votes of its farmers, its factory workers and its very soldiers what its future policy should be.

The election was a Lincoln 'landslide', only three Northern states voting against him. With characteristic magnanimity Lincoln invited all 'to re-unite in a common effort to save our common country', and turned his attention to the completion of the war and the preparation for peace. Military events moved fast. For all his apparent frustration, Grant had in fact imposed losses on Lee which he could not make good and which were bound to prove fatal. Blockaded by sea, devastated and disrupted by land, the Confederacy was slowly being strangled. From Savannah, Sherman turned North through the Carolinas, via Columbia and Goldsboro, until he linked up with Grant south of Richmond. On April 1st, at Five Forks, the final assault on Lee's besieged and weakened army began. Petersburg fell, Lee fell back in confusion, the Confederate President and his cabinet fled from Richmond. On April 7th, trapped and devoid of supplies, even of food, Lee asked for surrender terms at the village of Appomattox. It was a memorable scene, Lee immaculate and correct, Grant unkempt and mud-spattered. But the Northern leader was not lacking in generosity. Lee's army was allowed to disband freely, merely giving their word not to take up arms against the Union: they could take their horses back home 'to work their little farms'. As the Confederates moved away someone in the Union ranks raised a cheer.

After this the end came quickly. Johnston capitulated to Sherman, Montgomery, the original Confederate capital, surrendered soon after, and by the end of May the last embers of Southern resistance had burnt themselves out.

In March, Lincoln took office for the second time as President of the United States and on that occasion delivered his Second Inaugural Address. It is a speech which outranks all his other utterances in the perfection of its verbal form and it sums up within a few paragraphs Lincoln's own philosophy of history, his conception of the war and his attitude towards the peace.

> Fellow Countrymen: At this second appearing to take the oath of the Presidential office, there is less occasion for an extended address than there was at the first. Then, a statement, somewhat in detail, of a course to be pursued, seemed fitting and proper. Now, at the expiration of four years, during which public declarations have been constantly called forth on every point and phase of the great contest which still absorbs the attention and engrosses the energies of the nation, little that is new could be presented. The progress of our arms, upon which all else chiefly depends, is as well known to the public as to myself; and it is, I trust, reasonably satisfactory and encouraging to all. With high hope for the future, no prediction in regard to it is ventured.
>
> On the occasion corresponding to this four years ago, all thoughts were anxiously directed to an impending civil war. All dreaded it; all sought to avert it. While the inaugural address was being delivered from this place, devoted altogether

to *saving* the Union without war, insurgent agents were in the city seeking to *destroy* it without war – seeking to dissolve the Union, and divide effects, by negotiation. Both parties deprecated war; but one of them would *make* war rather than let the nation survive; and the other would *accept* war rather than let it perish. And the war came.

One-eighth of the whole population were coloured slaves, not distributed generally over the Union, but localized in the southern part of it. These slaves constituted a peculiar and powerful interest. All knew that this interest was, somehow, the cause of the war. To strengthen, perpetuate, and extend this interest was the object for which the insurgents would rend the Union, even by war; while the Government claimed no right to do more than to restrict the territorial enlargement of it. Neither party expected for the war the magnitude or the duration which it has already attained. Neither anticipated that the *cause* of the conflict might cease with, or even before, the conflict itself should cease. Each looked for an easier triumph, and a result less fundamental and astounding. Both read the same Bible, and pray to the same God; and each invokes His aid against the other. It may seem strange that any men should dare to ask a just God's assistance in wringing their bread from the sweat of other men's faces: but let us judge not, that we be not judged. The prayers of both could not be answered; that of neither has been answered fully. The Almighty has His own purposes. 'Woe unto the world because of offences! for it must needs be that offences come: but woe to the man by whom the offence cometh.' If we shall suppose American slavery is one of those offences which, in the providence of God, must needs come, but which, having continued through His appointed time, He now wills to remove, and that He gives to both North and South this terrible war, as the woe due to those by whom the offence came, shall we discern therein any departure from those divine attributes which the believers in a living God always ascribe to Him? Fondly do we hope, fervently do we pray, that this mighty scourge of war may speedily pass away. Yet, if God wills that it continue until all the wealth piled by the bondman's two hundred and fifty years of unrequited toil shall be sunk, and until every drop of blood drawn with the lash shall be paid by another drawn with the sword, as was said three thousand years ago, so still it must be said, 'The judgments of the Lord are true and righteous altogether.'

> With malice toward none, with charity for all, with firmness in the right, as God gives us to see the right, let us strive on to finish the work we are in; to bind up the nation's wounds; to care for him who shall have borne the battle, and for his widow, and his orphan: to do all which may achieve and cherish a just and a lasting peace among ourselves and with all nations.

But Lincoln was not destined to have the execution of his own high purpose. On Good Friday in the week following Appomattox, Lincoln held a Cabinet meeting in a happy mood. Last night, he said, he had a dream which invariably preceded good news. In his dream he was sailing in a strange, indescribable ship which moved at great speed towards a dark and undefined shore. The Cabinet meeting over, he and Mrs Lincoln that night attended a performance of 'Our American Cousin' at Ford's Theatre. In the midst of the performance shots rang out. They came from the revolver of a fanatical Southerner, John Wilkes Booth, leader of a conspiracy which aimed at killing all the principal figures of Lincoln's administration. Booth's own bullet inflicted a mortal wound on Lincoln: by the next day the President was dead. A week later a black-draped funeral train left Washington to take Lincoln's remains back to Springfield, Illinois, for burial. Wherever the train stopped people came to pay homage to 'Old Father Abraham', 'The Great Emancipator'. A nation's mourning attended his passing, and the greatest of American poets added his tribute:

> Coffin that passes through lanes and streets,
> Through day and night with the great cloud darkening the land,
> With the pomp of the inloop'd flags, with the cities draped in black,
> With the show of the States themselves as of crape-veil'd women standing,
> With processions long and winding and the flambeaus of the night,
> With the countless torches lit, with the silent sea of faces and the unbared heads,

With the waiting depot, the arriving coffin, and the sombre faces,
With dirges through the night, with the thousand voices rising strong and solemn,
With all the mournful voices of the dirges pour'd around the coffin,
The dim-lit churches and the shuddering organs—where amid these you journey,
With the tolling, tolling bells' perpetual clang,
Here, coffin that slowly passes,
I give you my sprig of lilac.*

CHAPTER XXIII

'*Reconstruction*'

THE consequences of the Civil War were great and far-reaching. The victorious North now controlled the destinies of the nation, and the cotton aristocracy was finally supplanted by the potentates of business and industry, the lords of the new machines and the ploughs that were breaking the western plains. The developments of the war years had already pointed the way to the tendencies of peace. The South emerged from the conflict to find riveted on the Union the protective tariff which she had so long by votes and by threats striven to keep off. The financiers, too, had passed a National Banking Act which was to keep control of the nation's purse-strings in the hands of a few men of the East. Similarly the farmers had their wartime success in the Homestead Act of 1862, with its promise of free western lands to any *bona fide* settler. Thus when peace came the masters of industry, finance and the free lands of the West were already in a position to take over the shaping of American life for the next generation.

By contrast, the war left the South a wreck. Out of the million or so casualties of the war it was indeed the North

* Walt Whitman, *When Lilacs Last in the Dooryard Bloom'd.*

which bore the larger share, but in proportion to its population the South was by far the worse sufferer. Over a quarter of a million of its manhood were killed, with the result that there is to-day barely a village in the South which does not bear its pathetic monument to 'Our Confederate Dead'. Moreover, it was on southern soil that the war was fought and in a manner peculiarly destructive – Sheridan turning large parts of Virginia into a desert and Sherman cutting a swathe of destruction through the Carolinas and Georgia. But more than losses in men, money or materials was the fact that defeat meant to the South the end of a way of life. It was not merely that slavery was abolished, never to return, but rather that a whole tradition and culture had fallen in and could never be restored as before. Suddenly a whole nation, for so the South had come to regard itelf, found its power forfeited and its pride humbled. Small wonder that to this day to Southerners it is not 'The Civil War', nor even 'The War Between the States', but simply 'The War'.

These were scars indeed, scars which even now have not properly healed. Lincoln had known this when he spoke of 'binding up the nation's wounds', but Lincoln was dead and his assassination had the grievous consequence of leaving the South like a dangerously wounded man in the hands of heartless and incompetent surgeons. As far as the peace was concerned, Lincoln died with his work only just begun. The political position was as follows: Lincoln had been re-elected in 1864 as head of a party which contained three elements – the 'Radicals' (fervent abolitionists), the more conservative Republicans, and a minority of 'War Democrats', who had deserted the rest of their party out of loyalty to the Union cause. It was the 'War Democrats' whom Andrew Johnson represented when he was chosen as Lincoln's running-mate in 1864 and when on Lincoln's death he stepped from the Vice-Presidency into the White House. His position, thus already weak by virtue of the size of his party, was made still more difficult by the fact that the Congress with which he had to work was several degrees more 'radical' than himself and was dominated by two of his most diehard critics, Sumner, Senator from Massachusetts, and Thaddeus Stevens, Congressman from Pennsylvania. Johnson himself, though well-meaning and honest, was wholly lacking in Lincoln's gifts of leadership. Alternately vehement and timid, curiously inept and seldom at ease in his office, he signally failed at a task which even a man of heroic stature would have had difficulty in mastering.

The task really fell into two parts. There was first of all the question of what was to be done with the emancipated Negroes. This was a social and economic problem which should have been considered on its own merits and by itself with insistence first and foremost on the interests of the Negroes themselves. Unfortunately it was confused, sometimes deliberately, with the second problem, namely what was to be done with the 'rebel' states. This was a political and constitutional problem which, given generosity of spirit and practical common sense, should not have been hard to solve. Unfortunately both were lacking.

The constitutional problem was twofold. Firstly, what was the legal position, now that the war was over, of the Southern states? One view was that since the war had been fought and *won* to preserve the Union, i.e. to prevent states seceding, the states as such must necessarily have been and must still be in the Union. As Lincoln said, 'No state can by its mere motion get out of the Union.' On this view only individuals could be rebels and so the only problem was that of seeing that state governments were restored to loyal hands. The Radical view, however, was that by seceding the states had put themselves outside the Union and so outside the protection of the Constitution. They had therefore forfeited all their rights and powers and should be administered like any other territory owned by the U.S.A. – directly from Washington, without any say in the determination of their own affairs.

Tied up with the first was the second problem. Was it the business of the President, or of Congress, to arrange for the rehabilitation of the seceded states? The President believed it was his, since he, as Commander-in-Chief, had imposed military law on the South and should therefore be responsible for its withdrawal. Congress contended that now that peace was restored it was their duty and privilege to settle this problem.

Thus, on the whole range of post-war issues there was a deep and sharp cleavage of opinion, each problem linking up with the next. The 'Radicals' had a majority in Congress. It was therefore hardly surprising that they advocated that Congress should have authority over the whole field of Reconstruction (the name soon given to the task of reorganizing the South). For the same reason they opposed the Lincoln-Johnson view that the states, as such, had never seceded at all. They were a party of mixed motives. They included men of high principle, ex-abolitionists who had believed that the war had been fought exclusively to end slavery and that the peace should be constructed solely with an eye to preventing the plantation South from ever reviving slavery in any shape or form. But they also included politicians of narrow and unscrupulous ambition who were only concerned with preserving for the Republican Party the complete dominance in the Government which it had won in the war and who cared nothing for the Negro, the Southerner, or indeed the Union except in so far as they served the interests of their Party. Thus they advocated votes for the Negro, not because they seriously believed that an ignorant Negro who had been a slave one day could be made into a responsible citizen the next, but because they were afraid that as long as the Southern states were controlled by white voters they would go Democratic. The Negroes, they thought, would vote Republican out of gratitude to their emancipators.

It was amidst controversy such as this that the task of Reconstruction was undertaken. Lincoln had made a start while the war was still on, with a proclamation in 1863 whereby if ten per cent. of the electorate in any state would take an oath of loyalty they could set up a state government which the President would recognize. Johnson continued this policy, and by the end of 1865 governments elected on this basis were in office all over the South, under State Constitutions which repudiated secession and accepted the abolition of slavery, though they restricted the vote to whites. Unfortunately the legislation these governments passed to solve the Negro problem looked, to Northern eyes, very much like an attempt to re-introduce slavery by the back door. 'The Black Laws', as they were called, were based on the principle of keeping an absolute bar between white and coloured and gave the Negro a status half-way between slave and citizen, with most of the burdens of the first and few of the rights of the second. Congress, which had all along refused to recognize the state governments which Lincoln and Johnson had set up, re-doubled its opposition to their policy. It extended the powers of the Freedmen's Bureau – an organization originally set up to assist the Army in dealing with the slaves emancipated by its advance – so as to make it almost a rival jurisdiction throughout the South wherever Negroes were involved, over-riding state governments and state courts. This was passed over Johnson's veto, and the battle between President and Congress rose to new heights of fury.

The Radicals increased their strength in the mid-term election of 1866 and pressed on with their programme by passing in 1867 the First Reconstruction Act. This did away with all Lincoln's and Johnson's work and put the South under direct military rule until such time as the states, with Negroes voting, should ratify the Fourteenth Amendment to the Constitution. (This was designed to guarantee to the Negro the same rights and protection as the white citizen already enjoyed under Amendments I–IX, the famous 'Bill of Rights'.) To achieve this against the opposition of practically the whole white South the Freedmen's Bureau 'organized' the Negro vote. It was ignorant, illiterate Negroes, understanding nothing of the issues involved, who, like pawns on a chessboard, were manipulated by a handful of carpet-baggers* and scallywags, to set up Southern

* Northern agents, so called from the carpet bags in which they carried their belongings.

governments which would do exactly what the Radical Representatives in Congress wanted.

Against this tide of post-war vengefulness and party bigotry Andrew Johnson could do nothing. Congress stuck at nothing in its efforts to reduce the President to a position of impotence. By a Tenure of Office Bill, of very doubtful constitutionality, they tried to deprive the President of his right to dismiss members of his own Cabinet. When, despite this, Johnson dismissed Stanton, his Secretary of War, the House in 1868 voted to impeach the President before the Senate (the only method, under the Constitution, by which a President may be removed). But this was going too far. There were no real crimes to be found and laid at the President's door and it was soon obvious that this was merely a shameful attempt to pervert the law into an instrument of partisan conflict. Nevertheless, it was only by one vote that the President secured his acquittal, and the trial marked the lowest point to which the power of the President has ever sunk in the United States. Later in the same year the Republicans nominated General Grant as their candidate to succeed Johnson in the White House, and although Grant knew nothing of politics his military reputation secured his election as a symbol of Northern sacrifices in the war and Radical aspirations for the peace.

If anyone hoped that Grant would moderate Radical excesses they were badly mistaken. He soon turned out to be a classic instance of the successful soldier who is a disastrous politician. Grant was putty in the hands of his party, a respectable figure who served to cover some of the dirtiest political deals in American history. The Radicals pushed on with their programmes unopposed. Their puppet governments in the South, supported by Northern troops, piled taxation and debt on to the already crippled Southern economy until at last they produced the inevitable hateful reaction. Foiled at the polls, the Southern whites took to extra-legal methods. Organizing themselves into secret armed bands – the 'Ku Klux Klan', 'Regulators', etc. – they terrorized the Negroes and intimidated the carpet-baggers until by 1870 the Democrats had recovered control, with white majorities, in four Southern States. Even in the North the price of Radical Reconstruction was beginning to look too high. The incompetence of the Grant regime, and the dishonesty of his lieutenants, which flowered in 1872 in a crop of political scandals, exposures of corrupt practices, and financial crashes unprecedented in American history, provoked a revolt of liberal Republicans which came very near to wrecking Grant's chances of re-election for a second term. Although he found his way back into the White House the power of the Radicals was sensibly weakened. The corruption and oppression which their policy in the South entailed became more and more disreputable. The Democrats re-asserted themselves in one Southern state after another and in the Congressional elections of 1874 actually won control of the House. By 1875 only three states were still under Radical rule and by 1876 the South was in a position to insist upon the final removal of the last of its Northern oppressors. In the Presidential election of that year the contest was so close that the election of Hayes, the Republican candidate, depended entirely upon the outcome in the South where some electoral votes were in dispute. A gentleman's agreement was arrived at by which the Democrats agreed not to press their claims to the limit in return for Hayes committing himself to ending Reconstruction. Hayes was pronounced elected, and one of his first acts was to withdraw the last federal troops from the South. Thus twelve years of Reconstruction came to an end in 1877.

The story of the Reconstruction years is not a pleasant one, yet in assessing this period of American history it is important to remember that it followed on four years of bitter and protracted civil war. Such wars always leave behind them passions which it is difficult to assuage, and the American Civil War, compared with others of modern times and considering the losses and bloodshed which it involved, left behind it a smaller legacy of irreconcilable hatreds than most. The divisions which the war so cruelly opened did in fact close again with remarkable speed and finality. The South accepted the decision of the war and resigned itself to re-incorporation in a Union in which it would always be in a minority. To Americans this has always seemed so natural a conclusion that they scarcely comment on it, but the historian who looks at comparable conflicts elsewhere can recognize it for what it is, a remarkable triumph for the healing powers of American democracy.

But if this is so it is not to the politicians of Reconstruction that the credit should go. Their work left harmful and lasting impressions behind. The South forgave the war sooner than it forgave Reconstruction, with all its bitter humiliation of subjection to a people of another colour, and former slaves. To remove this, the South had to resort to methods, such as the Ku Klux Klan, which were as objectionable as those of the Radicals, and the result was that the social emancipation of the Negro in the South was retarded for generations and a tradition of violence persisted long after any justification for it had disappeared. Furthermore, by inflicting such wounds on the defeated South, the Republicans made every Southerner into a Democrat, no matter what his political views might be. To this day, in consequence, the South has remained the 'Solid South' of the Democratic Party, nursing its memories of what a few years of Republican rule in Southern legislatures meant to every white Southerner. And although the South made good speed in healing the worst economic scars left by the war, it remained, by comparison with the North, an impoverished region. Reconstruction was not to blame for this – it was due to faulty agriculture, war losses, shortage of capital and other things beside – but Reconstruction made it worse by diverting the mind of the South away from its problems to its wrongs. While the North forgot the war and pressed onward, the South remembered and looked backward. The North could have its victory; the South would keep its memories.

CHAPTER XXIV

The Frontier

SOME, at least, of the American public's indifference to the crimes and follies perpetrated by the politicians of the Reconstruction decade may be due to the fact that it was not to the South but to the West that the nation's gaze was principally directed in the generation following the Civil War. The 'binding up of the nation's wounds' interested the average citizen much less than the extension of the nation's sway over prairie, desert and sierra. If you look at a map of the United States in 1865 you will find that white settlement stops at a line very little to the west of the Mississippi and the Missouri rivers. There is a strip of settlement along the Pacific coast, a few islands of scattered miners or prospectors in Colorado, Nevada or Montana, and a compact Mormon settlement around Salt Lake City. But the rest of the great Far West is still unsettled and often unexplored territory, where only the Indian and the buffalo roam. By 1890, however, the lines of settlement have closed in from both sides, from the Mississippi Valley and the California coast, until they have at last met, and the 'frontier', the moving boundary familiar to Americans ever since Jamestown, is officially described as 'closed'. Thus, at a time when the British, the French, the Germans and the Belgians were building overseas empires in Africa, the United States was completing its expansion on the continent where it had its home. The last stage of that expansion, the winning of the Far West, was the great pre-occupation of the post-war generation. It provided adventure, riches, romance and sport all in one.

One of the issues out of which the Civil War had sprung was, as the Kansas-Nebraska dispute indicated, the question of who was to look after the development of the West – the North or the South. Even while the war was still on, that issue, as we have seen, was virtually settled, and the rate at which the North poured migrants into the West actually increased during the war years. Small wonder, then, that with the obstacle of the war removed in 1865 the westward movement changed from a stream into a flood. It was a flood which was born at first on river steamers up the Missouri River and on freight wagons ('the prairie schooners') beyond. For fast trans-continental travel in the war and immediately post-war years there was the stage coach or 'Overland Express', run by such firms as Wells, Fargo & Co., which carried mails to and from California twice a week. But soon, from either side, the permanent way of the railroads came pushing into the wilderness, until that great day in 1869 when the Union and the Central Pacific, reaching out from Omaha and San Francisco respectively, joined their tracks at Promontory Point, Utah. By 1884 three other lines, the Northern Pacific, the Southern Pacific and the Santa Fé, had also reached the Pacific coast. (The adjacent Dominion of Canada had also constructed, by 1885, a trans-continental railway, the Canadian Pacific.) Though their finances were a playground for the unscrupulous and their construction provided opportunities for every kind of shady deal, the building of these railroads was a remarkable feat not only of engineering but also of human courage and perseverance. As Henry Adams pointed out, the energies which at other times or in other places men might have put into politics or diplomacy they put in the America of 1865–95 into building railroads. Their construction is truly part of the epic of America.

The importance which Henry Adams's contemporaries attached to railroads was not misplaced. The role they filled in American life was vitally important. Just as the railways of Britain which spread their network over town and country in the 1840's made it possible to mobilize the new power of the machine so as both to strengthen the nation and unify it, so the railways of the West tapped the great resources of the American prairies and mountains while at the same time binding the Union, new settlements and old alike, by bonds of steel and steam. And the railways were not merely communications; they were direct agents of colonization. The practice of financing the construction of these railroads very largely by grants of lands from Congress, on either side of the track, often to a depth of ten miles or more, meant that the railroads had a direct interest in populating the spaces through which they went. Settlers would pay for land, provide passengers and freight, and, best of all, attract others if they were themselves successful. How much this meant is indicated by the fact that the total acreage of land grants which the federal government gave to the railroads adds up to an area almost the size of the state of Texas. To settle these vast spaces the railroad kings competed with each other, advertising not only in the East, but even in Europe, shipping immigrants across the Atlantic, giving them free railway fares to the West, settling them and helping them, oftentimes, in the organization of their farms and communities. Thus it was that a great railroad king like James J. Hill of the Great Northern lines was as much a colonizer of Minnesota and the Dakotas as ever in the seventeenth century the Calverts had been of Maryland, or William Penn of Pennsylvania.

However, before advantage could be taken of the colonizing facilities of the railroads, the settlers, like their forerunners in the seventeenth and eighteenth centuries, had to dispose of the menace of the hostile Indians. The Indians of the Great Plains were dependent to an astonishing degree on the buffalo, an animal which provided them with food, clothing, housing and even fuel, and more almost than the conflict with the white man it was the destruction of the great buffalo herds, estimated at originally fifteen million strong, that subdued the Indian tribesmen. Deprived of their means of livelihood, they either became dependent on paleface charity or, the more savage of them, attacked white settlements in hopes of plunder and food. Such attacks provoked reprisals and from 1862 to 1886 there was almost continuous conflict, marked by savagery and deceit on both sides, often with heavy white slaughter (as at Custer's 'Land Stand', when the Sioux in 1876 massacred an entire regiment on the banks of the Little Big

Horn River). But there could, of course, be only one end to such an unequal contest, and by 1887 the Indian threat had virtually disappeared. The fiercest and most intractable had been killed, and the remainder had been confined to large reservations within which they could roam harmlessly at will. Since then, by degrees, the government has come to assume an ever greater responsibility for its Indian charges, giving them citizenship when their fitness was proved, assisting them to get a living and an education, and protecting them against commercial exploitation. The result is that the Indians are now making their own contributions to American life and culture and, so far from being exterminated, their numbers are now on the increase. (Since 1900 the Indian population of the United States has increased 53 per cent.)

As the Indian retreated across the Great Plains, the cowboy advanced. About 1865 someone discovered that cattle could survive the winter on the prairies, especially if they were driven up from Texas to the northern pastures of Western Kansas, Montana or Wyoming in the spring. As the railroad began to reach the confines of the 'cow country', it became possible to transport cattle to the towns of the East and sell them there for less than cattle reared locally. Then in 1875 there began the first shipments of dressed beef to Europe, particularly to Britain, where the population was growing so fast that it was increasingly dependent on imported food (without the wheat and beef of Western America the concentration of the British people on industry, rather than food-growing, would never have been possible). By 1881 over one hundred million pounds of beef was being shipped to Europe. Thus the prairie became as fertile a source of wealth as the gold or silver mines of the Rockies. Investors as far afield as England or Scotland put their money into ranches in the Far West.

By 1884 it was estimated that $30 millions of British capital had been invested on the Great Plains and British landowners like the Duke of Sutherland had holdings in Texas so vast that their ancestral acres were a mere farmyard by comparison. But the 'open range' system, by which vast herds wandered without fence or boundary, grazing over the largest common ever known in history, and herded only by a handful of cowboys – that could not long hold out against the westward march of settlement. The railroad which opened up the markets that made the range so profitable also brought the homesteader who was the cattleman's deadly rival. The cattleman wanted to keep the prairie *open*, to drive his herds where he pleased; the homesteader wanted to enclose it, to protect his crops against the coyote or the stampeding herd. In 1874 invention gave the homesteader the weapon he needed for victory – barbed wire, by which it was at last possible to fence the treeless plains cheaply and effectively. A vast guerrilla warfare ensued between cowboy and settler, centring round waterholes and river bottoms. But the settlers had the weight of sheer numbers on their side. By degrees the barbed wire criss-crossed the prairie, just as the railroads were doing, and the area of free movement for cattle on the range correspondingly diminished. The end came quickly. 1885 was the peak year of the open-range cattle industry, but by 1890 the end was at hand. In future, cattle, like wheat and sheep, would be raised only on enclosed land (though the enclosures might be the size of an English county) and the cowboy, like the Indian, would be only a picturesque relic of a nomadic culture which had disappeared.

How rapidly the homesteader moved into the West and filled up the vacant areas may be seen from the dates at which the new western territories were admitted to statehood. Nebraska (1867) was the first state admitted after the Civil War, and it was typical of the rest in that by 1880 its population almost quadrupled. Colorado came next in 1876 (Nevada, its mining rival, had been admitted in 1864). Political motives delayed the passage of bills to admit the next batch, but in 1889 Washington, Montana and the two Dakotas were included, to be followed in the next year by Wyoming and Idaho. Utah was long debarred because of the Mormon practice of polygamy, and its admission in 1896, when the Mormon leaders revised their creed, was, in terms of Utah's population, long overdue. In 1889 and 1893 the last remaining strips of the west, in what is now Oklahoma, were opened for settlement under the Homestead Act and before 1900 the territory had as much population as was needed for statehood. But here, as in the case of New Mexico and Arizona, the presence of large numbers of Indians delayed admission for many years. (Oklahoma, 1907, New Mexico and Arizona, 1912.) Long before then, however, the 'Wild' West had been tamed to the uses of the white man. In 1890 the Superintendent of the Census pronounced his verdict, 'Up to and including 1880 the country had a frontier of settlement, but at present the unsettled area has been so broken into by isolated bodies of settlement that there can hardly be said to be a frontier line'. The frontier was 'closed'.

The passing of the frontier was a landmark in American history. The frontier had meant, for millions of Americans, both an escape and an opportunity. It was an escape for the man who had been a disgrace or a failure; on the frontier he could forget his past and start all over again, pitting his own brawn and brains against the next man's. It was an opportunity for the young, the energetic or the adventurous. There everyone started equal and the handicaps of birth or poverty were eliminated. On the frontier anything could happen – the next hill might conceal the perfect site for a farm, the next gulch might hold an outcrop of gold, the next forest might conceal a wealth of skins or fur. Above all, as long as the frontier lasted there was always free land – land on which the settler need call no one master, land which was his to improve or spoil, virgin land, difficult but challenging. Thomas Jefferson, himself a frontiersman, had thought that democracy in America could not survive the day when 'vacant land' ceased to be available for the asking. Events proved him wrong, but although democracy successfully survived the passing of the frontier, it certainly underwent many changes and was confronted with new difficulties and strange threats. The post-1890 America could no longer dispose of its adventurers, its eccentrics, its criminals, and its unemployed by sending them out to the West. It had to make a society within itself in which all kinds of citizens could realize their rights to life, liberty and the pursuit of happiness.

CHAPTER XXV

The Immigrant

THE 'Conquest of the West', more remarkable in its speed and its extent than anything else previously seen in American history, could not have been accomplished without the aid of millions of men and women, immigrants from Europe, who supplied the muscles, the perseverance and the energy needed to build the railroads, defy the Indians, outlast the blizzard and the tornado, and people the vast spaces of the Plains. Between 1826 and 1930 over thirty-eight million people came to the United States. Such a figure is so huge that there is nothing to compare it with. It constitutes the greatest movement of human beings in history. In respect of the history of the United States of America its importance is overwhelming; one might almost say that the history of the United States *is* the history of American immigration. Throughout the nineteenth century, while the great powers of Europe were importing food, or raw materials or manufactures, the United States was importing people – old, young, rich, poor, of every nationality and type, the raw material of a new nation. This was a natural consequence of the facts that Europe had more mouths than it could feed and America had more space than it could fill.

By its willingness to receive Europe's unwanted millions the United States was in fact exercising a very important influence on European history throughout the nineteenth century. The Industrial Revolution, which began in Britain in the late eighteenth century and spread, with cumulative effect, over north-western Europe during the nineteenth, greatly increased the wealth and power of every country it affected – but, even so, the population increased faster than the means to feed it. (This was true of almost every European country except Spain and France, which did not recover from the vast blood-lettings of the Napoleonic Wars.) At the same time the progress of political and social reform loosened the restraints on the movements of the poor which had persisted from earlier centuries – e.g. serfdom in Russia, the grip of the commune in Europe, the Elizabethan poor law in England – and made it for the first time legally possible for them to leave their native soil. This coincided with the great nineteenth-century improvements in communications which made travel cheaper, safer and faster for the great mass of ordinary men and women.

The result of this was a great century of European migration. America was not the only destination of the travellers. Africa, Australia, even in some small degree Asia, received their European colonists. But nowhere were prospects so attractive as in America, and nowhere within the American continent was land so abundant, climate so tolerable and political freedom so certain as in the United States of America. As a result, of all the countries which received immigrants during the period 1820–1930 the United States took by far the largest share – over 60 per cent. (thirty-eight millions). Canada was a poor second with 11·5 per cent. (seven millions). For those who entered during the hundred years 1830–1930 we have fairly accurate records showing which countries they came from. There was not a country in Europe which did not contribute its share, but the leading countries are these*:

Germany	5,900,000
Italy	4,600,000
Ireland	4,500,000
Great Britain	4,500,000
Austria-Hungary	4,000,000
Russia (then including Poland) ..	3,300,000
Scandinavia	2,000,000

* The figures are correct to the nearest 100,000.

This great influx of assorted nationalities made the United States the most cosmopolitan nation in the world. It became, as Walt Whitman said, not so much a nation as 'a teeming nation of nations'.

This thirty-eight million flood of humanity did not come in an even flow, but rather like an incoming tide, in a series of waves, according as conditions in Europe drove people out and conditions in America attracted people in. If one looks at the dates of the peak immigration figures it becomes apparent how conditions in each continent acted on the other. The crests of the immigration waves were 1854, 1873, 1882, 1892, 1907, 1914, 1921. In 1848 the great unsuccessful wave of liberal revolution had swept across Europe and was followed in each country by the proscription of all those who had taken part. At about the same time there was a succession of poor harvests; thus hunger provided an added motive for emigration. From Germany in particular there was a large flight of political refugees who had failed in their efforts to win a democratic constitution, while in the case of Ireland, although dislike of British domination was widespread, the disaster which finally drove the Irish poor to mass emigration was the Potato Famine. It was America that had first given the potato to Europe and the coming of this cheap, easily-grown vegetable had meant a great deal to the rural labourer and his family. But in proportion as the poor agriculturalists relied upon it for their food, so their plight was calamitous when anything went wrong with such a staple crop. In the years 1846, '47 and '49 everything went wrong with the potato crop: blight virtually ruined it. The Irish died by their hundreds; the remainder, obsessed by hunger and the fear of hunger, did everything they could to get out of the country. Once started, the wave of emigration increased by its own weight. First arrivals wrote back home encouraging and inviting others. 'American letters' describing prospects in the new land were handed on from family to family, and dollars, earned by first arrivals in America, were sent back to Ireland to buy passages for poorer relations. (The Irish were so poor that the cost of passage was an all-important consideration; the present huge Irish population of Boston is largely due to the fact that the clipper ship fare was nine dollars cheaper to Boston than to New York.)

But in 1857 the American slump and the anti-immigrant activities of the 'Know-Nothing' party made the U.S.A. a slightly less attractive destination. This was followed by the Civil War years which, although they did not prevent immigration, certainly discouraged it. The new-comers did well in the Civil War; almost 500,000 foreign-born volunteers helped to fight the battles of the Union, and this did much to offset the anti-immigrant feeling which had grown up during the '50's. After the war the country needed immigrants again. The states of the Mid-West tumbled over each other to attract settlers – they offered them votes within as little as a year of residence, they advertised the charms and riches of their territory in European papers, they even sent commissioners to Europe to stimulate emigration. The Federal Government gave them its aid; in 1872 ten thousand copies of a *Special Report on Immigration* were printed in German and circulated in Europe by Congress. But perhaps the railroad and steamship companies were the biggest promoters. The steamship companies naturally wanted passengers and the railroads, who had western lands to dispose of, wanted settlers. Between them they opened offices and advertised in the principal cities and ports of Europe. The railroads, in order to make sure that the immigrant would not loiter on the eastern seaboard, would arrange for him to buy through tickets to the west, so that the German peasant from the Rhineland, for example, would be shipped right through to Wisconsin.

During the '60's the proportion of nationalities remained roughly as before, with the Germans and the Irish strongly in the lead. The German wars, with Denmark in 1864, with Austria in 1866, and with France in 1870, obstructed immigration while they lasted (because the Fatherland needed all available man-power for fighting its wars), but accelerated it once they were over, as demobilized soldiers, weary of fighting and conscription, responded to the appeal of having a farm of their own in the peaceful Mississippi Valley. Thus it was not surprising that 1873 was another peak year for immigrants.

Then followed the first of the post-war slumps in the U.S.A. and by a natural reaction immigration fell off again – only to rise again to new heights. The Scandinavian influx greatly increased, settling particularly in the states of Minnesota, Wisconsin and the Dakotas. There was a marked rise in the emigration from England, due principally to the coincidence of business and agricultural depressions in Britain with booms in the U.S.A. (Between 1870 and 1890 more Englishmen crossed the Atlantic than Scandinavians or Germans.) As the West was developed and industry expanded the flood of immigration rose to unprecedented heights. Although the '70's set a new record with 2,800,000 immigrants the '80's easily surpassed them with 5,250,000. Employers and contractors were so greedy for workmen that they were actually sending money to England to pay the passage of poor emigrants whom they could use as unskilled labourers. An Englishman, 'roughing it' in St. Paul, Minnesota, in 1884* found that his companions on a labourers' gang included 'some Englishmen, and a promiscuous crew of Canadians and European French, Germans, Swedes, Norwegians, Danes, Finns, Polanders, Austrians, Italians and one or two Mexicans'. His experience could have been paralleled a thousand times over.

Before the '80's, however, such a catalogue of nationalities would probably have stopped short of the inclusion of many Italians. Mention of them in such a connection is typical of a change which was coming over the immigration picture. Before 1883 about 85 per cent. of the immigrants came from the countries of northern and western Europe, the so-called 'Teutonic' nations who had been the principal sources of colonists for America since the founding of Jamestown. But by 1907 about 80 per cent. of the immigration stream (which had kept up, and even increased, its rate of

* Morley Roberts, *The Western Avernus*, p. 35.

flow) was coming from the countries of eastern and southern Europe. Thus from 1900 to 1914 the countries principally supplying American immigrants were, in order of numbers, Austria-Hungary, Italy, Russia (which then included Poland), England and Ireland. This 'new immigration', as it was called, created different problems from the old, in that it brought in people markedly different in language, habits and religion from the prevailing Anglo-Saxon-German strains which had previously dominated the U.S.A. The problem of grafting these new nationalities on to the existing stock was consequently a considerable one.

The change from the old to the 'new' immigration was due to a number of causes. In such eastern European areas as the Russian, Ottoman, or Austro-Hungarian Empires the governments had been so hostile to emigration and had so retained their hold on their subjects by legislation that relatively little movement was possible earlier in the century. But by degrees their hold weakened (e.g. in 1861 serfdom was abolished in Russia) and their unfortunate, impoverished peoples could take their turn in the queue of western travellers. Poverty, hunger and oppression were the principal motive forces of emigration. In Russia, for example, the assassination of Alexander II in 1881 was the signal for a wave of anti-Jewish violence and legislation which sent hundreds of thousands of Russian and Polish Jews seeking refuge overseas. This coincided with two developments in northern and western Europe which reduced the flow of the 'old' emigration just as the 'new' was rising. By about the 1880's the industrialization of northern Europe was beginning to be sufficiently advanced for countries like Britain and Germany to absorb their own surplus rural population and also to give their townspeople a considerably better standard of living – thus making the U.S.A. by comparison a less attractive alternative. Furthermore, the birth-rate in these countries began to decline, so that the problem of over-population began to look after itself. So by degrees the exodus changed its character, until the decade 1900–1910 showed such figures as 2,100,000 from

Austria-Hungary, 2,000,000 from Italy and 1,600,000 from Russia.

This vast transference of peoples had enormous effects on Europe and on America. Its effects on Europe were curiously similar to the effects which, inside America, were produced by the existence of the frontier. Just as the frontier took care of the shiftless, the jobless, the adventurous from the East, and gave them opportunity, land, work and thrills, so emigration took from Europe the hundred and one types of citizen which the existing society could not itself take care of. At the base of the Statue of Liberty in New York harbour the new-comer could read an inscription which expressed this aspect of the immigration story to perfection:

> Give me your tired, your poor,
> Your huddled masses yearning to breathe free,
> The wretched refuse of your teeming shore,
> Send these, the homeless, tempest-tost to me:
> I lift my lamp beside the golden door.

Emigration was an easy way for Europe to dispose of its 'wretched refuse', and it can be argued that America's readiness to accept them enabled European states to shuffle off responsibilities that they ought properly to have shouldered. Thus Britain was encouraged to persevere in an unjust Irish policy because, although disaster often threatened in Ireland, the safety valve of emigration always prevented a revolutionary explosion from taking place. The same was true of the subject peoples of the Austro-Hungarian Empire. In Germany, to the liberals of the '48 emigration offered an easy escape; consequently instead of staying in Germany to fight for democracy there they took their ideals across the Atlantic – to the great benefit of the U.S.A. but to the detriment of Germany. But however bad it may have been for Europe to be able thus to export its unemployed, its revolutionaries and its hungry, there can be no doubt that for the individuals concerned emigration was the doorway to opportunity and often to happiness. 'Amerika, du hast es besser',* wrote Goethe in 1831, and it was in that hope that

* "America, thou hast it better."

young and old wagered their all on life in the new land. The hope was not always realized, but rare indeed was the immigrant who, having once set his face westward, failed so signally in his expectations that he turned again to his European home.

For the period after the Civil War in America this great flood of European immigration had, of course, great consequences. The most obvious and immediate of these was that it made available a mass of manpower for the great nineteenth-century job of conquering the West. Then there was the incalculable contribution of skills and tastes and ideals which the varied nationalities made to the original American stock. To list all these would be impossible but to illustrate what this has meant for the enrichment of American life one need only mention Carl Schurz, the German who conducted vigorous crusades in the '60's and '70's for better government, Agassiz the Swiss authority on Natural History, Jacob Riis, the Dane who exposed the slum condition of the big cities, Andrew Carnegie, the Scottish steel millionaire and philanthropist, or Fiorello La Guardia, the famous Italian mayor of New York. Without these and thousands more America would have been in every sense a poorer country. But apart from the impact of individuals, however important, the mere presence of such numbers of foreign-born Americans created problems of its own.

In the first place it had an important effect on politics. Until 1906, when various tests, of literacy, etc., were imposed, the immigrant obtained citizenship, and consequently a vote, almost immediately after arrival. In the majority of cases he had never had a vote before, knew very little about the workings of American democracy and probably could not even read or write in his own language, let alone English. Such persons provided tempting prey for unscrupulous politicians, who built great political 'machines' on the basis of their ignorant votes. This was the period when Tammany Hall, the Democratic machine in New York, entered on its most notorious phase, William

Tweed, the boss, blatantly asserting, 'This population is too hopelessly split into races and factions to govern it, except by the bribery of patronage or corruption'. One set of immigrants were, however, so much superior to the rest in political ability that so far from being the victims of these machines they often themselves controlled them. These were the Irish. They were natural orators, had the great advantage of already speaking English, and, having suffered political oppression at home, meant to make the best of their new-found liberty in America. They soon acquired a reputation for political ability which their American descendants retain to this day.

In the labour field the effect of immigration was even more marked. If you compare the U.S.A. of 1870–1914 with the other democratic powers of that period you will find it notably behind in one respect – in the development of trade unionism. This is due to many causes, but a principal one is immigration. Trades unions, in face of employers' opposition, have always used the weapon of the 'strike'. But in America this weapon was seldom effective because with fresh immigrants arriving every year in search of work – some of them even imported by the employers – there was never a real threat of labour shortage. There was always available a reservoir of workmen to whom the lowest American wage was an increase on what they had left behind them. Moreover, being of so many nationalities, they did not easily make common cause with each other or with the native-born American worker who tended to despise the new-comer. Consequently their presence tended to depress wages and working conditions.

The immigrant's object was to become an American. But it took a long time, often several generations, to forget his roots in Europe. Sometimes he never forgot them. Consequently he tended to be divided, one half of him being more American than the Americans – learning English, anglicizing his name, serving his new country with passionate, self-conscious devotion – the other half still attracted by 'the old country' in which his habits and his tastes had been formed, where his parents probably still lived and to which he perhaps even hoped some day to return. This division often created problems. The Irish, for example, long continued to keep common cause with the old country in its struggle against Britain. After the Civil War many Irishmen who had fought for the Union retained their arms and organized themselves into 'the Fenian Brotherhood', a quarter of a million strong, with the object of establishing an 'Irish Republic'. In Ireland the conspiracy, financed from New York, caused many local disturbances but never assumed formidable dimensions. In America, however, the more militant group of Fenians conducted raids across the U.S. border into Canada. In 1866 and 1870 there were quite serious clashes with Canadian troops. Unimportant in themselves, these raids did have a harmful effect on relations between Britain and the United States, particularly because the United States Government, out of respect for the Irish vote, would not accept responsibility for these depredations while at the same time it protested against the Canadian Government treating Fenians whom it captured as rebellious British subjects. Fenianism in America died down in the '70's, but the American Irish did not lose interest in the cause of their old country. Organized in 'Hibernian' clubs or as 'Friends of Irish Freedom', they sent their dollars home to feed the flames of Irish resistance, to fight for Home Rule and Independence, and there can be no doubt that their moral support also counted for much in keeping Irish resistance alive. De Valera, it will be remembered, although condemned to death for his part in the Dublin rising of 1916, was reprieved by virtue of the fact that he was an American citizen. And although, as Americanization proceeded, the Irish immigrants and their descendants took a less and less active part in the struggles of their old country, those struggles left their mark in a long-cherished hatred of England. This Irish-American sentiment was something which, owing to the Irish rôle in American politics, often asserted itself extravagantly and many a flare-up of ill-feeling between Britain and the U.S.A. could be attributed to the tendency of American politicians to 'twist the lion's tail' in the interest of the Irish vote.

No other nationality looked back to their old homeland quite as passionately as the Irish, but few immigrant groups have been blind to the cries of their European namesakes in distress. Although the vast majority of Germans were loyal to the U.S.A. in 1914–18, most of them were opposed to America's taking up arms by the side of the Allies. After the first World War it was very largely the energies and subscriptions of American immigrants that organized and supported the new governments of Czecho-Slovakia and Yugoslavia. More often, however, the influence of the immigrant has been thrown in the other scale. He has come to America because he wanted to get away from Europe and he is consequently opposed to any course of action which would involve America in Europe's troubles. Thus in the main the immigrant has strengthened American 'isolationism', believing not only that Europe's wars are 'none of America's business', but also that for him in particular they belong to those 'old, unhappy, far-off things' which he came to America in order to forget.

CHAPTER XXVI

The Gilded Age

THE Civil War was the first big war to be fought with the full resources of an industrial age. Indeed, it was largely the industrial superiority of the North which gave it the victory. Industry, in return, received a great stimulus from the war – it expanded in response to war orders and made many discoveries and improvements in response to war needs. The result was to set going what was practically a second Industrial Revolution. From the pre-war period a great many inventions were taken over and given their first practical development – e.g. the telegraph, which

Morse invented in 1844, but which had to wait for the war before it was developed for general use. (The first successful transatlantic cable was not laid until 1866.) But more than this the generation which followed the war saw the exploitation of a great many resources which had previously been virtually unused – e.g. oil, the output of which mounted from 2,479,000 barrels in 1861 to over 100,000,000 barrels in 1900. New metals, such as aluminium, were developed, while new uses for old ones, such as copper, lead and zinc, were found. Electricity began to come into its own as a source of power; the inventions of the tram-car and the lift made possible larger cities and taller buildings. The gas-mantle and, soon after, the electric bulb (invention of Thomas Edison) brought about a revolution in the lighting both of buildings and of streets. Thousands of other discoveries of applied science were made available for general use in an astonishingly short space of time.

The effects of this were soon apparent. Between 1860 and 1900 manufactures in the U.S.A. (measured in terms of their dollar value) increased almost seven-fold, though they only employed four times as many people (so much was the machine effecting a saving of labour). The production of raw materials increased even more astonishingly – coal almost twenty-fold, copper forty-fold, lead sixteen-fold, iron more than nine-fold. Meanwhile the railroads (the arteries of industry) increased their mileage from 30,000 in 1860 to 192,000 in 1900.

All this had the effect, as industrial revolutions always do, of speeding up the shift of population from the country to the town. Whereas in 1860 five-sixths of the population lived on the country or in villages, by 1900 the proportion had dropped to two-thirds out of a total population more than twice as large.* New York had become a great city of three millions and Chicago, which at the time of Lincoln's first

* Even so, the U.S.A. remained a far more rural country than Great Britain. Already, in 1850, 40 per cent. of Britain's population lived in towns of 10,000 inhabitants and upward. By 1900 the proportion had risen to 75 per cent.

presidency was a frontier town of a hundred thousand, had become the capital of the Middle West with a million inhabitants to its credit.

This second industrial revolution was due to the combination of a number of circumstances. The swift development of applied science had a great deal to do with the emergence of new industries. One of the great figures of the period is Thomas Edison (1847–1931), whose name is linked with such mechanical devices as the telephone, the typewriter, the gramophone, the electric dynamo and the moving picture camera. But he was only the most outstanding of a number of figures working on the application of science to the needs of everyday life. More remarkable often than the actual inventions was the speed with which they were made available to the ordinary user. This was due in part to the enormous natural resources of the U.S.A. The coal deposits of Pennsylvania, the oil of Texas and Oklahoma, the iron ore of Michigan, the copper of Montana – these sources of wealth and power were larger and more accessible than any which had been tapped since large-scale industry first began. Alone among the great countries of the world the United States of America had all the principal raw materials it needed within its own borders.

It was notable that while Britain, whose industrial revolution was also still proceeding at a great pace, developed manufactures under an economy of free trade, the industrial expansion of the U.S.A. continued until 1913 under the shelter of a constantly heightening tariff wall. This was a direct consequence of the Civil War, when the Northern manufacturers converted the Republican party to the cause of Protectionism. But whatever the tariff may have done to promote this expansion of U.S. industry (and it is doubtful if it did very much) there was another consequence of the war which was far more important. The war disposed finally of the risk that the huge area of the United States would be split up into economically exclusive states, with the South keeping out the manufactures of the North, or the West being tied to the chariot of Southern agriculture. Although the war put up American tariffs against the outside world it guaranteed free trade *inside* the U.S.A., over the whole of this huge newly developing area from Canada to Mexico and from the Atlantic to the Pacific. There was thus created a vast market for the goods of American industry within the boundaries of the United States. Whereas Britain had to import her raw materials from overseas and sell her products abroad, the U.S.A. found her war materials under her very feet, her food supply in her back garden and her customers already on the premises. It was only her labour force that she had to import from abroad – and that Europe was only too delighted to send her.

Thus there developed that startling increase in America's national wealth which earned for this generation the title of 'The Gilded Age.' It is to these twenty or so years after the conclusion of the Civil War that the origin of most of the great American fortunes is to be traced. Until well into the nineteenth century the 'millionaire' was an unknown phenomenon in America, but after the Civil War he soon became famous as an American type. Many were the fortunes born of the railroad. Cornelius Vanderbilt, the founder of the New York Central Railroad, was also the founder of a great dynasty of wealth which persists to this day. The Central Pacific was the basis of three great Pacific fortunes – Huntington's, Leland Stanford's, and Crocker's – which made the San Francisco of the '70's and '80's a city of wealth and display. Edward H. Harriman and James J. Hill made their millions at a somewhat later stage when the first flush of railroad building was over and the time for 'mergers' had arrived. Oil, through the medium of the Standard Oil Company, made two of the greatest American fortunes, those of John D. Rockefeller and Stephen Harkness. Pierpont Morgan, the banker, was one of the few men powerful enough to constitute himself their equal. Each branch of industry and commerce created its own potentates, but it is interesting to notice that the alliance of industry and agriculture could also produce great fortunes. Cyrus McCormick, the inventor of the 'mechanical reaper' which did so much to increase wheat growing in the prairie country, died the possessor of millions, while the discovery that meat could be packed and preserved in tin cans laid the foundation of the great fortunes of the Swifts and the Armours. It was appropriate that these three fortunes should be located in Chicago which, as the Gilded Age went on, grew in importance as the meeting point of western agriculture and eastern industry.

To see what a typical magnate of the Gilded Age was like we cannot do better than glance at the life story of Andrew Carnegie, a man who indeed personifies much of the character and importance of the age, since his own industry, steel, has always been a good measuring rod by which to judge the industrial strength of a modern nation. Like many other 'self made' men of the period, Andrew Carnegie was an immigrant. Born in Scotland of very poor parents, he was brought by them to America at the age of twelve. He went to work immediately and rose by the age of eighteen to be a telegraph operator on the Pennsylvania Railroad. Promotion followed rapidly and by the outbreak of the Civil War Carnegie was Vice-President of the Company. To meet the war-time need for iron rails and railway bridges Carnegie started manufacturing companies of his own and so entered the steel business in which he was to become famous. In 1867 Carnegie visited England and was so impressed by the Bessemer process of steel-making which he saw in operation there that he erected a huge works at Pittsburgh to employ it. Thus, as he himself wrote, at the age of thirty-three he was making $50,000 a year; at thirty-five he would retire, go to Oxford, get an education and devote the rest of his life and his fortune to 'the improvement of the poorer classes'. But these intentions did not survive the impact of his own success. Thirty-five came and went and Carnegie remained in steel, becoming a greater figure in the industry each year until by 1881 he was the foremost iron-master in America. By 1888 his wealth had increased sixty times over. Then in 1899 he consolidated his various interests into the Carnegie Steel Company. His methods had been ruthless; competitors and employees had, when they opposed him, been treated very much as a feudal baron treated a rival or a rebel. In 1892, when a strike broke out in the Homestead works at Pittsburgh, there was a pitched battle between the strikers and the private detectives hired by Frick, Carnegie's colleague. It began to look as if Carnegie's word was law within his own domain. But one thing no one could dispute – the revolution he introduced in steel making. In 1870 the production of steel in the United States had been only 68,000 tons. By 1900 it had risen to ten million tons, more than the total production of Great Britain and Germany combined, a lead which America has never since surrendered.

It was then that Carnegie judged that the long-proposed time for retirement had arrived. But first of all Carnegie wished to make his empire safe against competition. So in 1901, with the aid of J. P. Morgan the great financier, a combine of the principal steel companies, including Carnegie's, was formed, to be called the United States Steel Corporation, which owned 149 steel plants, as well as all the iron ore, coal, ships and railways necessary for the conduct of its industry from start to finish. Having created this huge organization, Carnegie sold out his own share in it for £60,000,000, and, at the age of sixty-six devoted himself to disposing of it widely on the theory that 'the man who dies rich dies disgraced'. The Free Libraries bearing his name which have been set up with his endowments in towns all over Britain and the U.S.A. are his best known memorial, but Carnegie money has also been devoted to research, education, international peace and a variety of other causes.

The Carnegie story could be paralleled by many others in the Gilded Age. Many other magnates rose from 'rags to riches' by the phenomenal development of a new industry. They, like Carnegie, found this an all-absorbing occupation which left no leisure for anything else until they reached old age. And while very many of them turned their great fortunes to philanthropic uses few felt any compunction about employing 'strong arm' methods to build up their industrial empires. It was indeed, for the first time in America, an age of industrial 'bigness'. In the hands of these giants business concerns got ever larger and more impersonal. 'Combinations', 'organizations', 'corporations' – impersonal bodies such as these took the place of the old small company in which master and man knew each other by name and by sight. Such growth on the part of industry provoked a corresponding tendency on the part of labour. It, too, developed the large-scale organization in the years immediately following the war. There was the National Labour Union, founded in 1866, which reached a membership of over 600,000, but it only lasted six years. More successful was a big trade union organization called the Knights of Labour, which was the first such body to draw much of its membership from unskilled workers. In 1884 it won a great railroad strike and its membership mounted to 700,000. But two years later a strike in the McCormick Harvester works culminated in the Haymarket bomb explosion in Chicago and, although there was nothing to prove labour's responsibility, public revulsion against the Union was such that the Knights of Labour soon melted away. The truth was that the general public was sympathetic to business and hostile to trade unions, and in face of this a new union, the American Federation of Labour, which was born in the year of the Chicago 'outrage', decided to go slow, to steer clear of politics, and to restrict its membership to skilled workers. It was skilfully led by a British immigrant, Samuel Gompers, but first the great Homestead strike of 1892 and then the depression, 1893–7, worked against it and by 1900 its membership was only about 500,000 – at a time when in Britain, with a much smaller population, trade unionists mustered two millions strong.

The truth was that the years between 1865 and 1900 were the hey-day of business enterprise and it was the 'captains of industry' such as Carnegie who occupied the leading place in public esteem. It was business that offered the biggest excitements and the greatest rewards. By comparison even politics was dull and unimportant. Whereas in the generation before the Civil War the great popular names had been those of the politicians – Webster, Calhoun, Sumner,

Douglas, not to mention the Presidents – in the generation afterwards the great names were those of the industrialists and financiers. Even the Presidents of these years are unimportant compared with them. Grant, Hayes, Garfield, Arthur, Cleveland, Harrison and McKinley – those are their names in order, but with the exception of Cleveland's they are unimportant names, belonging to men of little influence or personality compared with such great figures as Rockefeller, Vanderbilt or Carnegie. The Presidents were colourless, short-lived figures who came and went leaving little impression behind, but a banker like Pierpont Morgan not only outlasted fourteen Presidents but was also able by his great financial power to exercise an influence on American history far greater than, say, President Harrison.

Indeed during the Gilded Age the role of politics was regarded as that of being handmaiden to business. There was a widespread conviction that if everything was left to the business man all would be well, prosperity would be guaranteed and everyone would have his share of the wealth which was being made on every hand. The function of politics was therefore in the first place not to get in the way of business by imposing restraints on it or passing too many laws, and in the second place to 'protect' business, principally by erecting tariffs against the goods of foreign competitors. Most important of all perhaps were the gifts which the politicians could grant the business men – the concessions to mine copper, or drill for oil on government territory, or the gifts of land to railoads to open up the West. In the low esteem in which politics was held, which made men of ability and probity loath to enter it, this opened the door to a good deal of corrupt practice. Thus the Union Pacific was convicted of corruption in connection with the financing of its construction – the famous Crédit Mobilier scandal of 1872 which rocked Grant's administration – and persons high in the councils of the Republican Party were shown to be involved. Businesses shamelessly sent contributions to both parties so that whichever one was elected its favour would still be certain. The ordinary citizen felt that his own vote counted for very little by comparison with the influence exerted by the great business companies. But perhaps the most remarkable feature of the Gilded Age was that while most people were conscious of this and many deplored it, relatively few voters did anything about it. There were reformers, of course, and energetic ones, but years went by before they attracted much of a following. Of the many reasons for this indifference one stood out in particular – the ordinary American in these years was proud of the achievements of American business, despite its ruthlessness and waste; he trusted the business men, with all their faults, more than he trusted the politicians. In fact, if he was not already a business man, it was almost certainly his ambition to become one.

CHAPTER XXVII

Politics and Reform

FOR twenty years after the Civil War the United States was administered by the Republican Party. The reasons for this were obvious. Although there were Democrats in the North who had remained loyal to the Union their main strength was in the 'rebel' South. It had therefore not been difficult for the Republicans to appear as the sole party of the Union, with a monopoly of patriotism and wisdom. Although in the South the policies of the Republican Party had only succeeded in driving every Southerner for good and all into the arms of the Democrats, in the North there was no doubt about it – the 'Grand Old Party' or 'G.O.P.', as the Republicans called themselves, was for a long time the only party which respectable people could join. Not everyone, of course, was 'respectable': in the big cities, in particular, the working classes and the immigrants tended to vote Democratic. But over most of the North and the West the Republican Party was the party to which ordinary, settled

Americans tended to belong, while in New England it had a monopoly as powerful as that of the Democrats in the South.

Both parties acquiesced in the secondary role which, as we have seen, the Gilded Age imposed on politics. They were both quite happy to be chained to the chariot of business enterprise. But as the party of victory, and the party which even before the war represented a union of eastern industry and western farmers, it was the Republicans who were most closely identified with the growing strength of American big business. It was the Republicans, for example, who made the tariff such an important plank in their platform. In return, it was the Republican Party whose coffers received the most handsome donations from business firms anxious that their interests should not be neglected when legislation was being considered.

But although these years were remarkable as a period of unbroken Republican ascendancy (rather like the period of Whig supremacy in England from 1714 to 1760) they were even more remarkable for the absence of any real difference in principles or in programmes between the two parties. Just as the Whigs and the Tories in eighteenth-century England had been merely the 'Ins' and the 'Outs', parties with different histories but with essentially the same policies, so the Republicans and the Democrats in the Gilded Age were little more than rivals for office whose appeal to the voter was essentially the same. Both accepted the decision of the Civil War, though the Democrats tried to forget it while the Republicans kept it alive, both believed in a free hand for business enterprise, both combined eloquent professions of 'reform' with much that was corrupt in practice. 'Reform', during most of this period, meant civil service reform. Ever since Jackson's time it had been regular practice to fill appointments in the government service on a strictly party basis, so that the vast majority of civil service posts changed hands whenever a new party won the elections. But as the century wore on and the civil service grew in numbers and its tasks grew in importance the Jackson system became more and more obviously unsatisfactory. In Britain it had been the practice since 1855 to have a qualifying examination for the Civil Service and in America a demand for something similar was raised. Both parties paid lip service to such a reform but little was done until in 1881 President Garfield, within four weeks of his inauguration, was assassinated by a disappointed office seeker. This produced a clamour for reform which even the politicians could not ignore and in 1883 Garfield's successor, Arthur, signed the Pendleton Civil Service Bill which empowered the President to insist on examinations for any civil service appointment. Presidents were often slow to employ this power, but by degrees the practice spread until it became the rule rather than the exception.

It was striking evidence of the low level of Republican politics that this trifling reform of Arthur's should have set the party against him. Yet so it was. For the election of 1884 they refused to renominate him and instead chose as their candidate the most typical 'regular' politician of the age, James G. Blaine, who as Speaker of the House had been associated with one scandal after another. But in doing so they went too far. The Democrats had a good candidate in Cleveland, the Governor of New York, and although the election was fought almost entirely on irrelevant personal issues, Cleveland's election did signify that honesty and public spirit were beginning to count for something again in politics. It also meant the end of twenty-four years of Republican rule.

The Democrats were able to win because at last they had formed an alliance which could challenge the Republican alliance of Eastern industry and Western farmers. The Democratic alliance was between the 'solid' South and the poor of the big cities. In organizing the latter the Irish had been of inestimable assistance to the Democratic party. Most Irish were Democrats – often for no better reason than that the Democratic politicians had been the first to enrol them as they came off the immigration ships. Whatever the reason, the Irish brought great strength to the Democratic party. They made such organizations as Tammany Hall in New York into efficient machines which 'brought out' the immigrant vote in its thousands and from the time of Cleveland to the time of Franklin Roosevelt two traditions have persisted among the foreign born in most of the big cities – to accept Irish leadership in politics, and to vote the Democratic ticket.

President Cleveland enjoyed two terms of office, interrupted by four years of Republican rule under the colourless President Harrison (1889–93).* They were less remarkable for positive achievements than for the firmness with which Cleveland resisted the corrupt tendencies in both his own party and in the Republican. He put a stop to the practice of raiding the public purse by Pensions Bills (bills purporting to relieve the distress of old Civil War soldiers, but in fact simply placing large sums at the disposal of the politicians for disbursement to their constituents), he temporarily checked the rising tariff and endeavoured to keep the country's finances on a reasonably sound basis. Harrison undid so much of the legislation of Cleveland's first term, that his second was largely devoted to further corrective measures along the same lines. When it ended, in 1896, there was general recognition of the fact that Cleveland had restored to the Federal Government some of the prestige and respect which it had been lacking ever since the death of Lincoln.

But despite the improvement which Cleveland represented, the election of 1896 found the country more discontented with its politics and its parties than at any time since Buchanan. The negative ideal of 'good government' which

* It is interesting, in passing, to notice that Cleveland's '88 defeat was largely due to the defection of that Irish vote which had installed him in '84. The Republicans, realizing that the Irish immigrants were even more anti-British than pro-Democrat, tricked the British ambassador, Sir Lionel Sackville-West, into saying that he thought Cleveland the better candidate, and then raised the cry of British interference in American politics. The Irish reacted as the Republicans expected and, in protest against this really quite innocent, but apparently most sinister, piece of British 'intrigue' deserted Cleveland in sufficient numbers to tip the balance. Thus Sackville-West's stupidity cost Cleveland four years 'in the wilderness'.

Cleveland represented was really quite inadequate to the needs of the nation. It was not enough for the Democrats to say that they would, if elected, do the same kind of things as the Republicans, but do them more honestly. There was a new spirit abroad in the land for which neither of the two great parties provided a home. The Gilded Age was over, to be succeeded by a period in which people would be less easily satisfied to take the achievements of business at their face value and would expect the state to intervene actively if the operations of business were harmful to the rest of the community.

The year 1890, which saw the official 'closing of the frontier', may be said to mark the starting point of this change. Then for the first time disappointed pioneers whose crops had been a failure turned back *East* in hopes of betterment instead of pursuing the traditional road of American migrants and 'staking out a claim' further *West*. The society which had raised them and sent them forth to try their luck was now having to accept responsibility for them when that luck failed. And between the years 1887 and 1893 many Americans' luck failed. Throughout the West there was a wave of agricultural distress. Prices, which had been forced to extravagant heights, suddenly came tumbling down. At the same time a series of summer droughts wrecked the crops. A spirit of revolt manifested itself throughout the prairie states – revolt against the railroads which charged too much for transporting the farmers' hard-earned crops to market and revolt against the 'money interests' of the East, which the West has always in American history held responsible for its economic misfortunes. Labour felt the impact of hard times as well. Although after the Haymarket affair of 1886, the American Federation of Labour was following a 'go slow' policy, the year 1890 saw more strikes than any other year in the century and in 1892 conditions in the steel industry led to the Homestead strike and Frick's brutal reprisals.

Out of these discontents on the farms and in the factories a new party, which called itself the *Populists*, was born. It was a party of the poor and the disenchanted from all over the country, but particularly from the agrarian West. It had no very clear programme. If you went to its meetings, which were scenes of camp-fire revivalism utterly unlike the sober-sided sessions of the two orthodox parties, you would hear tell of many grievances, but few remedies. In fact the Populists had only one remedy – reform of the currency. They had no very clear idea of the causes of their misfortunes, whether as farmers or as labourers, but they held strongly to the conviction that they were all due to the bankers of the East who exercised their control by making gold the standard of American currency. Consequently the principal plank in the Populist's programme was the free and unlimited coinage of silver.

The Populists first tried out their national strength in the election of 1892, but their candidate, a James Weaver of Iowa, secured only a million votes and did not seriously endanger Cleveland's victory. Then in 1893 the long drawn-out depression in farming began to recoil on industry and commerce. This coincided with a depression in Europe which had effects on the financial centre of Wall Street. Firm after firm in quick succession went bankrupt, the railroads, who had most over-capitalized their stock, suffering worst of all. The panic spread all over the country as bank after bank failed and people saw their savings lost just at the moment when unemployment stared them in the face. At the depth of the depression in 1894 the workers in the Pullman Company in Chicago struck against a cut in their wages. Their Union, the American Railway Union, was led by one of the few magnetic labour leaders of the century, Eugene Debs, and the strike soon spread until it held up railroad traffic through the Middle West. Cleveland here made a serious mistake and sent federal troops to Chicago who were used, not so much to keep order, which was scarcely threatened, as to break the strike. Debs was arrested, and became in consequence one of the martyrs of the American labour movement, and in the mid-term election of 1894 the Populists revealed new strength.

The Populists were in fact strong enough to do what every third party in America tries to do – that is, force one of the existing parties to adopt the principal features of their programme. The Republicans obviously would consider no Populist overtures, but the Democrats were in a different mood. There were already many 'silver Democrats' in their ranks, representing for the most part western states where silver mining was a principal industry; they were a lever by which the whole party could be swung over to 'free silver'. This was recognized by the Populists and in particular by William Jennings Bryan. Bryan was one of those remarkable crusading radicals of the West who, like Jackson and Lincoln, combined a warm humanity with a great gift of political oratory. The first quality was reflected in his title of 'The Great Commoner', while his early successes in Nebraska politics earned him fame as 'The Boy Orator of the Platte'.* He combined great political skill with a passionate sincerity and complete personal integrity. Coming at the end of a period when people had grown cynical of politicians, Bryan revived, with the fervour of an Old Testament prophet, men's faith in principles, in honest dealing, and in sympathy for the poor and the oppressed. In 1896 he brought this fervour to play on the Democratic Party Convention at Chicago. Three weeks earlier the Republicans had chosen as their candidate William McKinley, recognized as the creature of Mark Hanna, the great Republican 'boss', and notorious as the author of a tariff bill designed exclusively with an eye to the interests of big business. His nomination represented the operation of 'machine' politics at their most typical. By contrast, Bryan demonstrated the effect which one man of conviction and courage could produce on a convention. His weapon was his tongue – a 'silver' oratory in more senses than one. After the Convention had listened to the orthodox spokesmen, the 'safe' conservatives, Bryan took the stand. 'I come to speak to

* The Platte is a broad tributary of the Missouri River. Hence the criticism by Bryan's opponents that he was like the Platte – 'A foot deep and a mile wide at the mouth'.

you in defence of a cause as holy as the cause of liberty, the cause of humanity', he said. The speech listed the claims of the workman, the farmer, the 'common people' everywhere and reached its climax in its peroration. 'Having behind us the producing masses of the nation and the world, supported by the commercial interests, the labouring interests and the toilers everywhere, we will answer their demand for a gold standard by saying to them: You shall not press down upon the brow of labour this crown of thorns, you shall not crucify mankind upon a cross of gold.' The effect was electrical. The Convention, carried off its feet, nominated Bryan by acclamation.

But Bryan's oratory, so successful in the Convention hall, was not powerful enough to carry the country. McKinley refused to be drawn on the issue of the Gold Standard: while Bryan toured the land making whirlwind speeches, McKinley stayed at home, carefully non-committal on almost every controversial issue, leaving the campaign to Mark Hanna who spent three and a half million dollars to get him elected. Good harvests in the campaign year relieved the agricultural depression and took the edge off the 'revolt' of the normally Republican Middle West. The business East was frightened by McKinley into the belief that a vote for Bryan meant a vote for revolution. Consequently, despite the fact that the election stirred America as she had not been stirred since 1860, the established order held its ground and McKinley was elected by a small, but safe, margin.

CHAPTER XXVIII

Foreign Affairs, 1870 to 1900

AT home, McKinley's victory meant only a temporary check to the forces of reform, but in foreign affairs his Presidency saw new developments in American policy which had far-reaching results. The United States had had little cause to worry about foreign affairs during the Gilded Age. Since the end of the Civil War she had been too strong and too remote to invite attack from outside, while at the same time she had been preoccupied and absorbed in the consolidation and development of her own vast domain. Consequently foreign affairs had meant less to the ordinary American citizen than to the inhabitants of any other important country of the western world. The few developments of any importance during these years can be briefly summarized.

There were, first of all, the problems arising out of the Civil War, of which the most important were the *Alabama* Claims. The *Alabama*, built in a British dockyard and sold to the South, had been responsible for much damage to northern shipping, and the Union government demanded compensation from Britain for their losses. Britain was ready, indeed eager as a great naval power, to negotiate a treaty accepting the liability and laying down the general principle that in time of war neutrals should not be allowed to build or refit naval vessels for a belligerent. But the original figure of the American claims for the *Alabama* damage was soon inflated by reckless speeches in the Senate, where Sumner claimed that Britain had been responsible for prolonging the war by two years and implied that nothing less than the cession of Canada would be adequate compensation. It took time for tempers on both sides to cool, and it was not until Hamilton Fish succeeded Seward as Secretary of State and Granville succeeded Clarendon at the Foreign Office that an Anglo-American-Canadian commission was able to meet in a sensible atmosphere and settle the whole nexus of existing disputes – Canadian fisheries, North-western boundaries and *Alabama* claims. In the Treaty of Washington that followed in 1871 Britain made a frank apology for the *Alabama* escape and agreed to submit the figures of damages to international arbitration. The arbitration court met at Geneva and awarded 15 million dollars to the U.S.A. Britain promptly paid, and thus an issue which had great possibilities of mischief-making was amicably settled. Furthermore, it established arbitration as a peaceful and regular method of settling all important disputes between Britain and the United States. This was well illustrated twenty years later when the controversy between Canada and the United States over the seal fishing in the Bering Sea was decided – in this case against the United States – by a court of arbitration.

Three years later a more serious issue arose between Britain and America, as a result of a boundary dispute between Venezuela and the colony of British Guiana. Venezuela invoked the good offices of the U.S.A. and President Cleveland responded by asking Britain to submit the dispute to arbitration. It was his contention that the U.S.A. was interested as a guardian of the Monroe Doctrine, which forbade any European power to increase its holdings of territory on the American continent. Salisbury, who was then the British Foreign Minister, was not at first disposed to agree to such a view and both he and Cleveland indulged in unnecessarily blustering language over the dispute. Cleveland's bluster was by far the more successful of the two, principally because this was a moment when Britain could not afford the extravagant luxury of an American quarrel; the Transvaal crisis was approaching, with the folly of Jameson's raid and the implied insult of the German Kaiser's telegram to Kruger. Consequently Britain agreed to submit the dispute to arbitration, and two American Supreme Court justices sat with two English jurists and a Russian umpire to form the tribunal.

Cleveland's aggressive tone over the Venezuela controversy was, however, indicative of a new spirit permeating American policy, a spirit which was manifesting itself as American imperialism. Imperialism, the aggressive building of an empire by the acquisition of new territory, was a characteristic of all the great powers in the second half of the nineteenth century. Africa was the continent to which most of the European imperialist powers turned, but as that began to be divided up their attention turned also to the Far East and the Pacific. Unlike the nations of Europe, the

U.S.A. did not have to cross the seas in order to extend its territory: the West, which served as an outlet for America's colonizing energies during most of the nineteenth century, lay at her own back door. Nevertheless Seward, Secretary of State under Lincoln and Johnson, could not resist a tempting opportunity which was offered him as early as 1867 by the Russian government. They wanted to get rid of their American possession, Alaska, and Seward, like Jefferson half a century earlier over Louisiana, secured a bargain by buying it for $7,200,000. For a long time the new possession lay neglected, despised as 'Seward's folly', until in 1896 the discovery of gold in the Klondike brought thousands into the territory; they did not all find gold but in them Alaska at last found settlers.

Alaska apart, America's overseas expansion was more commercial than territorial, but the possible connection between trade and acquisition was presently illustrated by the case of Hawaii. In 1875 a treaty of commerce was made with Hawaii, and on its renewal in 1884 an important clause was added providing the U.S.A. with exclusive rights to a naval base at Pearl Harbour. Then in 1893 a rebellion broke out against the Queen of Hawaii, a rebellion in part engineered by American residents and sugar growers in the islands, and although Cleveland refused to annex the territory, the 'republic' which was established was American in all but name. Similarly in Samoa, the U.S.A. started off as a mere trading power which then secured special privileges in the harbour of Pago Pago, but at this stage she encountered the rival ambitions of Britain and Germany. The result was initially, in 1889, the establishment of a three-power protectorate over the islands. Eventually Britain withdrew and ten years later, in 1899, the islands were divided between Germany and the United States of America.

But these were small and isolated ventures. What faced McKinley, immediately on his entry into the White House, was an outbreak in the U.S.A. of something of the same kind of popular fervour for imperialist adventures as swept the Britain of the Boer War, the France of Jules Ferry and the Germany of William II. The frontier was 'closed', but the spirit of adventure was not dead. A naval strategist by the name of Captain Mahan was writing books to prove that the new frontier for America was on the sea, and that sea power was the key to national strength. At this moment a testing-ground for American sea-power offered itself and the national mood welcomed the opportunity of making the test. The testing ground was Cuba.

In 1895, for the second time since the American Civil War, rebellion broke out in Cuba against Spanish rule. The first rebellion in 1868 had been a failure, but since then American interest in Cuba had grown and popular sympathy in the U.S.A., fanned by the press and by Cuban emigrés, was strongly on the side of the rebels, although McKinley counselled caution. One newspaper owner in particular, William Randolph Hearst, was an adept in playing on popular emotion without very much regard for fact or principle and when in 1898 the U.S. battleship *Maine*, anchored in Havana Harbour, mysteriously exploded, his newspapers whipped the public into a frenzy of war-like indignation against Spain. 'Remember the *Maine*' became the popular cry, and Congress and nation demanded nothing less than Spain's immediate and unconditional withdrawal from Cuba. When Spain ignored the ultimatum, Congress declared war.

The war was fought on two fronts – in Cuba, where it was soon over, the Spaniards capitulating within a few months, and in the other large Spanish colony, the Philippines. The war in the Philippines began dramatically by an American naval squadron under Commodore Dewey entering Manila Bay and sinking the Spanish Pacific fleet at its moorings. An army of 100,000 men was later landed and with the capture of Manila Spanish resistance virtually ceased. By December, 1898, Spain had made peace and left American forces in possession of Hawaii (annexed in the course of the fighting with Spain), Puerto Rico and the Philippines, and exercising a protectorate over Cuba. The

United States of America suddenly found herself a colonial power.

These new responsibilities presented considerable problems, problems that cut across the traditional lines of division between the parties. To take the Philippines first – should the U.S.A. remain in these newly-occupied islands or give the Filipinos their independence? It was argued that the United States had no interests in the Far East important enough to warrant the retention of the Philippines; Chinese trade accounted for only a trifling percentage of American exports. On the other hand, it was pointed out that if the United States withdrew, the only result would be that some Far Eastern rival such as Germany, which had just seized Kiaochow, or Britain, which had taken Wei-Hai-Wei, would move into the Philippines and run up its flag in place of the *Stars and Stripes*. The anti-imperialists urged that whatever national interests might be involved the moral issue was plain – the United States had no right to annex the island without the consent of the native inhabitants. The issue was loudly and fiercely contested and the treaty which invoked annexation only just scraped through the Senate. Scarcely had it done so when the real complications of the Philippines problem revealed themselves. The Filipinos, so far from welcoming annexation, violently resisted it and proclaimed a republic. A war, marked by savageries on both sides, was fought in the mountains and jungles of the Philippines and dragged on until the last guerilla bands were rounded up in 1902. General MacArthur, father of the 1942 defender of the Philippines, was notable among the commanders of the American forces.

In Cuba American interests were much more obviously involved. It lay near American soil and American capital was invested in the sugar plantations. Before Congress declared war on Spain it had passed a self-denying ordinance with regard to Cuba, the Teller Amendment, which disclaimed any intention of annexing the island. So for two years after the war's end it was merely a protectorate, an efficient and beneficial protectorate, which was exercised by the American army. But when the time came for restoring Cuban rule the problem was how to reconcile Cuban independence with the protection of the valuable American properties on the island. The solution was found in 1903 by an agreement, known as the Platt Amendment, which the Cubans reluctantly accepted, which did in fact considerably limit Cuban sovereignty. It gave the U.S.A. a right to two naval stations on the island and also a right to intervene in Cuba whenever 'life, property or liberty' were endangered there. Moreover, it forbade Cuba to contract an excessive public debt. A commercial treaty, principally designed to benefit the sugar growers, supplemented the political one.

These developments in American policy, as might be expected, did not go unchallenged in the elections of 1900. In fact they provided one of the central issues of the campaign. Bryan, who once again received the Democratic nomination, was for making them the crucial issue. Although free silver and the menace of big business featured in his addresses it was anti-imperialism that he came back to in speech after speech, supported moreover by men of letters like Mark Twain and scholars like William James. (It is instructive to compare Bryan's attitude on the Philippines with that of Campbell-Bannerman in England at the same time on the Boer War.) But the Republicans would not give battle on that ground. Instead McKinley, who had been renominated, stressed the prosperity which had followed on his four years' administration, adopted the slogan of 'The Full Dinner Pail' and invited his opponents to deny that under the Republicans victories had been won, tariffs raised and wages increased. McKinley's appeal was successful. He won by an impressive margin and it seemed as if 'regular' Republicanism was impregnable. But within six months of his inauguration McKinley was assassinated by a young anarchist and into his place stepped the Vice-President, a Republican indeed, but one who wore his Republicanism with a difference. The new President's name was Theodore Roosevelt.

CHAPTER XXIX

Theodore Roosevelt

IN the spring of 1898, immediately on the declaration of war with Spain, Theodore Roosevelt had left his comfortable desk at the Navy Department where he was Assistant Secretary, and set about organizing a volunteer regiment to fight in Cuba. Within a couple of months he was leading his 'Rough Riders', as he called them, up the slope of San Juan Hill to storm the defences of Santiago. When, three years later, Roosevelt moved into the White House, he brought the spirit of the 'Rough Riders' with him. The youngest President in history, he brought energy, exuberance and courage to an office and a party which had grown timid and self-satisfied. Even his imperialism, which was orthodox Republican policy, seemed different from his predecessor's. McKinley's version of 'Manifest Destiny' had looked too much like a mere cloak for the interests of big business. Roosevelt trounced big business at the very moment when he beat the imperialist drum the loudest; no one could convincingly charge him with 'dollar diplomacy'. He represented himself, indeed, as accustomed to 'speak softly and carry a big stick', but the speech was never very soft though the stick was always big. And he was a born leader. Whether Americans supported 'Teddy's' imperialism or not they could be sure that he would never involve them in dangers that he would not himself share. Whether as President or as 'Rough Rider' he would always be where the fire was hottest.

The new President was not long in making his influence felt in foreign affairs. The Philippines, of course, were subjugated and in 1902 given the status of 'incorporated territory', i.e. territory under the control of the President and Congress and administered by a Governor, a status very like that of a British Crown Colony. But it was within the

Western hemisphere itself that events moved fastest. The Spanish-American War, fought in two oceans, had demonstrated the value to the United States of an Atlantic-Pacific canal which would provide the American navy with a shorter link than the route around the Horn. As long ago as 1850 a treaty with Britain, the Clayton-Bulwer Treaty, had provided for this and in 1901 the Hay-Pauncefote Agreement had attempted to guarantee that any such canal would be an international waterway, like Suez, not a merely exclusive preserve of the United States. But the Senate rejected the agreement in favour of one which permitted the United States to fortify any canal it constructed, and it was on this basis that Roosevelt went to work. The French had for two years been attempting to dig a canal through the Isthmus of Panama, but their company had gone bankrupt in the process. To buy up their rights was simple enough, but the government of Colombia, which owned the territory, contended that some of the cash payment should come into its coffers; arguing about this, it delayed ratification of the treaty which was to cede to the United States a zone ten miles wide for the construction of the canal. This was foolish of the Colombian government because there was already in existence in Panama a group who were only too ready to organize a 'revolution', in typical Latin-American style, the moment it seemed worth while. Roosevelt made no attempt to conceal his impatience and the impression gained ground in Panama that any uprising could count on United States support. On a dark November night the 'revolution' duly occurred and three American warships prevented Colombian troops from being landed to restore authority. An independent Republic of Panama was proclaimed, which speedily concluded a treaty leasing the Canal Zone to the United States.

Although the Colombian government was a corrupt and undemocratic assembly, there can be no doubt that the abruptness and irregularity of Roosevelt's behaviour administered a severe shock to the U.S.A.'s relations with Latin America. The effect persisted long after the immediate impact had worn off – and indeed even after the United States in 1921 had paid Colombia the sum of $25,000,000 in belated compensation. The canal itself was a triumph of engineering. In the face of every conceivable variety of tropical disease plus more than the normal run of constructional difficulties, the canal was driven through. Begun in 1904, it was opened to commerce in 1914. Its strategical importance for the United States is enormous; its commercial value to world shipping scarcely less so.

Concurrently with the Panama episode came another Venezuelan dispute. This, like that of 1895, involved Venezuela's relations with European powers. She was in default on debts to Germany, Britain and Italy, and Germany proposed to intervene and collect by force what was owing. At British instigation this was modified to take the form of a joint three-power blockade of Venezuelan harbours. This manifestation of European imperialism in American waters seemed to most Americans an implied threat to the Monroe Doctrine, and Roosevelt, rather in the style of Cleveland, put pressure on the disputants to agree to Venezuela's request for arbitration. The dispute was settled by the Hague Court. But Roosevelt's reasoning went further than this. If the Monroe Doctrine prevented European powers collecting their debts in American waters was it not up to the United States of America, as guardian of the Doctrine, to do their debt-collecting for them? Roosevelt concluded that it was, enunciated it to the Senate in what became known as the 'Roosevelt Corollary', and in 1904, when San Domingo defaulted, put it into practice by installing an American receiver-general to look after San Domingo's bookkeeping. But, as might be expected, the Corollary was not a popular principle south of the Rio Grande.

The enhanced prestige which this policy (backed by a modern navy) won for the United States among the great powers of the time enabled Roosevelt during his second term to play his part on the larger stage of world politics. His earlier activities, though they involved overseas powers, had their roots in properly American problems. Emboldened by success, Roosevelt decided to fish in more distant waters, acting as his own Secretary of State and dealing personally with the rival potentates of Europe and Asia. In the Far East, for example, the Russo-Japanese War was dragging on to a protracted conclusion. America had always advocated what was called 'the open door' in China, meaning free access to China for all foreign business and commerce, and to that end always sought to prevent any single power gaining a dominating position in the Far East. Japan's success in her war with Russia looked like giving her something of a dominant position; Roosevelt consequently threw his weight into the other scale and tried to arrange a peace which would not be too harsh on Russia. He eventually succeeded and in 1905 the Treaty of Portsmouth brought the war to an end without Russia having to pay the heavy indemnities which Japan had been demanding. For this Roosevelt was awarded the Nobel Peace Prize, but in Japan he was widely execrated as a busybody who had come between the victor and the legitimate fruits of victory. Japanese feeling was further roused when the State of California, giving way to racial prejudice, refused to allow Japanese school children to attend the same schools as whites, and it was not until Roosevelt got an agreement with Japan checking Japanese immigration into the United States that California eased its rules. Even so, in 1907 Roosevelt judged it wise to send the American fleet to visit Yokohama while on a world cruise, ostensibly as a gesture of friendship, actually as a demonstration of strength.

In Europe, meanwhile, the rivalry of the Great Powers, governed by no law other than their own, often inadequate, sense of prudence, had produced one of diplomacy's periodic crises. French and German claims clashed in Morocco and war was threatened. Directly, it was none of America's business, but Roosevelt was right in realizing that, since no one could tell how far a war would spread, America had an interest in keeping the peace. He consequently used all his influence to bring the disputants into a conference at Algeciras in 1906, out of which came an agreement on the future of Morocco such as would probably not have been possible without the mediating efforts of the American representative. It was not an ideal settlement, but it rendered a real, if short-lived, service to European peace.

These ventures in war and diplomacy, whether of the buccaneering kind as in Panama, or of the more statesmanlike order as at Algeciras, were departures from the old path of American foreign policy. Yet the opposition they met with amongst the American public was small. This was partly explained by the dash and charm of Roosevelt's personality before which criticism often melted like snow in the sunshine, but also by the fact that those elements in politics who might most have disapproved of Roosevelt the Imperialist were committed to the support of Roosevelt the Social Reformer. Roosevelt was like Joseph Chamberlain in the skill and sincerity with which he played both these rôles at one and the same time.

Roosevelt had his first experience of social problems when he was police commissioner of New York City from 1895 to 1897 and Governor of New York State from 1899 to 1901. Here he saw how the problems of the big cities, of which New York was only one, the poverty, the overcrowding, the sweated conditions of labour, could not just be left to solve themselves. Contrary to the prevailing philosophy of the period, which held that the State had no business to concern itself with social and industrial conditions, Roosevelt became convinced that unless the government took some action the cities of America would become the breeding spots of dirt, disease and crime. Many of the needed reforms at the beginning of the century were carried out by city or state governments and were not even matters for federal regulation at all, but Roosevelt's interest and enthusiasm created a volume of public support without which other reformers could not have achieved much success.

Thus Roosevelt's handling of the great coal strike of 1902, in which he threatened to take over the mines and thus forced the stubborn owners to arbitrate with the United Mine Workers' Union, was a landmark in labour history.

Labour began, almost for the first time, to have a recognized and respectable voice in industrial disputes. Again it was Roosevelt who got Congress to authorize the establishment of a new Department of Commerce and Labour, and although it was left to his successors to use the instrument which he created, its mere creation served notice on everyone that commerce and labour were activities in which government might take a legitimate interest. During his second term he tackled a menace which affected everyone alike, but which had hitherto evaded treatment because regulation of it had been regarded as 'socialistic' – namely, impure food. He secured legislation which gave officials the right to inspect meat and check the sale of harmful patent medicines – commonplace operations now in every civilized country but novel in 1906.

But Roosevelt was by temperament a giant-killer, and what he most enjoyed was attacking what he called 'the malefactors of great wealth'. By 1900 something of a revulsion of feeling had set in against big business. It was too big, men felt. Too much of the wealth was concentrated in too few hands. Nor were the methods by which this wealth had been acquired such as would bear close inspection. Lastly, as successive financial crises showed, these industrial and financial 'lords of creation' could not even prevent their own gigantic machinery of business from breaking down with disastrous results for millions of people. In the widespread belief that the way to check these evils was to make the formation of 'trusts' or monopolies a legal offence, Congress in 1890 had passed the Sherman Anti-Trust Act, but no significant prosecution had been attempted during the regimes of Cleveland and McKinley. Big business almost openly dared the government to act against it. Its attitude as a kind of rival power within the realm was well illustrated when J. P. Morgan, the great financier, was threatened with a prosecution. He called on President Roosevelt and said, 'Send your man (meaning the Attorney-General) to my man (naming one of his lawyers) and they can fix it up.' But Roosevelt was determined to show that the State was supreme and that the law was not to be adjusted like the figures in a business deal. In 1903 prosecution under the Sherman Act began with a suit against the Northern Securities Corporation, a 'trust' which had gathered into its control practically the entire railroad system of the North-West. The government won its case to the astonishment of Wall Street and the defeat of Harriman, the great railroad king who had been planning to bring every railroad in the United States under his control.

There was indeed no form of business that so much needed regulation as the railroads. They were the arteries of the country and the rates they fixed for carrying goods determined whether the country's life-blood circulated freely or not. Without any competitors they had been fixing the rates they liked, granting 'rebates' to such favourites as the great Standard Oil Corporation (who paid them handsomely in other ways), and penalizing small farmers and business men throughout whole states and regions. The establishment of the Interstate Commerce Commission in 1887 had made available the necessary machinery of control, but as originally appointed the Commission lacked the necessary regulatory powers. What was first needed was to make the railroads fix definite rates and publish them. This was provided for in the Elkins Act of 1903. Then, in his second term, Roosevelt secured the passage of the Hepburn Act which took the next step and enabled the government to fix rates, with penalties for railroads which exceeded them. At last the sovereign people of the United States were securing some return for the generous gifts of their land which an earlier generation had made to the railroad pioneers.

Not all Roosevelt's 'trust-busting' was successful, because companies found ingenious methods of circumventing the law, and it was not always possible to 'unscramble' a combine or business alliance by a mere prosecution. Indeed, Roosevelt himself denied that he was an indiscriminate foe of trusts and claimed that he was only opposed to 'bad' ones. Nor can it be pretended that wealth was dispersed into very many more hands at the end of his regime than it was at the beginning. But he did much to destroy the notion that business should be a law unto itself; in its place he re-established the principle that the common weal comes first and that business should be the servant of the community, not its master.

Less spectacular, but almost more valuable, was the work Roosevelt did in preserving the natural resources of the United States. The natural wealth of America, in fields, forests and mines, had been exploited recklessly. Now that there were no more lands beyond the frontier it became more imperative than ever to preserve from wastage those which remained. Cleveland had made a start by setting aside some forest land as a government reservation. But Roosevelt, who had the West in his blood, who had punched cattle on his own ranch and cared enormously for nature and wild life, went much further. He withheld huge areas of the West from sale and saved whole forests from annihilation at the hands of prospectors. At the same time he promoted irrigation and tried to teach the farmer how best to conserve his soil. Above all, he did this with such enthusiasm and effect that he awakened a national interest in conservation which persisted after he had gone.

He left the presidency in 1909. His re-election in 1904 had been easy, but he chose to stand down in 1908 (perhaps with a view to a later return) and endorsed his Secretary of War, Taft, for the succession. With such endorsement Taft beat Bryan, still the Democrats' leader, and Roosevelt went off to Africa, characteristically on a big game expedition. Taft's rule meant a respite from 'reform' and buccaneering and a marked renewal of strength in Congress for the 'Old Guard' of the Republican Party. Naturally this resulted in a tariff revision. Taft called it 'a revision downward', but by the time Congress had finished with it the Payne-Aldrich Bill of 1909 had raised the tariff wall by at least one brick all round.

In normal times, perhaps, Taft's presidency, which was honest and introduced many useful small measures, would have been judged a mildly reforming administration. But it was his misfortune that the Progressive movement around him was going so fast that by comparison he seemed to be standing still. 'Progressivism' was in the air on every hand, a movement which was not content with the gentle pace of Taft's Republicanism. Roosevelt returned from his world tour more radical by far than when he went away, and was soon pronouncing himself 'disappointed' with Taft. And in New Jersey, a state noted for its corrupt politics, the Democrats had a house-cleaning and elected as the new Governor a noted Progressive – and, what was more significant, a man who had been professor of government at Princeton University. His name was Woodrow Wilson. These were the portents when the election year of 1912 came round.

CHAPTER XXX

Woodrow Wilson: War and Peace

WHEN 1912 began, Theodore Roosevelt at first bent his efforts on capturing the Republican nomination. He made speeches announcing that he stood for 'the square deal' and advocated radical reforms. But at the Convention the Old Guard would have none of him. Taft was re-nominated, and Roosevelt, rather than abide by the choice, led his supporters out of the party. At a separate Convention, amid scenes of almost religious enthusiasm, the 'Progressives', as they called themselves, chose Roosevelt as their candidate and Roosevelt accepted the nomination with crusading fervour. 'We stand at Armageddon', he told his followers, 'and we battle for the Lord.' Meanwhile the Democrats had also felt the call of radicalism and reform, and had chosen for their candidate the college-bred Governor of New Jersey, Woodrow Wilson.

Wilson was Roosevelt's real opponent. It was a battle of rival progressives, with Taft and the Republican regulars in the background. Roosevelt called his programme 'The New Nationalism' and Wilson called his 'The New Freedom', but their proposals were much the same. Roosevelt would very probably have won, had it not been for the split in the Republican Party. Wilson had a united party to give him strength and consequently won almost as many popular votes as his two opponents combined, as well as a sweeping majority in the electoral college. At last, Bryan felt, the Populist movement had elected a President they could trust.

Aided by a Democratic Congress, Wilson lost no time in fulfilling the promises of the 'New Freedom'. At long last a real reduction in the tariff was effected (the Underwood Tariff of 1913). Income tax was introduced, even though the Constitution had to be amended to do it. Furthermore, the long-nursed ambition of the Populists was realized; by the Federal Reserve Act the domination which the Eastern bankers exercised over the nation's money was broken and the government assumed a large measure of control. Lastly, trusts were attended to – by a Clayton Act which blocked many loopholes in earlier measures, and by the creation of a Federal Trade Commission to advise on prosecutions.*

Then suddenly, across the path of this 'New Freedom' there fell the shadow of the World War. America at first did not appear to be much affected. It seemed a 'European' War, which was no more the business of the United States than the Franco-Prussian War of 1870 had been. Wilson had none of Theodore Roosevelt's desire to cut a figure in foreign affairs, and Bryan, who was his Secretary of State, had strong pacifist leanings. The country was in a similar mood; when Wilson announced that the United States was neutral in the conflict scarcely anyone dissented. There were few who saw what a menace German militarism could be to a democratic America and there were many, apart from those with German blood in their veins, who doubted if Germany was to blame.

Then in 1915 there came the sinking of the *Lusitania*, and immediately many Americans who had previously heeded

* The Federal Trade Commission has also rendered valuable service in reducing such practices as false or misleading labelling and advertising of goods, commercial bribery, etc.

Wilson's injunction to be 'neutral in thought as well as in deed', realized with a shock that Germany was determined to stick at nothing in order to win. Opinion moved markedly in favour of the Allies. Wilson protested strongly both at this and at subsequent violations of international law, but German sinkings continued. Even so, when the elections of 1916 came up and Wilson was re-adopted as the Democratic candidate, one of the slogans employed by the Democratic machine was 'he kept us out of war'. It was a close election, with the Republican candidate, Charles Evans Hughes, losing only at the last moment when the vote of California was counted.

By the time Wilson entered on his second term of office in 1917 the European War presented to American eyes an appearance very different from that which it had worn in August, 1914. American opinion increasingly favoured the Allies and criticized the Germans, and the American ambassadors in London and Berlin went even further than opinion in their home country. Walter Hines Page in London spoke to Grey, the British Foreign Secretary, more as an ally than as a diplomat, while Gerard in Berlin made no attempt to smooth ruffled German sensibilities. Meanwhile in Washington, Bryan, who disapproved of what he regarded as Wilson's increasingly un-neutral course, was replaced by Lansing, an uninfluential figure whose appointment signified that Wilson was going to be in effect his own Secretary of State.

During these years of American neutrality, American products, including munitions, had been on sale to all belligerents, but in fact, since the Allies had command of the seas, the volume of Allied purchases had increased enormously while the Central Powers obtained practically nothing. To finance these huge purchases the Allies raised loans from American bankers, particularly from the house of J. Pierpont Morgan. An attempt has since been made by one or two students and a number of United States politicians to show that the munitions trade and the Allied loans were responsible for involving the United States of America in the War; in support of this it has been argued that the

Allies were so short of funds that they would soon have had to stop their purchases and default on their loans, with the result that the war-time boom would have turned into a crash. To prevent this, the argument runs, America came into the war herself. There is, however, no evidence that either Congress or Wilson were swayed by such considerations, and in fact the theory ignores the most potent cause of American intervention, the developments in the war at sea.

On January 31st, 1917, the Germans, feeling the fearful pinch of the Allied blockade, broke their earlier promise to Wilson and announced that henceforth they would torpedo all ships, naval or merchant, Allied or neutral, at sight. This broke all the laws of naval warfare, and the Germans knew that such behaviour would utterly shock the United States; they calculated, however, that their U-boats would reduce Britain to starvation before America could act. (In this they were very nearly right. In April, 1917, Allied merchant shipping losses rose to 840,000 tons, and it was estimated that British food stocks were not sufficient to feed the country for more than a few weeks.) The U.S.A.'s reply to Germany's new submarine campaign was to break off diplomatic relations. Hardened as we have become in World War II to every kind of German atrocity, it is not easy for us to recapture the indignation aroused by this deliberate campaign of sinking merchant ships. But in 1917, so relatively civilized was the world then, this was something new and peculiarly horrific in warfare and Wilson felt, not without reason, that a people which could engage in it would stop at nothing to achieve victory. Moreover, next to Britain, the U.S.A. as a naval power had the greatest stake in the freedom of the seas and knew that if Germany succeeded in dominating the Atlantic the very shores of America would be endangered.

While the U.S.A. was digesting the implications of the new submarine campaign a fresh development occurred. A telegram was intercepted between Zimmermann, the German Foreign Minister, and his Minister in Mexico. It instructed him, in the event of war between Germany and the United States of America, to offer Mexico the territory of Texas, Arizona and New Mexico if only she would intervene on the German side. If the submarine warfare had shocked the Eastern seaboard, this ran like an electric charge up the spine of the Middle West, who realized suddenly that their boasted security was an illusion if this came to pass. But Wilson still held out against war. Then in March the Russian Revolution broke out and the Western Allies were deprived both of an asset (for Germany was now free to concentrate all her might on the West) and of a liability (for the U.S.A. had distrusted an alliance which included autocratic Tsarist Russia). On the heels of this came the sinking in quick succession of five American merchantmen. On April 2nd Wilson read his War Message to Congress:

> It is a fearful thing to lead this great peaceful people into war ... But the right is more precious than peace, and we shall fight for the things which we have always carried nearest our hearts – for democracy, for the right of those who submit to authority to have a voice in their own governments, for the rights and liberties of small nations, for a universal dominion of right by such a concert of free peoples as shall bring peace and safety to all nations and make the world itself at last free.

These were high ideals. Wilson, who had thought deeply about war and peace, advocated them sincerely. The country accepted them equally sincerely as its own, but it had not thought so deeply about the implications. Congress was frankly divided. Fifty-six members voted against war, although their opponents, 455 strong, easily carried the day.

America's role in the remainder of the war belongs more to the history of the war itself than to the history of the U.S.A. Her intervention was decisive, although it was eighteen months before German collapse ensued. But although American military fatalities numbered only 126,000, the fact that untold millions of Americans were ready to reinforce the units who fought so bravely and well at Chateau-Thierry and Belleau Wood was a vital factor in breaking

German morale and convincing the General Staff that defeat was certain. Besides, American naval assistance had spelled the doom of the U-boat, while American production, mobilized by Bernard Baruch, provided the Allies with a wealth of munitions which surpassed anything that Germany could muster.

On the home front the war meant a great production effort, the introduction of a certain amount of rationing, the entry of women into all sorts of new employments (from many of which they never retired), and the introduction of a measure of conscription. There was a Selective Service Act, by which every male of military age had to register, and then those called to the colours were selected by lot. At great speed an army was fashioned, of whom about half, approximately two millions, actually went overseas under the Commander-in-Chief, General Pershing. No such merging of American and Allied commands was achieved as in World War II; indeed it was only for a brief period in the darkest days of 1918 that Pershing consented, as a special concession, to put his men under Foch. But this distinction between military commands was really the reflection of a distinction on the political level for which Wilson was partly responsible.

Wilson always felt that the U.S.A. was in some sense different from the other belligerents, who, he argued, had been in the war earlier and had become compromised by secret treaties, diplomatic deals and the like. The U.S.A., although it had now entered the war, ought not, he thought, to involve itself any more than was absolutely necessary in their politics. Using its fortunate and privileged position, it should remain as independent as possible and set an example of high-principled dealing in international affairs. In line with this the U.S.A. never became one of the Allies, but called herself an 'Associated Power'. This did give Wilson some of the freedom of action he desired, but it also meant a great loss of confidence between the Allied and Associated powers and prevented the U.S.A. learning much that was going on in Europe. In these circumstances, however, it was natural that Wilson should take the lead in formulating the principles on which peace should be made, and indeed the forcefulness of his reasoning and his high idealism gave him an enormous following not merely in the U.S.A., but throughout the world. He drew up his programme in January, 1918, under the now famous title of the Fourteen Points, and for the first time in the history of the world the United States was on record, not merely as participating in a European war (for that had happened in 1812), but as setting out the basis of a European peace. The Fourteen Points had a great effect in Germany, where people increasingly asked themselves whether there was any point in going on fighting against such reasonable and indeed generous terms. Eventually, in November, 1918, with the weight of Allied arms added to the war-weariness of the German home front, they gave in, and in December, again for the first time in the world's history, an American President set sail for Europe to represent his country at the peace table.

Unfortunately, before Wilson ever left for France, certain things had happened which were to make his task more difficult than he himself realized. Although the Fourteen Points commanded a wide measure of general agreement, understandings – some of them secret – already arrived at between the Allies cut across many of the principles as well as the details of the programme. And although the last of the Fourteen Points – the one which envisaged the creation of a League of Nations – won general acceptance among all the delegates to the Peace Conference, there was much difference of opinion as to what the new League should be like. Moreover, the absence from Versailles of Russia, then only just emerging from the Bolshevik revolution, meant that a vital force in Europe was virtually ignored throughout the proceedings. Lastly, although Wilson's own eloquence, energy and idealism exercised a great sway at the council table, the European delegates, particularly the French, never felt confident that Wilson's voice was the voice of the American nation as a whole. For this Wilson was himself partly to blame. In the mid-term elections of November, 1918, Wilson issued a statement which made it appear as if only the Democrats could be trusted to support his policies, abroad as well as at home. The Republicans made much of this implied slur on their loyalty and won a handsome majority in both houses of Congress. Nor was the tension between the President and the Republican leaders made any easier when Wilson took with him to Paris a delegation which contained not one single Republican politician, although there were Republicans of standing who had endorsed his policy.

In London, in Paris and in Rome, Wilson received a popular welcome such as no other American leader had ever been given: a welcome which expressed the people's desire for peace and their admiration for Wilson's ideals. Then came the hard months of deliberation at Paris where Wilson, with his confidential assistant Colonel House, laboured at the Peace Treaty and the constitution of the League. By degrees it became apparent that Wilson could not have exactly the kind of peace he wanted, but he consoled himself for compromises and concessions by the thought that the League, if only he got that, could take care of the imperfections of the Peace Treaty. This was a reasonable point of view, the more so because it was not immediately apparent what America's attitude to the League would be. The French wanted a 'strong' League with power immediately to go to war against any country which disturbed the peace. Neither Britain nor the U.S.A. was prepared to delegate so much authority to a new international organization, but what Wilson did agree to went almost as far. In addition to Article X of the League Covenant, the famous Article which promised to preserve intact the territory of every member, he agreed, jointly with Britain, to guarantee military aid to France in the event of another German invasion.

This was an astonishing move of Wilson's. The United States had never in its history undertaken any alliance which involved a promise to send its forces abroad, even within the American continents, much less to Europe. It was wildly improbable that the Senate, even if it ratified the League, would ratify the Security Treaty with France and Britain. However, Wilson staked his all on it and in return for the alliance Clemenceau gave up his demand for the annexation of the west bank of the Rhine. Then in June, 1919, after completing his work on the Covenant of the League and signing the Treaty of Versailles which embodied it, Wilson turned for home, to secure for the League and the Security Treaty that support of two-thirds of the United States Senate without which his promise and his signature would be meaningless.

Wilson returned to an America in many ways changed. The idealism of the war years had given way to a mood of cynicism and revenge. Many thought the Versailles Treaty had given Germany too lenient a peace, many criticized it for its injustices, most were indifferent to what kind of a peace it was, provided it was peace. The Irish-Americans were busy generating animosity against Britain for her conduct in suppressing the Sinn Fein revolution in Ireland, and argued that under Article X of the League Covenant 'the British Empire can demand American blood to subdue Ireland'. And hundreds of thousands of American soldiers were returning from overseas service war-weary and disillusioned. Wilson set about combating this spirit of hostility, cynicism and indifference. But he faced a hostile Congress led by three particularly able Senators: Lodge of Massachusetts (who had a powerful personal detestation of Wilson), Borah of Idaho and Johnson of California. The Security Treaty they just ignored: that was pigeon-holed and left to die. As far as the League was concerned, they concentrated their attacks on Article X, which promised the use of force, if necessary, to restrain aggressors, and they achieved as much by delay as by criticism, because with every day that went by the public mood cooled. Wilson for his part refused to consider any alteration in the Treaty – had he done so, some argue, he could have won the Senate round; but others contend that, given one concession, Lodge and his confederates would merely have asked for more. However, turning from Congress, Wilson decided to appeal to the people and set off in September on a speaking tour, making speeches every day and every night, and each one fresh and carefully prepared – perhaps the most remarkable oratorical feat in United States history. Wilson put his heart into it because he was fighting for all he held dear. As he said at St Louis, 'I would like to get together the boys who fought in the war and I would stand up before them and say: "Boys, I told you before you went across the seas that this was a war against wars, and I did my best to fulfil the promise, but I am obliged to come to you in mortification and shame and say I have not been able to fulfil the promise. You are betrayed ... You fought for something you did not get ... and there will come some time, in the vengeful Providence of God, another struggle in which not a few hundred thousand fine men from America will have to die, but as many millions as are necessary to accomplish the final freedom of the world."' But the strain was too much for the already ailing President. Within less than a month he suffered a collapse, from which he never properly recovered, and from October, 1919, to March, 1921, the government of the United States was headed by a sick man.

In November the Treaty of Versailles was defeated in the Senate by a vote of 39 to 55, and although the Senate reconsidered its decision in March, 1920, when, with certain alterations in the Treaty, the vote was 49 for, 35 against, this still fell short of the two-thirds majority needed. Lodge had beaten his Presidential rival. Wilson tried to make the impending Presidential election a 'solemn referendum' on the League. His health would not permit him to stand, but Cox, the well-meaning Governor of Ohio, who was the Democratic nominee, accepted Wilson's principles as his own. The Republicans, however, took care to confuse the issue. Their candidate, Senator Harding, also from Ohio, was for 'a League, but not the League'; for the League with reservations in one speech and for no League in the next. So the 'solemn referendum' was never really held. But as the Republican vote came crowding in to give Harding a six millions majority it was soon obvious that the fight was lost. The League, to use Harding's words, was pronounced 'deceased'.

CHAPTER XXXI

Boom, Slump and New Deal

ONE of the consequences of Wilson's tragic illness, which removed virtually all direction from the course of public affairs, was that the U.S.A. simply drifted back from war into peace, without any plan or control. This drift was not in any way checked by Harding, who in fact pursued a conscious policy of non-interference, letting each department of government look after itself, with the White House doing as little as possible, while big business was given a free hand to organize itself as it wished. This was what Harding meant by his famous phrase, 'Back to Normalcy'. In fact there was very little that was normal about it. As a result of the Prohibition Amendment which became effective in 1920, the United States had for the first time made the sale of alcoholic drinks a federal offence; the result unfortunately was not so much the stoppage of drunkenness as the increase of crime, 'bootleggers' and other violators of the law flourishing all over the country. The short-lived war and post-war boom was succeeded by a wave of strikes, involving more than four million workers. This, coupled with a good deal of nervousness over the spread of 'Bolshevism' (due to the unpopularity in America of the new Communist regime in Russia), led to a wave of arrests and prosecutions by Wilson's Attorney-General, Mitchell Palmer, which for a brief period constituted a serious threat to American civil liberties. (It was in 1927 that Sacco and Vanzetti, two anarchists charged with complicity in a bomb explosion, were put to death for a crime which the consensus of opinion agreed they did not commit.)

This constituted a state of affairs unhappily reminiscent of the years which followed the Civil War sixty years earlier. (Indeed in the South the Ku Klux Klan even made bold to 'ride again', terrorising Negroes and Catholics.) There was that same slackening of public standards which had marked the end of the earlier war. Harding appointed his friends to public offices without much consideration of their fitness to govern. The result was that his Presidency is principally remembered for a crop of scandals such as the U.S.A. had not known since Grant. The most notorious of these, the Teapot Dome* affair, involved Albert Fall, Harding's Secretary of the Interior, who was convicted of profiting from the sale of the nation's oil reserves. The Secretary of the Navy, Denby, was dismissed for complicity, while Daugherty, the Attorney-General, was dismissed at the same time for other frauds and misconduct.

Under the impact of these exposures Harding's health broke down and in August, 1923, he died of ptomaine poisoning, to be succeeded by his Vice-President, Calvin Coolidge. Coolidge was a tight-lipped, puritanical Yankee from Vermont, as different in appearance and temperament from Harding as could be imagined, but there was little difference in their views on public affairs. Coolidge was as hostile to the League of Nations and to anything that savoured of 'progressivism', and as friendly to high tariffs and big business as Harding had ever been. In the existing mood of the Republican Party 'silent Cal' was the obvious candidate for 1924, and in the existing mood of the country he was the easy victor in the election. His Democratic opponent, Davis, was a weak rival and Coolidge's victory was made even more certain by the emergence of a fresh 'Progressive' Party, built largely on local groups in Wisconsin and neighbouring states. The Progressives nominated Bob La Follette, the Governor of Wisconsin, who tried to make a party out of a coalition of the Middle-Western rural radi-

* So called after the 'Teapot Dome' oil-bearing hills in Wyoming.

cals and the labour elements of the cities. The attempt was even less successful than Theodore Roosevelt's earlier 'breakaway' Progressive Party had been, La Follette winning less than five million votes; with his defeat the Progressive Party virtually disappeared from the national scene. In the next election the spirit of reform found its principal expression once again in the Democratic Party. In 1928 the Democrats chose Al Smith, the popular liberal Governor of New York, as their candidate, and under his banner carried most of the big urban areas. But victory in the big cities was not enough: the country at large had been well content with the uneventful years of Coolidge's regime; business was booming, wages were high – there seemed no reason to abandon the Republican Party. The Party's candidate, Mr Hoover, was a distinguished engineer with a reputation for his organization of relief in Europe after the Great War; he was supported by a campaign fund which recalled that of McKinley, and he won a resounding victory of 444 electoral votes to 87.

Although Hoover was more able than Harding and more positive than Coolidge, his policies were in a true line of descent from theirs. Where Harding had authorized the Fordney-McCumber tariff, the highest in United States history, Hoover in 1930 signed the Hawley-Smoot bill which raised protection to still greater heights. The practice of tax reduction begun in 1921 under Harding, and continued in 1924 under Coolidge, was carried still further in 1929, despite the constantly rising level of incomes and profits. The principle that government should not enter into or compete with private business, which was one of the most blindly held tenets of the period, had been powerfully exemplified by Coolidge when in 1928 he insisted on the Muscle Shoals Dam in Tennessee, built during the war for making munitions, being turned back to private industry; in 1931 Hoover similarly denounced as 'degenerate' the proposal that government should build a second Tennessee River dam and sell the electric power which it would manufacture. At the same time, however, large subsidies were paid to shipping, aviation and agriculture without any satisfactory scrutiny of their efficiency. In one respect, however, Hoover was an innovator. Under Harding and Coolidge big business had been growing bigger, 'consolidating', 'merging', 'combining' – in fact ignoring the anti-trust laws almost at will. But Hoover was unique in using the Department of Commerce for the purpose of positively promoting and facilitating that process; as an engineer he was shocked by the waste which seemed to be entailed in competition, and he sincerely believed that the bigger the unit the more efficient its operation.

From the economic practices of Hoover and his predecessors some very remarkable results ensued. The tariffs, for example, had a double effect: they prevented the payment by America's allies of the debts which they had contracted in the United States by their war-time and post-war purchases, because they prevented imports of goods at a time when the allies could not pay in gold; secondly, they helped to strangle world trade and to foster the drive in every country towards economic nationalism. Such tariffs were particularly out of place now that America was a creditor country; positions had been quite reversed since the '80's, when foreign capital was pouring into the U.S.A. Now it was American capital that was flowing outward – into Latin America, into Europe, and particularly into Germany, where it financed at first reconstruction and later rearmament. Meanwhile inside the U.S.A. the concentration of wealth and financial power into fewer and fewer hands meant that a shock to any part of the economic structure was felt throughout the whole frame. In 1929 the first of those shocks was felt. Hoover's election had been the signal for a business boom and a tide of speculation on the Stock Exchange which rose to a feverish height previously unknown in United States history. Then, in October, 1929, 'the bottom fell out of the market'. Within three days over 12,000,000 shares changed hands and a crash ensued in which Americans everywhere lost their savings or their jobs. Unemployment leapt up and 'breadlines' – queues of hungry men waiting to be fed by private charity – appeared in the streets.

The United States had known 'crashes' before, and at first it was thought that this was just another stock market panic which would right itself once 'confidence' returned. For a few months there was a movement of recovery, but it was short-lived. The Hawley-Smoot Tariff did nothing to help matters in the U.S.A. and soon it was evident that it only served to accelerate economic collapse elsewhere. In 1931 the Viennese bank, the Credit-Anstalt, closed its doors and in one European country after another economic disaster followed. American investments in Europe turned to worthless paper overnight. Although in face of this Hoover arranged for a year's stoppage of all debt payments, he was powerless to protect the already shaken Wall Street from the further impact of its European losses. More and more bankruptcies, more and more unemployment, longer and longer breadlines followed. The 'crash' had turned into the 'depression', a spreading economic plague which no one seemed to be able to understand or arrest.

It was in these circumstances that the rival parties prepared for the Presidential elections of 1932. In Germany another economic crisis in many ways similar was providing the excuse for a fanatical political gangster, Adolf Hitler, to seize the reins of power and establish himself as a ruthless dictator. In America the Republicans followed the obvious and traditional course of re-nominating the existing President, though Hoover's name nowhere commanded the enthusiasm it had provoked in 1928. The Democrats also followed a familiar recipe; as they had done in 1928 and 1892, they chose a Governor of New York. He had a famous name, that of Roosevelt, but he came from a branch of the family which was only distantly connected with the great Theodore. He had been Assistant Secretary of the Navy under Wilson, and in 1920 he had been the Democratic nominee for the Vice-Presidency. But close on the heels of the 1920 defeat had come a personal disaster which was literally crippling. In the prime of life Roosevelt was struck down by infantile paralysis and for seven years was absent from public life. But, assisted by his devoted wife Eleanor, herself a Roosevelt, he so far conquered his infirmity as to be elected in 1928 to the governorship of New York State, and from this vantage point he emerged in 1932 to win the Democratic nomination. He electrified the country with an unconventional campaign tour, in which he promised depression-ridden America a 'New Deal', a phrase which evoked memories of an earlier Roosevelt's 'square deal' and of a pre-war Wilson's 'New Freedom'. The same forces of progressivism, reform and poverty, which had rallied to those earlier banners now answered Franklin Delano Roosevelt's call. He won a clear mandate from the electorate – a popular majority of seven million and a lead of 472 to 59 in the electoral college.

When the new President assumed office in March, 1933, the Depression had reached its utmost depth. Despite Hoover's Reconstruction Finance Corporation, belatedly established in 1932 to make government loans to firms in financial difficulties, the financial crisis had become so acute that two-thirds of the banks of the country had closed their doors. It seemed as if the United States was on the point of economic paralysis. Roosevelt's first task was to instil confidence. Using the new medium of the radio, he spoke to the people at their own firesides, telling them that there was nothing insoluble about the nation's problems, that, in essence, 'the only thing we have to fear is fear itself'. The people and their Congress responded equally to the stimulus of his courage and warm humanity. He asked Congress for broad emergency powers, and got them. For a Hundred Days he was a democratic dictator of the United States. He immediately declared a banking holiday and allowed banks to re-open only as and when they were certified to be sound. To meet the joint problems of idle men and empty jobs he immediately arranged for the expenditure of $3,300,000,000 on public works, and for the men in the breadlines he arranged immediate federal relief, since state finances were obviously unequal to the demands of the situation. Noisiest and most revolutionary of all his measures was the 'N.R.A.' – the National Recovery Act. Under this Roosevelt virtually suspended the anti-trust acts and by a gigantic publicity campaign whipped business up to establish 'codes' for itself – i.e. to restrict wasteful competition, shorten hours, raise wages. The idea was self-government for business, but with the government scrutinizing the 'codes' and claiming the right to prosecute businesses whose codes did not come up to the government's standards.

These emergency measures saved the social and economic structure from the immediate danger of collapse. The corner was turned, but when Congress adjourned in June the long-term programme of recovery had still to be put into operation. To assist him in this the President had brought with him to Washington a team of economists, administrators, lawyers and social reformers who came to be known collectively as his 'Brains Trust'; their composition changed continually, but they constituted in total the greatest infusion of fresh blood and reforming zeal into the American government system which it had known in 150 years. The body of reforms known loosely as the New Deal was their creation and remains their monument.

The New Deal comprised several principles. First of all, it aimed at providing jobs, not relief, wherever possible. To this end it embarked on a huge programme of public works – dams, roads, schools, every manner of enterprise, all over the States, a programme which immediately took care of four million unemployed, involved expenditures hitherto considered gargantuan, and left behind it a legacy of very valuable achievement. Unemployment, however, could not all be taken care of thus, and the second aim of the New Deal was to establish a system of social security which would remove the haunting fear that loss of a job meant total impoverishment. Many states had such systems of their own, but the problem was really a national one which needed to be tackled federally. Hence in 1935 the passage of the Social Security Act which provided for both unemployment insurance and an old age pension.

Looking back on the 'twenties and 'thirties, it seemed to Roosevelt and his New Dealers that part of the explanation of the crash lay in the fact that the fabulous wealth of the Harding-Coolidge era had not been shared out as it deserved. Although business and often labour had done well, agriculture had been a depressed industry even in the boom years. The farmers, it was felt, were not receiving their proper share of the national income. So the Agricultural Adjustment Act was designed to give Wallace, the Secretary of Agriculture, the power to raise farm profits by a system of subsidies, while at the same time the farmer was discouraged from over-producing and from ploughing up land which was not suitable for use. Much of the land of America was being ruined through bad farming by growing one persistent crop, such as tobacco or cotton, which impoverished the soil, or by ploughing up grassland or deforesting dry mountain sides. This was resulting in the fertile top soil being blown or washed away, at the rate of millions of acres a year. To check this a youth 'army', the Civilian Conservation Corps, planted trees and organized irrigation, while in Tennessee, where Coolidge once frowned on Muscle Shoals, a gigantic programme of dams, electrification, and crop control, was planned by the Tennessee Valley Authority.

Nor was labour forgotten. Since the far-off '80's, trade unionism had certainly made strides and the American Federation of Labour had become a large and wealthy federation of unions. But business still permitted unionization only on its own terms, and they were often harsh and uncompromising terms. Labour's position in the U.S.A. was still far behind that of its brothers in Britain and Europe. Thus, not the least revolutionary of the provisions of 'N.R.A.' was a certain 'clause 7A', which guaranteed to labour the right to organize and bargain collectively. In 1935 this was written into a separate Act, the Wagner Act, which gave labour additional safeguards. Behind these bulwarks unionization proceeded apace – too fast indeed for the long-established American Federation of Labour, which was slow to admit members of newer industries and workers from the lower ranks of labour. To organize them John L. Lewis, the impulsive miners' leader, left the A.F. of L. and created a rival body, the Committee of Industrial Organizations. Soon, to the four million of the A.F. of L., the energetic C.I.O. was able to oppose a membership of only a million less.

Not all of the New Deal legislation was well considered and not all of it needed to be permanent in order to serve its purpose. By 1935 the Supreme Court had begun to scrutinize the constitutionality of some of the more sweeping enactments. The N.R.A., it found, had wielded a power considerably in excess of what the Constitution intended in enforcing such sweeping regulation of industry. But in fact by 1935 the N.R.A. had done its work and its passing was little regretted. More serious was the invalidation of the Agricultural Adjustment Act in 1936, though that could be re-enacted, and was, with some slight modification. But when the Court threw out a New York State law fixing minimum wages for women, people began to ask themselves whether the Justices were not confusing their own economic and political views with their task of interpreting the Constitution. Business, having recovered from the shock of '29 to '32, began to dislike the New Deal medicine which in the moment of its sickness it had welcomed, and soon embarked on a vigorous criticism of the President and his policies.

This criticism found expression in the elections of 1936, when the Republicans under the leadership of Alfred Landon, Governor of Kansas and himself a business man, asserted that the New Deal threatened an end to liberty and to 'the American way of life'. It was a shrill campaign, in which, as one wit remarked, 'everyone but the voters' seemed opposed to the President. Landon's defeat was catastrophic. Out of the whole nation he only carried the states of Maine and Vermont.

Disappointed Republican diehards began to mutter that 'the only bulwark' left now was the Supreme Court.

Tempted perhaps by the intemperance of such opponents, Roosevelt determined to carry even this last citadel. Most of the anti-New Deal decisions of the Court had been given by a six to three vote on the bench. Roosevelt proposed a bill which would have the effect of increasing the Court's membership sufficiently to provide a majority of liberal-minded Justices (the appointment of Justices is a Presidential prerogative). This was bitterly contested in Congress and denounced as 'wrecking the Constitution' and 'packing the Court'. The bill never went through in its original form, but whether by coincidence or not, the Court's rulings began to show a markedly more liberal trend and before long enough old and conservative Justices had retired to give the President an opportunity of appointing a majority of liberal successors. The great Court battle was, however, won at a price, because the conservative wing of the Democratic Party developed a bitter hostility to the President's domestic policy which was to cause him many a setback in subsequent years. Such was the state of domestic policy when the spreading shadows of war brought foreign policy into a prominence which it had not enjoyed since the death of Wilson.

CHAPTER XXXII

Isolation and War

ALTHOUGH President Harding was totally opposed to Wilson's conviction that the United States should play a leading part in world affairs, he nevertheless chose a man of considerable ability for his Secretary of State, the Charles Evans Hughes who had run against Wilson in 1916. Once the decision had been taken that the United States should not join the League of Nations, it was a natural corollary that she should withdraw from any political or diplomatic activity in Europe, and in fact fifteen years elapsed without the United States taking any important part in the settlement of European affairs. But even the opponents of the League had recognized that America had responsibilities in the Far East, and it was not long before Hughes found himself obliged to take some positive action in the Pacific.

The war had afforded Japan a remarkable opportunity to strengthen her position on the Asiatic mainland while all the Great Powers from Russia to the United States were engaged with Germany. Japan seized Shantung from China and several Pacific islands from Germany; both these gains were legalized at Versailles at the same time as the weakness of the new Russia and the new Republic of China enabled Japan to strengthen her hold over Manchuria and Mongolia. During all this time Britain was still a party to the Anglo-Japanese treaty of 1905, which might have obliged us to support Japan in the event of Japanese-American conflict. Both Britain and the United States had a common interest in correcting such a trend of events and in trying to construct some sort of stable order in the Far East.

Accordingly when Hughes proposed a Conference on Naval disarmament to take place in Washington in the winter of 1921, Britain gave it her warm support. The Conference, unlike most others of the 'twenties and 'thirties, did succeed in achieving a real measure of disarmament, because it also worked out a political settlement for the Pacific. Britain, the United States, Japan, France and Italy agreed to scrap enough ships to leave their battleship strengths in the ratio of 5, 5, 3, 1.7 and 1.7 respectively. Though this left Japan with a smaller navy than the first two, it was judged fully sufficient for the needs of her defence because the United States agreed not to construct any further fortifications on her Pacific islands – such as the Philippines, Guam or the Aleutians – which might conceivably menace Japan. Britain gave a similar pledge. Then the Conference went on to replace the Anglo-Japanese Alliance by a Four-Power Treaty (Great Britain, the United States, France and Japan) by which each Power undertook to respect the other's rights in the Pacific. Lastly, a Nine-Power Treaty (which included China and the smaller European powers with any naval strength) attempted to stabilize the situation in China – all nine Powers pledging themselves to respect the integrity of China and the principle of the Open Door.

Next to the Far East it was Latin America which principally exercised American diplomacy during the 'twenties. Even Wilson, with his careful regard for the rights of small nations, had been led to intervene in Mexico when civil war rent the country into two opposing factions. Coolidge, with fewer scruples, used American troops in 1927 to restore order in Nicaragua with a readiness which led many Latin Americans to accuse him of intervening on behalf of American commercial interests. This – coupled with disputes with Mexico over oil and mineral rights – led to a serious deterioration in United States-Mexican relations, until in 1927 Dwight Morrow was appointed United States ambassador at Mexico City. He substituted diplomatic compromise for the 'big stick' methods of his predecessors and the result was the beginning of an improvement in Pan-American relations which was to be carried even further in the 'thirties.

It was Hughes's successor as Secretary of State, Kellogg, who was principally responsible for this spirit of conciliation in American diplomacy. Nor were his efforts restricted to the Western Hemisphere. Although the United States was no more prepared to become a member of the League than she had been in 1920, the traditional policy of the United States embodied one strand which might be woven into the new fabric of international order – arbitration. It seemed natural that the United States should support the great international arbitration tribunal, the World Court, especially since the Court was not tied to the League. It was an American Secretary of State, Elihu Root, who had been one of the formulators of the World Court idea; an American jurist, John Bassett Moore, was one of the Court's first judges. Yet such was the mood of Congress that the Senate rejected every effort to have the United States made a member of the Court. Rebuffed in this endeavour, Kellogg in 1928 concentrated on the Pact of Paris which bears his name. It was a declaration of sixty-three nations, including the United States, that they 'renounced war as an instrument of national policy' – a well-sounding, well-meaning profession, which was wholly deprived of practical value because it contained no sort of provision for its enforcement. But in the America of the 1920's this was as far as any spokesman for the nation could go.

How inadequate such devices were, and how weak the League of Nations was without American membership, was well illustrated in the next few years. Hoover had succeeded to Coolidge and Stimson to Kellogg when, in the autumn of 1931, Japan invaded Manchuria. This was a violation of the Kellogg Pact, the Four-Power Treaty and the Nine-Power Treaty, not to speak of Japan's obligations as a member of the League. But neither in Britain nor in America was public opinion disposed to take the serious measures necessary if Japan was to be restricted. Stimson reminded Japan of her treaty pledges and sent an American representative to observe, but not participate in, the discussions at Geneva. The Geneva discussions led to little more than the despatch of the Lytton Commission which investigated the situation and found Japan guilty of aggression. But by this time Japan's conquest of Manchuria was virtually complete: the most the United States was able to do was to register her moral condemnation by announcing that she would not recognize changes brought about by Japan's aggression. Nor would the League go further: in fact its own non-recognition resolution was very similar in its wording to Stimson's own note.

The impotence of the League in face of the Manchurian problem greatly strengthened the isolationists in the United States, who argued that world co-operation achieved no results and only involved America in needless quarrels. As further proof of this, isolationist spokesmen pointed once again to the history of the 'War Debts' of the first World War. These were the debts which the Allies had piled up with the United States after her entry into the war. There was $7,000 million which had been spent on military purchases and $3,350 million which had been spent, after the Armistice, on reconstruction. Of these totals Britain's share was about $4,000 million. Post-war Europe found these debts more than it could pay and very soon a difference of opinion developed between debtors and creditors. The debtors said they could not pay in gold because they were short of gold and could not pay in goods when the United States was raising higher and ever higher tariffs in order to keep their goods out. The Americans, as creditors, contended that alone among the belligerents they had won no territorial or other gains at Versailles and that it was for Europe to find a means of meeting its obligations: 'They hired the money, didn't they?' said President Coolidge. Moreover, all the debtors wanted to make payment dependent on their receipt of German reparations, while the British wanted to link their $4,000 million debt to the $6,000 million which they in their turn were owed by their allies. America refused to accept any such connection, and the only compromise achieved between the differing groups was a scaling-down of the rates of interest on the debts, with payment maintained slowly and intermittently. This was the state of affairs when the financial crash in America made further re-consideration imperative, and in 1931 Hoover arranged a twelve months' moratorium or suspension on all international debt payments. But by the time the elections of November, 1932, had made it clear that Roosevelt would succeed Hoover, six nations, including France and Belgium, had defaulted outright and in 1933, when the next payments fell due, Britain and Italy made only a 'token payment', i.e. a small sum pending an agreed final settlement.

This coincided with the virtual failure in London of the World Economic Conference, the first big international event in Roosevelt's Presidency. Its failure was due fundamentally to the fact that each nation, frightened by the sudden collapse of its economic system, was trying to put its own house in order no matter at what cost to international collaboration. The United States, faced with its

'Depression', was no more exempt from this tendency than anyone else, and when the American delegation refused to consider any programme for stabilizing currencies the Conference soon petered out. The American Congress next passed the Johnson Act forbidding any more loans to countries already in default on their debts and defining 'token payments' as defaults for this purpose. So in 1934 the last of the debtors, including Britain, defaulted outright. The debts were dead, leaving only a legacy of resentment, recrimination and disillusion behind.

This marked the peak in America of that hostility to international co-operation in trade, finance and politics which the 'twenties and 'thirties called 'isolationism'. Born of the war, nourished by disillusion and the deceptive prosperity of the 'boom' years, isolationism found its prophets both among the demagogues who appealed to timidity and selfishness, and among the idealists who thought that American democracy ought to be protected at whatever cost from involvement in another war. But the new President, Franklin Roosevelt, who had been Wilson's colleague and disciple, and Cordell Hull, his free trade Secretary of State, were convinced that the United States could make no lasting security for herself in a world of tariffs, dictators, aggression and international lawlessness. Believing this, they were also convinced that the United States must play her part in curing these ills.

It was in accordance with these convictions that the new Administration secured from Congress in 1934, by the Trade Agreement Act, power to cut tariff rates by as much as fifty per cent. with nations who were prepared to make similar concessions. At last a reversal of the high tariff policy got under way. Similarly liberal objectives were aimed at in the political field. One of the first acts of the new Administration was to arrange for the long overdue recognition of the U.S.S.R. This was followed in 1934 by an Act which reversed McKinley's decision of 1898 – by fixing 1946 as the date when the Philippines should recover their independence. In 1934, by a similar reversal of the earlier policies of imperialism, Cuba was freed from the operation of the Platt amendment – a practical application of the 'Good Neighbour' policy which soon won the Roosevelt regime high praise in Latin America.

But Congress was thinking of United States' security in negative terms – trying, as it were, to build for the United States a bomb-proof shelter in the midst of a war-like world. Senator Nye, who had created a considerable sensation by investigating the history of the armaments industry, induced Congress in 1935 to pass a Neutrality Act which materially limited the President's power in foreign affairs. Nye and his supporters, asserting that it was the sale of munitions to the Allies which had involved America in war in 1917, succeeded by this Act in making it illegal to sell munitions to any countries at war. The only immediate effect of the Act was to prevent Abyssinia, then attacked by Italy, from buying arms to defend herself. When the fires of war spread to Spain in 1936 the Act was amended to apply to participants in a civil war – with the result that Republican Spain was penalized as Abyssinia had been. Then in 1937 the Act was re-enacted in an amended form with the addition of the 'cash-and-carry' formula – which still further reduced the possibilities of American involvement by enabling the President to ban even raw material exports to belligerents unless they paid cash down and transported them in their own ships.

The President had little faith in such measures and in October, 1937, in face of the increasing threats of the dictators, he proposed at Chicago that the United States should join with other law-abiding powers to 'quarantine' nations who were contributing to 'international anarchy'. But the criticism which the speech provoked showed that public opinion was not ready for such a bold move. Roosevelt had perhaps hoped that public opinion would support a stronger policy in the Far East, where Japan, emboldened by her success in Manchuria, had now proceeded to a direct attack on China, aimed at the capture of Peking. Taking advantage of the fact that Japan had never made a formal declaration of war on China, the President refrained from applying the Neutrality Act to the Far Eastern conflict, thus leaving China free to draw on the United States for arms and materials. A conference was also summoned at Brussels of all the signatories to the Nine-Power Pact to consider what action should be taken. But just as Britain had her hands full and her nerves worn with events in Europe, so the United States was clearly unable to embark on any course of action which would not be repudiated by a largely isolationist public. The Brussels Conference accordingly petered out without taking any measures to repair the Nine-Power agreement which the Japanese had violated. Not even the sinking of the American gunboat *Panay*, while on patrol in the Yangtze, aroused the American people to demand punitive steps against Japan. The United States seemed stricken by the same paralysis of will which was afflicting the European democracies faced by the challenge of the dictators.

But as the shadows of war thickened, the Roosevelt administration gave fresh evidence that, after doing so much to save democracy on the home front, it did not propose lightheartedly to abandon the struggle abroad. By degrees the efforts of world-minded Americans to mobilize the nation to a full awareness of its dangers and its duties began to show results. In newspapers, on platforms, over the radio, around the firesides and on the floor of Congress a great national debate took place, in which the American people looked afresh at the darkening picture of the world they lived in and tried to make up their minds about the course of action their country should pursue. In this debate the internationalists started with a great advantage; by and large the sympathies of all Americans were on the side of the democracies and against the dictators and the aggressors. But ranged against these sympathies were the fear of war and the hope that, protected by her ocean, America could somehow escape, no matter what befell the rest of mankind. The Administration's policy therefore wisely concentrated on educating the nation to realize that geography alone could no longer bring security, at the same time as it mobilized

Americans' sympathies to support all measures 'short of war'.

It was in line with this that Cordell Hull in June, 1938, announced a 'moral embargo' on shipments of aircraft to all countries – such as Japan and Italy – who bombed civilian populations. The embargo had no legal basis: the administration merely used its influence to shame manufacturers from exporting their wares. In December of the same year a more practical step was taken, of advancing a credit to the Chinese government. The Pacific Fleet was built up with energy and by midsummer the commercial treaty with Japan was broken off.

By this time, however, it had become apparent that Europe was in an even more explosive condition than Asia. In the spring of 1938 Hitler took Austria: by the summer he was menacing Czecho-Slovakia. American verbal disapproval of such behaviour was strong, but scarcely any American felt it was America's business to intervene forcibly and prevent further aggression. The President's notes to Hitler at the time of Munich confined themselves to expressing the hope that a peaceful settlement would be found (and to conveying the implication that it would be Germany's fault if it were not). The shame of Munich added fresh fire to the arguments of the internationalists, but their work of persuasion and education was still woefully incomplete when 1939 brought the seizure of Albania and the threat to Poland. Denunciations of the Jewish persecutions, refusals to recognize the annexations of Czecho-Slovakia and Albania, were excellent methods of showing the dictatorships that America disapproved of their behaviour but, they left open the question of what, if anything, the United States would do in face of the mounting risk of war.

The President tried to secure an answer to that question. In the summer of 1939 he asked Congress to revise the Neutrality Act so as to lift the embargo on the export of arms. The implications were clear: he wanted the democracies to know that America's arsenals would be at their disposal. But Congress would not act, and when the President warned Senator Borah that war was imminent the Senator said that he preferred his own sources of information which assured him of the contrary. Within less than two months of their conversation Hitler had invaded Poland and World War II had broken out. President Roosevelt's first act, like Wilson's in 1914, was the discharge of his legal obligation to issue a formal proclamation of neutrality. But unlike Wilson, he did not ask for neutrality in thought. So far, at least, the United States had come since 1914. Moreover, before the end of November the President had secured from Congress the long-desired revision of the Neutrality Act, lifting the arms embargo, so that at least the Allies could draw arms from the United States so long as they could pay cash and carry them in their own ships.

The great debate of isolationism versus interventionism hung fire while the war persisted in what Americans called the 'phoney' phase, with little fighting, persistent peace rumours, and frequent blockade incidents which, as in 1914–17, brought the Allies as sea powers into friction with America's view of her maritime rights. It seemed to be, after all, a war which held few threats for America and which the Allies, given time, would certainly win. But with the *blitzkrieg* of May-June, 1940, both these suppositions were exploded. The United States suddenly realized how inadequate were her own defences against warfare waged on the Nazi scale and how much her own safety depended upon the resistance of Britain and the strength of the British Navy. The Administration, strengthened by the addition of two Republicans, Stimson and Knox, to head the Departments of War and the Navy respectively, made no secret of its sympathies for the Allies. With the nearest Ally, Canada, it set up a Joint Board on Defence. With Britain it negotiated the deal by which Britain secured fifty over-age destroyers and the United States obtained ninety-nine year leases on strategic bases in Newfoundland and the West Indies. In August, Congress at last passed a conscription measure, while rearmament was pressed on with speed.

Unfortunately this fateful year 1940 coincided with a Presidential election, an event which necessarily weakened Roosevelt's leadership and confused the public mind. Although fresh New Deal measures had been passed during Roosevelt's second term, the continuing liberal tendencies of the Administration had proved increasingly galling to conservatives of every kind. When the President announced that, contrary to all precedent, he was proposing to stand for a third term the cry of 'dictator' was added to the well-worn accusations of 'radical' and 'war-monger'. Fortunately for the United States, however, the interventionists were by no means confined to the Democratic Party and the choice by the Republican Convention of Wendell Willkie, a warm advocate of Allied aid, meant that in large measure foreign policy was kept out of the campaign. But with most of the voters the President's known sympathies and large experience in foreign affairs counted for a great deal, and his re-election by a large majority in the electoral college (though a small margin of the popular vote) was rightly regarded as an endorsement of his policy of 'all aid short of war'.

In December, 1940, in one of his famous radio 'fireside chats', the President asked the American people to make themselves the 'arsenal of democracy' that would give the Allies all the aid they wanted 'short of war'. And when in the spring of 1941 it became apparent that Britain's purchases from the arsenal might have to stop because she no longer had the cash to pay for them, the President announced the great concept of Lend-Lease, by which the United States government was empowered to provide 'any defence article' to Britain or any other country 'vital to the defence of the United States', leaving the form of repayment, if any, to be settled later.

The long debate in Congress on the Lend-Lease Bill was really the final stage also in the American people's debate on the pros and cons of interventionism. For when the Lend-Lease Bill was finally passed in March, 1941, the United States, for all its formal neutrality, in fact became a participant in the war, pledged to the Allied cause and committed to using all its resources to prevent a Nazi victory. Thus in rapid succession United States forces occupied Greenland, Germany announced a policy of unrestricted sinkings similar to 1917, and the President, denouncing it as 'piracy', demanded the repatriation of all German officials in the United States. The pattern of approaching war was clear. And the joint interest which Britain and the United States had shared, since the time of Jefferson, in keeping the Atlantic safe, at whatever cost, from the domination of an aggressor, was dramatically reaffirmed when in August Roosevelt and Churchill met off the coast of Maine and promulgated the Atlantic Charter. In this document, while still technically at peace, the United States and its great Atlantic partner made public their war aims and the principles upon which they proposed to build the peace.

It was soon clear that the Atlantic lifeline, without which the Atlantic Charter would become an unrealizable scrap of paper, would need American force for its defence. Allied shipping losses were heavy and Nazi submarines were not hesitating to attack American ships as well. In September the President gave the fleet instructions to 'shoot at sight', and in November Congress authorized a further revision of the Neutrality Act to permit the arming of American merchant ships and their entry into belligerent ports. The 'shooting war', though still undeclared, had in fact begun. How soon would the inevitable consequences ensue? The answer, to most Americans' surprise, came from the Pacific.

So long as American armaments at sea and in the air remained inadequate and the menace of Germany was so portentous and huge, the United States government, like the British, had played for time in the Far East. It had given what help it could to China, but had refrained from gestures which would unduly provoke Japan. But when Japan, immediately after Hitler's invasion of Russia, began to move into Vichy-French Indo-China, the United States showed its displeasure not only by word but also by imposing a virtual embargo on the export of materials to Japan. The Japanese retorted, in August, 1941, by attempting negotiations with Washington for 'a Far East settlement'. The negotiations were protracted, but when it became apparent that by a 'settlement' the Japanese meant that the United States should abandon China and give Japan a free hand in Asia, the State Department replied by restating its old principles of law and order and the 'open door' and demanding that Japan completely reverse her policy. Finally, on December 6th, the President made a last appeal to the Japanese Emperor to abandon his aggressive designs in Indo-China. While on the following day the Secretary of State was awaiting the Japanese envoy's return visit and reply, the news came over the radio that Japanese bombers were attacking the American fleet at its base in Pearl Harbour. The Japanese bombs which thus precipitated the Pacific War also exploded the last pretences of non-belligerency in Europe. Within four days of Pearl Harbour Germany and Italy declared war on the United States. President Roosevelt's reply was swift and confident: 'We are going to win the war and we are going to win the peace that follows'.

CHAPTER XXXIII

Total War

THE lightning change from hostile neutrality to deadly belligerency which was produced by Pearl Harbour found the United States only half prepared for the demands of a world-wide, total war. The foresight of President Roosevelt had maintained a large, two-ocean navy, but the Japanese surprise attack had momentarily crippled it as an offensive force. The army, as a result of the previous year's Selective Service Act, had expanded to something over one and a half million men, but in addition to being still far too small it was under-equipped and ill-experienced. The munitions industry was already at work turning out weapons for Lend-Lease, but production was wholly insufficient for an all-out war against the Axis.

In this period of semi-preparedness, therefore, it was not surprising that Japan and Germany made great gains at the expense of the U.S.A. and her allies. During the first six months of 1942 the United States was in greater peril than at any time in its history; it was saved by its relative remoteness from its enemies, by the tenacity of its allies and by the fighting resolution of its citizens. At first the Japanese flood flowed over allied possessions in the Pacific virtually unchecked. In rapid succession American bases at Guam and Wake were overrun, the Philippines were occupied, British possessions in Malaya and the whole of the Dutch East Indies collapsed. The resistances of American troops at Bataan and Corregidor evoked the admiration of the world for their heroism and endurance, but it was not until the Battle of the Coral Sea in May, 1942, that any serious check was administered to the Japanese advance – by which time it was at the very doors of Australia.

But despite the spectacular successes of the Japanese, President Roosevelt, with remarkable strategic foresight, recognized that it was Germany which constituted the most immediate menace to the Allied cause. Consequently not only did the bulk of American supplies continue to go to the European theatres, where the Russians were fighting desperately on their own soil and the British were battling along the shores and in the waters of the Mediterranean, but also, in November of 1942, a great allied invasion of North Africa was organized, under an American commander, General Eisenhower, and with a decisive weight of American troops, planes and armour. The operation, brilliantly successful, demonstrated to the world that America had corrected the unpreparedness of Pearl Harbour. It demonstrated, too, the distinctive contribution which the U.S.A. would make to the defeat of the Axis – organization and production. In the war against the Axis, America was to be what Britain had been in the wars against Napoleon – the organizer of victory.

Putting her massive strength at the disposal of her allies, she also played an important part in welding them into a united whole. With Britain in particular her links were close. Combined commands were set up for every theatre of operations and Combined Boards in Washington and London planned the gigantic business of war as a joint enterprise. The friendship between Roosevelt and Churchill set the tone for the war-time collaboration of the two peoples, and soon at every lower level links were established which grew closer the longer the war went on. The machinery of Lend-Lease, originally devised simply as 'aid short of war' from a neutral U.S.A. to her belligerent friends, was adapted to fit this new unity of design. 'Reverse Lend-Lease' came into play as American forces moved into allied theatres and needed in their turn local supplies or assistance. Soon, for the multiple munitions of modern war, from aeroplanes to 'Spam', a pooling of supplies became the rule, the test being no longer 'Who owns it?' or 'Can you pay?' but how, in the old Civil War phrase, you could 'get there fustest with mostest' – get material to the place where it was most needed and to the hands that could best use it. So out of the difficulties of the common struggle the idea of mutual aid was born.

Of all the warring Powers the United States had the greatest industrial plant, and the one most immune from enemy attack. Consequently, above all the others, she contributed an overwhelming weight of production to the common pool. By the end of 1942 alone she had turned out 46,000 aeroplanes and 56,000 armoured vehicles. American shipyards were mobilized to produce the merchant and naval shipping which in some ways was the allies' sorest need. The genius of Henry Kaiser designed and produced the *Liberty* ships, in speed and numbers sufficient to defeat the Axis submarines in the critical battles for the supply lines in the Atlantic and Pacific. Meanwhile, in the hills of Tennessee a mysterious factory was in process of erection about which nothing was known save only (and that only to a restricted few) that it was part of something called the Manhattan Project.

But the production achievement of 1942, remarkable as it was, was only the beginning. By 1944 it had been almost doubled. That year saw the manufacture of 95,000 planes and more than twice the previous tonnage of merchant and naval shipping. An army of nine million and a navy of two and a half million men was being equipped and supplied with a completeness in relation to its size unknown in history. Inventiveness went hand-in-hand with quantity: the Jeep, that miracle of mobility; the Superfortress, farthest-ranging bombing plane; the aircraft-carriers designed for an aero-naval war of vast distances – these were only instances of the application of American industrial science to the purposes of war. Most remarkable of all, however, as indicating the industrial strength of America, was the fact that this huge output of goods of war was achieved without any serious decline in the output of goods of peace. Although some items were short and a measure of rationing had to be introduced – notably for petrol, rubber, fats and sugar – the average American civilian was able to enjoy throughout the war a higher standard of living than in 1929 or 1940.

That did not mean that the war was an easy time for Americans. Soldiers and sailors apart, the American knew at first hand nothing of the physical horrors of war: his country was neither bombed nor invaded. But this very immunity created peculiar difficulties for him: he lacked the stimulus of visible danger. The war for which he was asked to work and sacrifice was thousands of miles away. It required no small effort of imagination and will to recognize it for what it was – a struggle for survival. The American constitutional system makes impossible the formation of a coalition government such as Britain enjoyed from 1940 to 1945. Consequently, although the country rallied loyally behind Roosevelt in his capacity as Commander-in-Chief, there were elections to be fought, criticisms and delays in

Congress, business and labour struggles involving strikes in coal-mines and on railroads, and many other distractions which countries nearer the fighting line were spared. But through all the differences and diversions one increasing purpose manifested itself – to win the war and to make after it a lasting peace.

By degrees the weight of the United Nations began to tell. The expulsion of the Axis from Africa was followed by the allied landings in Sicily and Sardinia. In the gruelling battles up the backbone of Italy, American soldiers learnt battle experience which was to stand them in good stead in 1944 and 1945. At the same time, while the Russian resistance blunted the edge of the great German war machine in successive battles of attrition, British and American bombers, flying from British bases, accelerated their crippling of the German home front. Meanwhile a vast American army was massed in Britain, a peaceful khaki invasion, pouring in from every ship and into every port, filling towns and villages all over these islands – an organized trans-Atlantic immigration greater even than Europe's emigration to America in the peak years of the nineteen-hundreds. Never, to adopt Canning's famous phrase, had the New World been so visibly called in to redress the balance of the Old. Out of the strains and stresses of this great influx was born a new intimacy between the two nations, a larger knowledge and understanding of each other's way of life than could ever have been won from the normal intercourse of peace. Presiding over the whole operation, welding American and Briton alike into a single striking force, was the large-hearted genius of General Eisenhower, who as Supreme Commander displayed not only a remarkable mastery of the science of war, but also a selfless devotion to the ideal of United Nations unity.

In consequence, when on D-Day, June 6th, 1944, the blow fell and the liberation of Europe began, it was a thoroughly planned and unified operation which resulted, and although the American forces greatly outnumbered those of their allies, all equally subordinated national pride to the demands of allied teamwork and all equally shared in the glory of the common victory. Some names and incidents of the campaign will, however, by reason of their particular association with American arms, long retain a bright place in American memory. The landing at Omaha Beach, where the heaviest losses were suffered, General Patton's break-through from Avranches, the checking of the Ardennes counter-offensive at Bastogne and the capture of the Remagen bridgehead over the Rhine – these will remain vivid to those who knew them and will survive as great American legends to those who did not.

On May 7th, 1945, General Eisenhower saw the reward of his labours in the surrender of the German government to the Allies at Rheims and the world breathed at last with the realization that Nazi might was broken. But Americans, more sharply perhaps than any other of the fighting allies, still had their eyes fixed on the other enemy in the Far East. The struggle there had been no less bitter than in Africa and Europe; indeed, the climate and terrain of the jungles of Oceania had added difficulties of their own. But, as in the West, a unified strategy was adopted for the Eastern war which by degrees overcame the disadvantages under which the allies had to fight. The vast distances involved necessitated several commands, but over-arching them all there was a common allied plan. China, so long a combatant, held on with desperate gallantry, with the aid of every ton of supplies that could be flown in to her over the mountain 'hump' from India. From Ceylon the South-East Asia Command under Lord Louis Mountbatten organized the attack on Burma, designed to be a running sore in the far-flung flank of the Japanese advance. From Australia General Macarthur, as Commander-in-Chief for the South-West Pacific, organized, in collaboration with the U.S. fleet under Admiral Nimitz, the long struggle to evict the Japanese from their island conquests. Under his command American, Australian, and New Zealand troops fought to win back, one by one, the stepping-stones to Tokyo.

As they progressed, America learnt a new geography of

the Pacific, in which hitherto obscure spots in island jungles became as familiar as place-names in Kansas or New England because of their association with the struggles and victories of American arms – Buna, Rabaul, Bougainville, Guadalcanal, Tarawa, Kwajalein, Saipan. Then at last came the happy day when the scenes of earlier defeats became the setting of new victories – when the Philippines were re-conquered and Guam re-occupied. Meanwhile American bombers were within striking distance of Japan itself, mounting tornadoes of destruction which were ripping the heart out of the Japanese homeland at a time when Japanese troops were still vainly fighting their useless conquests overseas. Thus before even the fall of Germany it became obvious that for Japan a net was closing in from which there was no escape.

Already, while the prospect of peace was little more than a pin-point of light at the end of the long tunnel of war, Americans, in common with their allies, had been working at plans for a new world order. The revolution in American thinking which, beginning in the debates of the 'thirties, had been spurred by the catastrophes of 1940, now proceeded to work itself out under the pressure of total war. When factories in Detroit were making tanks for use in the Ukraine and young men from Iowa were fighting in the jungles of New Guinea, the old catchwords of isolationism obviously lost all meaning; Americans everywhere, whether Easterners or Mid-westerners, Republicans or Democrats, had no choice but to endorse the discovery of Mr Willkie that they, in common with the rest of mankind, were living in 'One World'. The problem was no longer how to escape from the rest of the world, but how to organize it for peace and liberty. Mr Roosevelt and Mr Hull shared the conviction that any future league or organization must grow out of the war-time collaboration of the United Nations and that it must have as its foundation the unity of the great powers who had combined to defeat the Axis. The old League of Nations had failed largely because the U.S.A. and the U.S.S.R. had remained outside it; its successor must build upon their strength from the start. With this purpose the United States summoned a preliminary conference to meet at Dumbarton Oaks, in Washington, in the summer of 1944, at which a draft plan for a United Nations organization was hammered out between the great powers. Moreover – and this was of crucial importance – Mr Roosevelt, unlike his predecessor, Woodrow Wilson, was careful and able to get the support of the Republicans, as well as the Democrats, for the plans which the U.S. delegation put forward.

It was largely owing to this statesmanlike policy of taking the opposition party into the administration's confidence that the presidential election of 1944 passed off with so little harmful effect on the plans for either the war or the peace. Within these patriotic limits the Republicans, under Mr Dewey, the Governor of New York State, fought a vigorous campaign, but the country showed itself in no mood to change its leader at so crucial an hour, and Mr Roosevelt enjoyed the unprecedented distinction of being re-elected for a fourth term. It was observed, however, by those who accompanied him to the last 'big three' conference with Mr Churchill and Marshal Stalin at Yalta in the following February that he was in poor health and that the strain of the journey obviously told on him considerably. Then suddenly, on April 12th, 1945, while American troops in Germany were crossing the Elbe and Japanese suicide planes were raiding the U.S. navy at Okinawa, the President died at Warm Springs, Georgia, of a cerebral hæmorrhage. He died with his work unfinished, but with the certainty of victory in sight; truly, no less than President Lincoln before him, he died as a soldier in a war which his leadership went far to win.

It was fitting that Mr Roosevelt's death was not allowed by his successor, Mr Truman, to interfere with the holding of the San Francisco Conference which opened, as arranged, on April 25th, for this might appropriately be regarded as the coping-stone to Mr Roosevelt's work for world peace. At San Francisco the United Nations, great and small, took the draft which had been prepared at Dumbarton Oaks and fashioned out of it the Charter of the United Nations. The result was the establishment of an organization for world peace in whose shaping every country had had a hand, but it might fairly be claimed, to the credit not only of Mr Stettinius, the U.S. delegate, but also of Mr Roosevelt and Mr Hull, of Mr Stimson and Woodrow Wilson – indeed of every American who in hard times as well as in good had fought for the cause of world order – that the United States had made a contribution second to none.

Hardly, however, had the Senate endorsed the San Francisco Charter, thereby triumphantly reversing its treatment of the League of Nations twenty-five years before, than a force was released upon the world whose use, for good or evil, would strain the resources of world statesmanship to the uttermost. On August 6th an American plane dropped an atomic bomb on the Japanese city of Hiroshima. The atomic age had begun. The world heard, with incredulity, the story, at last disclosed, of the Manhattan Project and of the mysterious factories in the hills of Tennessee and the deserts of Washington State and New Mexico. This was the last miracle of American industrial production – the wresting from nature of the secret of the atom and the mastery of a force which in one second could obliterate a city and destroy a hundred thousand lives. Thus was realized, almost in a flash, the objective which Americans had feared would take months of fighting and heavy casualties to win – the collapse of Japan. But it also brought into existence a power which, as men slowly grasped its potentialities, was seen to be capable of re-making or obliterating civilization. Its existence posed a challenge to the wisdom of the entire world, but especially to the wisdom of the United States, in whose hands this power was temporarily deposited, in the words of President Truman, 'as a sacred trust'.

In December, 1862, at the height of the Civil War, Abraham Lincoln had reminded the Congress that in that struggle nothing less than the future of the American Union was at stake. 'Fellow-citizens, we cannot escape history. We of this Congress and this Administration will be remembered in spite of ourselves. No personal significance or insignificance can spare one or another of us. The fiery trial through which we pass will light us down, in honour or dishonour, to the latest generation. We say we are for the Union. The world will not forget that we say this. We know how to save the Union. The world knows we do know how to save it. We, even we here, hold the power and bear the responsibility ... We shall nobly save or meanly lose the last, best hope of earth.' There was nothing that Lincoln had to say of the struggle of 1862 which was not even more truly applicable to the struggle of 1946, save that now it was not the American Union merely, it was world civilization which was at stake. Looking back on their history, all could see the answer they had given then; looking forward, they could resolve not to shirk the answer now.

PRESIDENTS OF THE UNITED STATES

			Date of Inauguration
1.	George Washington	Federalist	1789
2.	John Adams	,,	1797
3.	Thomas Jefferson	Republican	1801
4.	James Madison	,,	1809
5.	James Monroe	,,	1817
6.	John Quincy Adams	,,	1825
7.	Andrew Jackson	Democrat	1829
8.	Martin Van Buren	,,	1837
9.	William Henry Harrison[1]	Whig	1841
10.	John Tyler[3]	,,	1841
11.	James Knox Polk	Democrat	1845
12.	Zachary Taylor[1]	Whig	1849
13.	Millard Fillmore	,,	1850
14.	Franklin Pierce	Democrat	1853
15.	James Buchanan	,,	1857
16.	Abraham Lincoln[2]	Republican	1861
17.	Andrew Johnson[3]	,,	1865
18.	Ulysses Simpson Grant	,,	1869
19.	Rutherford Birchard Hayes	,,	1877
20.	James Abram Garfield[2]	,,	1881
21.	Chester Alan Arthur[3]	,,	1881
22.	Grover Cleveland	Democrat	1885
23.	Benjamin Harrison	Republican	1889
24.	Grover Cleveland	Democrat	1893
25.	William McKinley[2]	Republican	1897
26.	Theodore Roosevelt[3]	,,	1901
27.	William Howard Taft	,,	1909
28.	Woodrow Wilson	Democrat	1913
29.	Warren Gamaliel Harding[1]	Republican	1921
30.	Calvin Coolidge[3]	,,	1923
31.	Herbert Hoover	,,	1929
32.	Franklin Delano Roosevelt[1]	Democrat	1933
33.	Harry S. Truman[3]	,,	1945

[1] Died in office. [2] Assassinated. [3] Elected Vice-President.

INDEX